Out of the Mist

Demystifying and Understanding Other Cultures

To Improve International Business

An Anthropological Perspective

by

Don E. Post, Ph.D.

Two Bytes Publishing, Ltd.
Darien, Connecticut

1996

Produced and Published by:
Two Bytes Publishing, Ltd.
P.O. Box 1043
83 Old Kingshighway South
Darien, Connecticut 06820

ISBN: 1-881907-09-0 (*soft cover edition*)

*Printed in
the United States of America*

Dedication

*To my wife, Victoria
and our children,
Darren and Lenora*

Foreword

Every society functions within a marketplace environment, and the integral workings of such an environment can be largely defined by the phenomenon known as *culture*. Any culture is *a composite of all the mental rules or codes shared by a group of people which identify unique behavior patterns*. We group people on the basis of these shared sets of mental rules known as culture. We know that Americans think, and therefore act, differently from French, Russians, Chinese or other international peoples. While all groups share a number of stereotypes about those other people, some accurate, some inaccurate, the basic contours of these differences elude our grasp because they reside in the mind and are not easily accessed by our senses. We can see cultural products but not culture itself.

Further, one's culture includes a defining or all-encompassing set of value codes that are so deeply held they are generally unconscious baggage. Those value codes weave a tapestry that defines all of human existence. We are so much the product of our culture that we find it very difficult to understand how anyone else could view life differently. This is where the problem begins. The inability to understand those who are culturally different has often triggered war. It is also a fundamental reason for, or at least a contributing factor to, inferior international business results and unhappy foreign travel experiences.

The overriding message for the international business person is this: *even if one has the most elite MBA degree available, has been domestically successful and garnered significant profits in many countries over a number of years, but cannot read, decode or demystify another culture accurately, then one's* <u>maximum potential</u> *is diminished.* This principle is simultaneously applicable to cross-cultural political and diplomatic relations, international travel in general, and even to the most fundamental of human social relationships of those living in a culturally pluralistic America! Due to technological and communication advances, people of different cultures are increasingly thrown against each other economically, politically and socially so it is important that we learn how to more efficiently and accurately comprehend those who are culturally different. An accurate cultural portrait of another can lead to productive relationships which, in turn, can lead to increased international business opportunities for one's company, more harmonious diplomatic relations between nations and more enjoyable experiences for the casual international traveler.

Although this book's focus is upon international business activity, the *tool* or *device* outlined in the following pages will enable business personnel, traveler or vacationer, and diplomat to *read* and *demystify* other cultures more accurately. Its use will reduce the confusion and anxiety of working, living or traveling cross-culturally.

The device set forth in this book enables one to sketch a more accurate cutural portrait of others by viewing and organizing all cross-cultural experiences into a specific set of scenes: economic, political, religious, social, technological and environmental. Most importantly, each scene is discussed from a basic anthropological perspective. The cultural history sketched in most of these scenes will make some readers wonder what such former socio-cultural patterns or life-ways have to do with understanding contemporary people. To those people I would suggest that most of the world's people are still tradition oriented. On closer self-inspection we, Westerners, probably may find that we are not as modern, sophisticated and secular as we claim to be. One has only to scratch the cultural skin of most of the world's people to find former cultural patterns emerging. An understanding of these basic contours adds clarity to any contemporary cultural portrait.

D.E.P.

Acknowledgments

There were many who contributed heavily to this work. A great debt is owed Henry Selby, Ph.D., Professor of Anthropology and formerly Director of Mexican Studies at the University of Texas in Austin, Texas, for sharing his time in critical reflection over many months. Our discussions were always rich and enjoyable. Special thanks is also due Jim Koch, Professor of Economics, and Richard Hughes, Ph.D., Professor of American History, both of St. Edward's University in Austin, Texas, for their critical comments (Richard Hughes died in October, 1993 and his friendship will be greatly missed); to Neil McFarland, Professor (ret.) of Comparative Religions at Perkins School of Theology, SMU, for his help with the religion chapter; and to the many American and foreign businessmen and women with whom I have worked over the years for their insights. Each taught me a great deal, and I am greatly indebted to all. I am also most appreciative of the support received from the library staff of St. Edward's University, Austin, Texas.

Finally, I am extremely grateful for the support and patience of my wife, Victoria, and our children, Lenora and Darren. Although they traveled with me to many places over the years, they tolerated an absentee husband and father more than one should.

Don E. Post
Huntsville, Texas
January 30, 1996

Table of Contents

Foreword v

Acknowledgments vii

Table of Contents. ix

List of Charts and Illustrations xi

Chapter I: Our Need To Understand Other People. 1
   A Foreign Advantage. 7
   The Cross Cultural Perspective:
     What It Is And What It Does 11
   Summary 15
   References Cited 19

Chapter II: Obstacles To Cross-Cultural Understanding 21
   Traditional and Modern Classifications. 21
     World Views/Mythic Structures 22
     Change and Progress. 23
     Viewing Life Constraints .25
     Social Identities. 25
     Summary: Traditional Versus Modern World Views .25
   The Lure of Modernism. 26
   Some Valued Traditional Culture Traits 28
   American Ethnocentricism 30
   American Individualism: Our Navel Focus 31
   Our Offensive Body Language 37
   The Way Americans Talk. 39
   Impatience and Bluntness 40
   Summary 42
   References Cited 43

Chapter III: The Cultural Perspective. 46
   Building A Useful Cultural Perspective:
     The Need For A Skeptical Mind 46
   The Culture Concept: The Main Focal Lens. 48

A Look At Cultural Relativity. .53
A Strategy For Accessing Cultural Meanings 54
The Seven Cultural Scenes. 54
Associated Issues. 56
References Cited 60

Chapter IV: The Social Scene. 61
Basic Socio-Cultural Organizational Building Blocks. .63
The Intimacy Continuum 64
Mexican Family and Kin. 65
First Tier Intimacy: Kinship. 65
Jose's Business Relations and
Some Western Comparisons 68
Second Tier Intimacy: Fictive Kin 70
Building Relations Beyond The Kin. 71
Compadrazgo. 71
Patron. 72
Other Tiers of Intimacy:
Emphasis On The Outsider 72
The Universality of Social Distinctions 75
Groups In The Marketplace .79
Social Tension-Releasing Mechanisms. 80
References Cited 83

Chapter V: The Religious Scene 85
Some Thoughts On Christianity. 88
Hinduism. 90
Buddhism. 92
Taoism and Confucianism. 94
Yin-Yang Creation Principles 95
Feng-Shui. 96
Confucianism. 97
Ahinto: A Japanese Phenomenon. 98
Islam. 102
Islamic History 103
Traditional or Folk Religions 105
Summary. 106
References Cited 108

Chapter VI: The Environmental Scene. 109
Nature and Culture. 111

Our Historic American Culture 111
The Inuit Case 114
  The Habitat 114
  Cultural Responses 114
  Implications For Doing Business 116
  Summary 117
The Japanese Case 117
  The Habitat 117
  Cultural Responses 118
  Implications For Doing Business 119
  Summary 120
Chapter Summary 121
References Cited 122

Chapter VII: The Technological Scene. 124
Historical Technologies 126
  Hunting and Gathering (Includes Fishing) 126
  Pastoralism (Herding) 127
Contemporary Technologies 130
  Horticulture 130
  Intensive Agriculture 134
Industrial To Modern High-Technology 138
References Cited 145

Chapter VIII: The Economic Scene 149
The Economy and The Rest of Culture 150
Some Economic Differences 151
Reflections and Additional Nuances 157
Traditional Modes of Exchange 159
  Marketless Economies 160
  Peripheral Markets Only 163
  Market Dominated Economies (Peasantry) 163
  Implications 165
Modernism and The Market .167
Some Suggested Strategies .171
References Cited 175

Chapter IX: The Political Scene 179
Pressures On Current Political Systems 180
Political Culture 181
Power and Its Exercise 183

Historic Political Systems 185
    Tribes 188
Today's Political Cultures 189
On Political Risk Analysis. .191
Summary 191
References Cited 192

Chapter X: Time and Space 193
    Time 195
    Space 204
    Modern Technologies:
        Annihilation Of Space Through Time 204
    References Cited 211

Chapter XI: Completing the Cultural Portrait. 213
    Danger In Romanticizing The Foreign. 215
    Reading The Literature: Pursuit Strategy One. 216
    Home-Stays: Pursuit Strategy Two 217
    Sensitive Questioning: Pursuit Strategy Three 220
    Observation: Pursuit Strategy Four. 222
    References Cited 223

Appendix to Chapter VI. 227
    References Cited. 237

Bibliography 241

Index 247

List of Charts and Illustrations

Cover and Title Page

Bridging Cultures . . . . Cover
                                    by Jonas Sanchez

Bridging Cultures - close-up. Title Page
                                    by Jonas Sanchez

List of Charts and Illustrations (continued)

Chapter I

Basic Focal Lens for Demystifying Other Cultures 13

Chapter III

The Complete Cultural Reading Device 55

Chapter IV

A Social Organization Structure 62

Tracing Social Bonding in Mexico 65

Mexican Intimacy Scale 75

Devices Creating Social Boundaries 79

Chapter V

Buddha 92

by Jonas Sanchez

Lao-Tzu 95

by Jonas Sanchez

Confucius 97

by Jonas Sanchez

Chapter IX

Historical Political Systems and System Attributes 186

Chapter X

P-Time and M-Time 201

The Globe Has Shrunk! 205

Personal Space Zones 208

Out of the Mist:

Demystifying and Understanding Other Cultures
To Improve International Business

Chapter I:
Our Need To Understand Other People

"...Where do we stand in terms of the economic strength of this country? We're in a very different position from where we stood in 1950, at the beginning of the Cold War. Then we had nine of the ten largest banks in the world; now we have none of the top twenty. Then we had a seventy percent share of world assets and world markets; now we are down in the eighteen and nineteen percent range. It follows that we have an urgent need to restore the economic strength of this country if we're going to play a leadership role in the next century–if we are to have as great an impact on the world as we did in this century."

– Speech by Senator David L. Boren
National Press Club, April 3, 1990

It is reported that a man in Kentucky who loved to hunt fox was invited to his state's most prestigious annual hunt. Participants were asked to bring only male hounds. Unfortunately his fine young male had just died, leaving him with one young, but talented female and an old male that could barely walk, much less chase a fox. To his relief he received permission to bring his female hound and hoped that he could get one last hunt out of the old male dog.

He arrived at the hunt and turned his hounds loose with the rest of the dogs. The pack took off like a flash and was soon out of sight. The hunters pursued the pack and had a difficult time catching up. They finally came across a farmer working in his field and asked if he had seen a pack of dogs go by.

"Yep," he said.

"Did you see where they went?" asked the hunters.

"No," he replied, "but it was the first time I ever saw a fox running in fifth place!"

Whereas our Nation's industrial strength should be leading the pack, we are running "about fifth."

We all agree that re-exerting our Nation's global economic leadership is a critical challenge. No day passes without media reports of our foreign trade dilemma. We may argue the causes, and they are numerous, but not the fact that we are having difficulty coping in the foreign market place. So what's happened to us? Why are we so inept in serving foreign markets? Many explain our current predicament by blaming others. There is a mass of accusations that others do not play fair, that most foreign laborers are paid less thus leading to lower manufacturing costs, that other governments are in collusion with their business sector and that our Nation's lawmakers are incompetent.[2] In the midst of all this is a pervasive charge that average American business persons do not understand foreign people. Here and there, now and again, there is truth to each of these charges.

There is plenty of blame to go around. The purpose of this book is not to argue the relative importance of one cause versus another; they all contribute to our predicament. Instead, there is a great need to show how business people can most efficiently understand people of another culture. This understanding will lead to more productive cross-cultural business relationships. The cultural perspective outlined in the following chapters equips one to sketch an adequate portrait of any culture, which is the essence of better understanding any group.

It should be clearly understood: This is NOT another book on "How To Do Business in Bongo-Bongo." *A person who possesses all the business skills and experience possible and has been extremely successful internationally, but does not have the ability to decode or to accurately understand other cultures, is most likely failing to maximize his full potential!* The ability to decode other cultures should be seen as an essential prerequisite to "doing business" in a foreign country.

This cross-cultural perspective presents a way for business people, or anyone else with an interest in international affairs, to more accurately read, demystify, decode, interpret or make better sense of any other culture. It is an anthropological perspective which should be seen as a necessary augmentation to conduct international business and other relations successfully.

Of course, one does not have to be doing business to use the cross-culture perspective. It will lead to more rewarding visits to other countries for the seasoned traveler, the first-time tourist and the occasional visitor. Lasting impressions gained by countrymen on both sides will help to bring about more fruitful social and business contacts for American businessmen and women. Who has not felt anxious as they packed for a trip to a foreign land? We worry about not understanding the language and behavior of another people. Who has not felt relief as the plane landed back on United States soil after the trip abroad?

This perspective should reduce one's anxiety about working abroad, improve one's foreign relationships and equip America's business associates to develop more profitable cross-cultural relations. More intimate relations with one's foreign associates is directly proportional to the amount of accurate knowledge one has about the foreigner's culture and language as well as other factors. This knowledge of another's culture must be joined by deep respect and appreciation. The economist Lester Thurow, among others, has noted that cross-cultural misunderstanding significantly impedes increased foreign profits.[3]

Our relative inability to understand other cultures gets little attention. How can we do something about this situation? We must start by making a conscious, or intentional decision to understand how our foreign associates uniquely view their world. The benefits of more accurately understanding another's culture are several:

First, such knowledge on our part is quickly communicated to foreign business people and has the effect of enhancing their self-esteem and dignity. *Second,* it is likely that it will inspire greater trust, deeper interpersonal devotion and increased cooperation. *Lastly* and most essential: it will result in profits for all parties.

It follows that better foreign relations will lead to the resolution of hundreds of trade issues that now plague us. The benefits go a step further as better impressions left by tourist, traveler and visitor lead to greater understanding on the social level. As far back as 1778, Samuel Johnson quoted a Spanish proverb to emphasize this point:

> "He who would bring home the wealth of the Indies, must carry the wealth of the Indies with him, so it is in traveling, a man must carry knowledge with him if he would bring home knowledge." [4]

Our need to understand our foreign business associates was demonstrated quite dramatically in Singapore during July 1983. The following dialogue took place between a Singapore politician, whom I shall call Mr. Teng, and a president and CEO, whom I shall call Mr. Clark, of an American company, the revenues of which were in the $100 million range annually. Mr. Clark's firm had lost a large government contract and Mr. Teng had been a member of the final evaluation panel.

Mr. Teng diplomatically explained that business in Southeast Asia is conducted on the basis of trust and past history of business relations. The chosen firm was Asian and the government believed this company understood the region and its people better than Mr. Clark's group. Mr. Clark diplomatically countered by reciting his firm's fifty-year history, much of it international. Mr. Clark's rigid and tense posture, creased brow and steely stare communicated to Mr. Teng suspicions that the bid was awarded on the basis of race and nationalism, not technical competence. Mr. Teng's aide responded by saying that they were all impressed, but they were more comfortable with those who had been working in the area longer. They hoped Mr. Clark's firm would set up a local office and take the time to become acquainted with the local culture.

As the meeting progressed, Mr. Clark's American, no-nonsense, "tell-it-like-it-is-and-take-no-prisoners" attitude, came to the fore. The following reflects the conversation which took place:

Mr. Clark: "Well, we've done well in Europe without having to expend a great amount of funds. I do not understand why you people make it so difficult for non-Asians to do business. Have you stacked the deck against us like the Japanese? I thought you would jump at the chance to use our knowledge and ability."

Mr. Teng: "No, we are not prejudiced against non-Asians. Many Asians believe American and European markets are difficult for Asians to enter. We tend to believe this difficulty is a matter of difference in cultures, not prejudice."

Mr. Clark: "Ah, Asian companies are taking over the United States market. We do not shut out anybody, and maybe that is our problem."

Mr. Teng: "Yes, I agree that Asians have a relatively easier time in America and Europe. Your markets are more open, but you are so much larger and more highly developed. We are constantly striving to balance our own people's need to develop with the interests of foreign firms. It is difficult. Governments in developing states must manage business relations more strictly than you do."

At this point a somewhat lengthy conversation regarding governmental roles in the marketplace ensued.

This conversation has been repeated over the years in a variety of forms in Latin America, Asia, Africa and the Mid-East—although perhaps not as dramatically. Mr. Clark was confronting the fears that stalk every American company's staff as they seek to do business overseas. How can we compete where business is so obviously stacked in favor of indigenous firms? Unfortunately, Mr. Clark's pride was hurt. It was tough for an old line quality company to be beaten by an upstart group of Asians! He decided to write Asia off for the near future.

Tom Peters, the author of *In Search of Excellence,* spent a month lecturing in the People's Republic of China in 1988 and his reflections emphasize our problem with other cultures.[5] After citing a number of issues that effect America's current trade problem, such as corporate fat, slovenly manufacturing processes, a strong United States dollar, and some protectionist markets, he views the general discomfort of American business with Asian cultures as the main culprit.

We all admit that Americans are more comfortable doing business with European cultures for obvious historic reasons. We share many cultural similarities. Our own cultural strategies are uniquely our own. But they do not transplant well. We have had problems in Europe, too. Peters states that European trade relations have not been as smooth as they should because we refuse to learn other languages and are too impatient. Peters believes that the total, radical contrast between Asian and United States cultures, the whole world view, has exacerbated our differences to a degree far more serious than problems with Europe and have hurt our ties with that area. He labels the inability of Americans to understand Asia's cultures the largest stumbling block to healthier trade relations.

A Hong Kong businessman is quoted as saying,[6] "You Americans have to realize that we do not need you. To succeed in Asia, you need us." Columnist Ina Corinne Brown further supports these views when she quotes Carlos P. Romulo, former President of the Philippines, as saying:

> "It makes little difference whether the penguins of Antarctica know anything about the squirrels of Rock Creek Park. But it makes all the difference in the world whether the American people understand the crowded millions who inhabit Asia. Your destiny, Asia's destiny, the world's very survival, may depend on such an understanding on your part."[7]

Our business interests in the nations of the world depend upon understanding other cultures. The preceding views pose serious challenges to America's business community. Some serious people accuse us of being insensitive to other cultures. We are shocked to discover that this view of Americans is shared by most of the world's people.

A FOREIGN ADVANTAGE

Whenever foreign business persons voice their opinions about America's trade imbalance and lackluster competitiveness, they unfailingly list our ignorance of other cultures as the prime culprit. Some use this line of reasoning to hide their own protectionist policies, but the charge is voiced too often and in too many private settings by too many people who want to see us improve our international market penetration. Those who have worked in the international sector for any significant length of time affirm the relative authenticity of the charge. Our lack of basic geographical and cultural insights is often shocking.

In 1981, a company that was a client of mine decided to hold a seminar in the Philippines for its Pacific Basin distributors. When this plan was reported to the home office, the college-degreed, international vice-president asked the question: "Where's the Philippines?"

Again, in 1987 I accompanied the vice president of another client company to a luncheon where the Ambassadors to the United States from six Asian countries spoke. Each Ambassador emphasized that Americans operating at the international level lacked basic cultural knowledge. As we left the meeting, I sought my client's reaction. He retorted, "I tell everyone that *culture just is.*" I was stunned! He had not understood the Ambassadors.

Our predicament is increasingly recognized throughout our own country. The head of an American executive search firm cites the need to develop what he calls "global executives" in an article in the Houston Chronicle:

> "...and nowhere is an eroding comparative advantage more evident than in the case of the American executive, who as a senior manager of a multinational corporation, must often compete against the superior international prowess of a for-

eign-raised executive who is well-versed in dealing with a variety of cultures." [8]

America's cross-cultural illiteracy extends far beyond the business community. It afflicts our political leadership as well. An example of our political ineptness surfaced in Seoul, Korea, in August, 1990, when the Asia Foundation sponsored a seminar for the Pacific nations' Attorneys General. America's Attorney General angered his foreign colleagues by walking out after his presentation. As one of the Asian participants told me, "He did not stay to hear what others had to say." He left the conference without notifying the organizers or recognizing the common courtesy of apologizing to the other conferees for his sudden departure, further exacerbating the situation. The incident reflected negatively on America.

We have all made such mistakes, even in our own culture. Of concern is that such incidents can be detrimental not only to business interests but also to American political interests. For while business and government may be viewed as separate spheres of activities in the United States, they have a singular impact at the international level.

America's international business influence wields great impact on the global economic order. This fact is sufficient incentive for business persons to acquire a high degree of cross-cultural literacy. The foreign interests of our nation's business community preceded the current democratization movements around the world. A culturally literate business community can have a positive impact on both its own interests and those of the world community at large.

The world's marketplace possesses more cross-cultural contacts than any other sphere of human endeavor. Here images and views of people from other societies are formed and reformed for good or ill. It is important for the business person to understand that his or her mission may be specific in its intent; but every foreign business relation has a serious ripple effect on all other economic, social and political aspects of the involved nations. This should be highly sobering to all business people.

We can meet the challenge. America's corporate sector spends millions on helping employees upgrade their personal and relationship skills in a variety of areas. There are seminars on stress management, human relations sensitivity, goal setting, motivation, and many other topics. Corporate America has recognized that these human relations skills are as important as technical ones when realizing productivity and profit. We are a nation of people who have painfully realized that even such seemingly natural and taken-for-granted skills as parenting and marriage need special attention. If these basic human relations areas are in need of special schooling, how much greater the need for cross-cultural training or cross-cultural engineering? (Engineering used in this context refers to the act or acts of skillful or artful maneuvering in another culture.)

Cross-cultural literacy training is important for a number of reasons: *First:* if we do not improve, we could face the gradual eroding of our global economic leadership which will have significant implications. *Second:* there is overwhelming evidence that a high degree of cultural literacy is necessary for conducting what could be characterized as the maximization of a company's international business goals in the world's market place. *Third:* a high degree of cross-cultural literacy is critical to our nation's political leadership on the world stage.

Effective cross-cultural engineering skills promote the ability to understand and interpret the most important cultural features shaping the thoughts and actions of foreign business associates, in other words, those differences that so often mystify us. We must not only understand these differences, but also appreciate them. We can best appreciate another's way of life if we know the historic context of their most basic cultural patterns. That knowledge should allow us to accommodate or maneuver our American thought and behavior accordingly. Such cross-cultural "adjustment" is an essential prerequisite to good communication and personal acceptance, conditions vital to any business interest.

But where does one begin? There must be a starting point. There is no detectable gene that equips one for cross-cultural understanding. We know that cultural knowledge is not a virus that one can catch by "having been there." Just walking the streets of other people's towns and cities, breathing their air or haggling over prices with merchants does not provide us sufficient information to sketch a decent outline of their culture.

Essentially, we must know what a culture is and of what it is comprised. We Americans learn from our elders a whole set of "do's and don'ts" that govern our behavior in a whole variety of social settings. Some are understood, some are not; some are accurate, some are not. Our culture, as any culture, is composed of a thick and complex pattern of meanings. We tend to watch and ask others to either affirm our definition of correct behavior or to define it for us. The discussion of our own cultural views, our codes or meanings, can comprise a good part of our daily conversations. Such encounters serve to culturally transform us.

More than a few people have been ushered out a company's back door for failing to understand the prevailing culture. A good friend, who is also a well-trained environmental engineer, recently called to inform me that he was fired from his Dallas-based company. He was told that he "did not fit in."

It is likely that many of us have had at least one experience of "not fitting in," which is a slang expression for "one does not share the world views held by the rest of the group". We all have a perspective, or point of view, as to acceptable behavior in all kinds of social situations, such as family, friendship, government, religion, business and so forth. To understand other's views of this same type of social construction, we need something that allows us to put our own views and commitments in neutral. We need a unique way of looking at other people's cultures.

THE CROSS CULTURAL PERSPECTIVE:
WHAT IT IS AND WHAT IT DOES

The cross-cultural perspective developed here is a way of effectively viewing and thinking about cultures. Most people have their own perspective on culture. Every business person, tourist, and government official leaving the United States carries a set of images about the people to be visited that act as a "lens" for interpreting what they see, hear and feel.

These images are often inaccurate because the lens is flawed. The recent movements to affirm minority rights have made Americans aware of how easy it is to view others through flawed lenses, whether speaking ethnically, racially, religiously or of gender. By using such flawed viewing devices, we create and maintain distorted images or stereotypes of others. Such images or stereotypes compose one's perspective of another group. Business people too often enter the international arena with "flawed cross-cultural lenses" and operate on the basis of distorted images of those other people upon whom their success or failure is determined. The lens is shaped by rumor, innuendo or media based on similarly blemished information. We err profoundly when we register experiences while working in one foreign culture and expect those experiences to be universally applied.

American business persons *need to be equipped with the tools necessary for better understanding another people.* These tools are analogous to a blueprint or template for more accurately assessing how members of another group view themselves and their world. *This cross-cultural device provides an American with a resource to demystify any culture, thereby developing a better grasp of one's business associates.* As Clifford Geertz states:

> "Understanding a people's culture exposes their normalness without reducing their particularity. (The more I manage to follow what the Moroccans are up to, the more logical, and the more singular, they seem.) It renders them accessible; setting them in the frame of their own banalities, it dissolves their opacity." [10]

For our purposes, it may be more effective to think of culture as the main focal lens of the device to define culture as: *those sets of meanings, codes, or symbols which reside in the minds of a people and serve to interpret the world.*

Through this lens one can see culture as a tool with which a people build reality. A person's concept of reality is a gift of their culture. Everything a person believes, feels, and thinks is a product of culture as we have defined it here.

Sketching a reasonably useful cultural portrait includes the ability to filter out what is not culture. Since culture is a set of meanings in the heads of a group of people, it follows that foods, for example, are of peripheral interest.

Traditional folk dances, on the other hand, may enhance one's cultural knowledge. The value of traditional dances, if they are in fact traditional, is found in their substance—not the loveliness of the dancers. It is more important to ask what meanings or codes a dance is attempting to communicate. Mexico's *Ballet Folklorico* reflects a series of regional cultural traditions that deserve attention for understanding regional cultural variations. Most cultures have similar productions.

These examples show how a very tight notion of culture can serve one's quest to more correctly understand another culture. It significantly clears away the conceptual debris to think of culture as a set of meanings or codes in people's minds. Culture, in this strict sense, is analogous to a computer software's source code. It programs people's thought and behavior and explains most basic human behavior. We should understand that our cultural codes are so deeply embedded in our psyche through the learning process that we act very unselfconsciously in most situations. We laugh, cry, recoil in horror, grieve, greet others, and act out our family, political, religious, economic and social lives as though all was natural, or instinctive. Because culture is so indelibly etched at the deepest recesses of our minds, every group argues that their view of reality is the ultimate one.

This use of culture leaves items such as tools, houses, paintings, books, and all other human output in a separate category as products of culture; not culture in the qualified way used above.

To view culture as a complex, dynamic and fairly fluid type of program, as opposed to reducing the concept of culture to a tangible product, is essential. One can rarely grasp it totally. People are constantly exploring new ways to cope with their specific social situation, so there are always additions, changes, and manipulations of the general rules. About the time you believe that you have a significant grasp of another people, you will meet one whose views of their culture force you to adjust your understanding.

This specific idea of culture is the most critical tool to have when attempting to understand a people's way of life – even our own. In the same way we use the aids of microscopes, telescopes, binoculars or spectacles to see the physical world more clearly, we need a clarifying tool to enable us to more accurately focus on another people. To continue the optic analogy, it is the basic focal lens of the cross-cultural perspective that helps one to construct a more accurate cultural portrait.

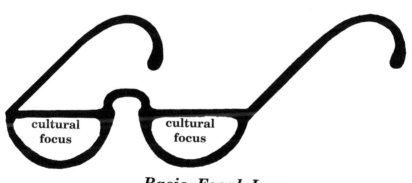

Basic Focal Lens
For Demystifying
Other Cultures

This concept is borrowed from the writer Richard Critchfield.[11] He rightly argues that non-academics seeking to operate cross-culturally are engaged in sketching a portrait of a culture.

The more accurate one's portrait of another culture, the more profitable his or her relationships in that culture.

Americans, whether engaged in business, government or other endeavors, need not take a back seat to any other people in cross-cultural understanding. Given the current world global economic incentives combined with the proper tools, we can compete with any people. It is hard to grasp something as traditionally elusive and complex as culture, if the idea is conceived and used in broad and amorphous ways. A proper perspective is necessary to mentally create a useful portrait of any culture.

American business people with any significant experience abroad are usually aware of how cultural differences affect their company's business posture. Sadly, we often fail to do our homework and stumble over important cultural differences in a painful way. A junior executive of a leading Texas company traveled to Japan with one of his company's attorneys who happened to be female. The legal profession has not yet permeated Japanese culture as much as it has in America. Had this executive more fully appreciated the nuances of Japanese culture, the business situation could have been dealt with more effectively and diplomatically. A great deal of face is lost by bringing an attorney into the fray, especially a female. The female, as yet, does not hold an acceptable role in the Japanese market place in comparison with America. The executive did not do his homework! He had only made a few trips to Japan and became, "abra kadabra", an instant expert.

There are numerous ways a good cultural portrait serves a company's international operations. *First,* and foremost, a more accurate understanding of our foreign business associates increases the probability of smoother cross-cultural personal relations. A company's success and profitability can be adversely affected by the lack of attention given to these issues. For example, if one understands what another person believes about critical aspects of life, then one can more successfully anticipate that person's responses to a number of real life situations. This is true whether that other person be a wife, parent, business partner or customer.

One can also measure one's own actions in order to get the most profitable response from one's counterparts. For example, the relationship between a secretary and a manager can be enhanced by the secretary's knowledge of the manager's style of management and his typical reactions to various situations.

Second, a good cultural perspective provides the business person with a mental guide for framing questions that will lead to a more accurate cultural portrait and not merely learning about the best restaurants or shops.

Third, a good perspective enhances one's ability to more clearly understand one's own culture, a useful by-product that also contributes to a more accurate understanding of others.

Fourth, a more accurate understanding of others allows one to experience being at relative ease in another culture. There is no need to operate in anxiety or to experience undue cultural shock. One can see and hear things previously hidden and place them in a meaningful framework.

One can be invested with a confidence inspired by a good grasp of the culture in which one has to work. A good cultural perspective equips one to paint a more accurate and useful portrait of another culture. International business becomes far more productive. The mystery most business people speak of is dispelled! A good cultural perspective can "demystify" those cultures about which one may not be familiar.

SUMMARY

Business people need a tool that overcomes past deficiencies and enables them to efficiently discover the most critical characteristics of a foreign culture. Using the optic analogy of spectacles (see page 13), the basic tool for focusing on others and subsequently building their cultural portrait, is a cultural perspective whose main focal lens is a definition of culture that directs one's attention to the cognitive symbols of a people. This perspective equips one to better understand any other culture.

The use of the cultural perspective as set forth is dependent on several preconditions. First, a cultural perspective is useful only if one approaches another culture with a posture of ignorance which is a learner's attitude. Second, it must be recognized that our own culture has a number of elements that too often prevent us from understanding others, in spite of our best intentions. These impediments should be acknowledged and managed. The recognition and knowledge of their role in distorting our cultural perspective is the first step toward their management. This, then, is our starting point and the focus of *Chapter II*.

The conceptual schema starts by describing people as either modern or traditional in orientation, a very broad generalization but useful for orienting business people to a world of cultural complexity. These contrasts certainly should not be used to fuel anyone's feelings of cultural superiority, because there are none. We will see that traditional life styles are to be greatly admired and appreciated.

Chapter III presents the mental instrument that business people should use to sketch a more informed portrait of another culture, the key to understanding others or the cultural perspective. *Chapters IV* through *IX* explore the six foci or scenes that comprise this analytical instrument. The emphasis is on ways cultural histories can impact the behavior of our foreign business associates.

The many ways humans organize and codify human social relations is discussed in *Chapter IV,* including key organizational features of group life and why it is important for business people to grasp other people's basic social codes.

Chapter V provides a brief, critical orientation to the most prominent religious views. The chapter's most important contribution is to show the powerful and dramatic impact religious codes have on all other parts of a culture, especially non-Western cultures. It is very important for American business people to understand other people's religious codes.

Chapter VI explains why it is so important to understand how a people's physical and social environment (their habitat) has contributed to their present world view or culture. This is an aspect of a people's cultural history that is often neglected. For illustrative purpose, two case histories, The Inuit and The Japanese, are included in the *Appendix to Chapter VI*.

Chapter VII explores how a people's technological history molds particular world views and ways of acting and how beneficial it can be to understand these differences.

Chapter VIII sets out how non-Western cultures have historically solved their economic problems and explores ways in which these traditions might affect our current business relations.

Chapter IX traces how political cultures have evolved and examines ways these histories affect one's ability to do business in many traditional countries.

Time and space meanings uniquely permeate all aspects of human thinking and behavior. *Chapter X* describes some of the basic time and space differences one can encounter in business activity throughout the world.

Chapter XI concludes the presentation by stressing the features discussed in earlier chapters and presents some ideas for implementing the cultural perspective to develop more profitable cross-cultural relations.

In conclusion, it is important to re-emphasize that *Out of the Mist* is not another how-to-do-business book. *Out of the Mist* presents a perspective that is an augmentation to the mechanics of good business in enabling one to decode or to better read another culture. The most profitable business relationships result from accurately understanding others. The relationships built through a more accurate understanding of one's foreign business associates can compensate for weak business skills. Conversely, even if one possesses excellent business skills but does not accurately understand the other culture, a loss of market share and profitability can result.

Some of the cultural history material reported may seem to have little or no direct bearing on understanding contemporary peoples. Most people are products of the totality of their cultural history even though some traits have ebbed and others flowed. If one scratches the surface of anyone's present cultural skin the most critical features of the cultural past are revealed. For most non-Westerners that top layer of cultural skin may seem very thin. What we would agree to call a modern skin is only an alluring cosmetic. The modern European cultures certainly maintain allegiance to a deeper cultural tradition than Americans. The Japanese provide a good case of how some of the key features of modernism can be successfully blended with tradition. Traditional codes and views of the world still dominate human life on this planet.

The chapters of the book contain what may be considered exotic cases to exemplify certain cultural characteristics. These cases are used as illustrations of the issue at hand. There is sufficient research to cite in support of each case, and these enrich our overall knowledge of the world's people.

The main issue at stake for American business people is to remember that to accurately understand others, we must understand their cultural past. The future of our business endeavors may depend on it.

References Cited

1. Related to author by Faulk Landrum, Houston, Texas; a similar version found in Loyal Jones & Billy Edd Wheeler, *Hometown Humor, USA* (Little Rock, AR: August House Publishers, Inc., 1991), p. 127.

2. Paul Craig Roberts, "Problem Isn't Tokyo, It's Washington", in <u>Houston Chronicle</u>, Outlook Section, November 27, 1991, p. 10C.

The argument is presented that foreign acquisitions are high because United States government policies have made it impossible for Americans to finance. He states that "The 1986 tax reform bill greatly reduced real estate values by raising capital gains tax rates, by reducing depreciation allowances and by denying normal tax deductions to most investors... The subsequent collapse in real estate values wiped out loan collateral and impaired the capital of financial institutions. This, together with tougher regulations, has made it almost impossible for most banks to lend to risky high-tech ventures...The United States cannot compete because it has the wrong values. We punish success by overtaxing capital and rewarding failure with subsidies...In truth, we have become a nation of juveniles. Blacks blame whites, women blame men, unions blame management, business blames foreigners and politicians blame each other."

The data describing America's industrial decline is well reported, e.g.:

Ramon Bakerjian and Patricia P. Mishne, "A Whole New Ball Game", <u>Manufacturing Engineering</u>, Vol. 101, Issue 4, October, 1988, pp. 61-62;

Donna Brown, "The High-Tech Debate: Can America Keep Pace?", <u>Management Review</u>, Vol. 78, Issue 12, December, 1989, pp. 30-36;

Michael L. Dortouzos, et al, *Made In America* (New York: Harper Collins, 1990);

Clyde V. Prestowitz, Jr.,"Trading Places", *How We Are Giving Our Future to Japan and How We Can Reclaim It* (New York: Basic Books, 1988), p. 333f;

3. Lester Thurow, *Head to Head: The Coming Economic Battle Among Japan, Europe, and America* (New York: William Morrow and Company, Inc., 1992).

4. John Bartlett, *Familiar Quotations* (Boston: Little, Brown and Company, 1980), 15th Edition, p. 356.

5. Tom Peters, "Our Real Trouble Is, Asia is Asian", <u>Houston Chronicle</u>, Outlook, Section 4, July 31, 1988.

6.   Marlene C. Piturro, "How to Blow a Billion-Dollar Deal", <u>World Trade</u>, June/July, 1991, p. 56f.

7.   Ina Corinne Brown, *Understanding Other Cultures* (Englewood Cliffs, New Jersey: Prentice-Hall, 1963), p. 1.

See also an interesting, if somewhat caustic, article describing our claims to be country experts after a short time; John E. Ullman, "From Bubble Traveler to Country Expert: Knowledge, Ideology and the Conduct of International Business", Cheryl R. Lehman and Russell M. Moore, <u>Multinational Culture: Social Impacts of a Global Economy</u> (Westport, CT, 1992), p. 81f.

8.   George J. Donnelly, "Global Executives? America Doesn't Have Them", <u>Houston Chronicle</u>, September 25, 1989, p. 11A.

9.   George A. Ricks, *Blunders in International Business* (Cambridge, MA: Blackwell Publishers, 1993).

10. Clifford Geertz, *The Interpretation of Cultures* (New York: Basic Books, 1973), p. 14.

11. Richard Critchfield,*Villages* (New York: Harper & Row, 1981), p. 204.

Chapter II:
Obstacles To Cross-Cultural Understanding

It is one of the conceits of most people in highly mod-
ernized contexts that somehow what we do, if not
proper and good, is at least normal, reasonable, and
easily intelligible. The non-modernized parts of
human experience tend to be regarded as dubiously
rational and above all as exotic and bizarre.

Marion Levy

Most Americans would like to understand local customs and behaviors as they travel around the world. Our ability to understand others is crippled by lack of a useful *cultural perspective* and by *our own cultural baggage.* The most accurate cross-cultural decoding device is of little help if it is "fogged" by one's own cultural biases.

The destructive effect of American traits varies from culture to culture. There are several that tend to be our most universal impediments. Careful observation of a specific culture will enable a person to decide how seriously our traits impede the ability to form profitable relationships. Throughout the world the author's own experiences suggest that most foreign cultures have significant problems with specific American traits.

TRADITIONAL AND MODERN
CLASSIFICATIONS

It is essential to first show how so-called *traditional* and *modern* peoples differ.[1] "So-called," because these generalities obscure variations and nuances; and if applied too mechanically, these generalities can create the notion that all non-Westerners are *traditional* and, conversely, that all Westerners are *modern*. Japan and a number of other Asian populations certainly exhibit some basic modern world views while successfully maintaining their core cultural traditions. It will be necessary to view Japan and several other Asian communities as hybrids bridging modernism and traditionalism. There is no intention to either romanticize or demean non-Western cultures by labeling them traditional nor to elevate modernism to an undeserving pedestal of superiority. A variety of criticism can be leveled at current Western cultures, notably our own!

The ultimate value of any culture is in the eye of the beholder. There is no better way to conceptualize cultural differences in order to frame the conceptual playing field than to use traditional and modern as macro-level categories. Any concepts used to generalize about cultures on a global basis will be fraught with similar danger. For the purpose of sketching brief, useful portraits of another culture, it is helpful to think of a continuum where modernity is one ideal type and traditionalism is the other. The following describes these polarities as, first, differences in world views or mythic structures as they relate to interpreting the universe; second, valuing cultural change and defining progress; third, interpreting the future as open or closed; and fourth, defining self either communally or individualistically.

World Views/Mythic Structures

The *first* and most critical difference between a traditional and modern view of the world has to do with the myths used to interpret the self as the self relates to one's world. The term, myth, used in this fashion does not mean something is unreal as in "Alice in Wonderland". Instead, *myth refers to the symbolic images all people use for interpreting the world.* All human life is driven by such significant myths. Man, the culture creator, and man, the symbolic myth maker are one and the same.

Joseph Campbell, the foremost authority on mythology, believes symbolic myths serve four functions: (1) the *mystical,* which refers to the feeling of awe one senses in being part of the universe; (2) the *imaging,* which has to do with the way we picture ourselves in relation to the universe; (3) the *validating,* or imprinting, which means that every human being must reflect the rules or codes of a particular culture, and lastly; (4) the *guiding* function, that leads one through the various stages of his or her life in "health, strength, and harmony of spirit."[2]

Campbell points out that much of Western man's myths have not caught up with the late 20th century. In spite of this fact, however, it is still possible to characterize a modern view of the world for the present comparative purpose.

Modern myths paint a portrait of the universe as an intricate system of wheeling galaxies, composed of inorganic and organic matter operating according to orderly and mechanical laws of physics. Humans function as an integral part of the organic part of the universe. There is no mystical intrusion. Supernatural beings do not dabble in human affairs. Things are either organic or inorganic and behave according to natural law.

Traditional myths are quite the opposite. The world is limited to one's own village or region and everything in it is alive including rocks, hills, volcanos, trees and so forth. Human life is subject to the whims and desires of a pantheon of beings who inhabit everything, everywhere and in many dimensions.

Change and Progress

The *second* critical difference between traditional and modern peoples has to do with how change and progress are viewed. Moderns are relatively more innovative. This does not mean that traditionalists cannot innovate. It only means they generally prefer to think and act by reference to the past which is often beyond a Westerner's comprehension. Although most nations are composed of a mixture of modern, traditional and people on a continuum in between, it is still important to realize which mentality generally drives the cultural system. In traditional cultures most of the people intensely believe in most of their traditions. Deviation from traditional ways of thinking and acting are socially unthinkable.

Several examples can be cited. Despite years of rule by the Pahlevi dynasty which imposed Western culture on the people of Iran, many Westerners were surprised to find that the people of Iran were still deeply rooted to a traditional Islamic culture.

Also, a study of pottery makers in a Mexican village found that potters changing traditional designs were pressured to stop.[3]

And again, American agricultural agents after World War II tried to convince some of the Indian groups along the upper Rio Grande River in New Mexico to change the breed of corn grown for centuries. The new hybrid seed the agricultural agents were pushing produced more bushels per acre and would promote more efficient use of land and provide the Indians with a cash crop. The Indians reluctantly changed. Even after increased production was realized, the Indians returned to growing the old corn much to the chagrin of the agricultural experts. Investigation revealed that tortillas[4] made with the new corn did not have the *traditional* coloring or texture. So the Indians returned to growing the traditional corn.

Lastly, about this same time government agricultural agents tried to prevent Navajo sheepherders from overgrazing the land and to take up farming, thinking that it was more advantageous to the Navajos. The Navajos refused to change. The large herds of sheep represented a family's status and prestige in society. Economic considerations were less important than the social gains. One can also point to Africa and other parts of the world where herding is the basic economic operation. Western experts have tried time and again, in vain, to introduce a more efficient breed of cattle. Again, modern rationality collided with a cultural element that overrode the economic interest.

There is a vast repertoire of cases like these where traditional people refused to take their modern cousins' advice. The rejection had to do with historical Western imperialism, but most objections are driven by their own strong traditional beliefs.

Most of the world's cultures have traditional beliefs that override modernity. Religion, kinship, status and prestige and a host of other cultural ideas often dominate market concerns. *The profits of American companies abroad depend greatly upon their representatives understanding these critical differences.*

Viewing Life Constraints

Third, in contrast to moderns, traditional people believe their lives to be highly constrained. The world view is fatalistic. They do not believe they control their own lives. The future is limited and relatively closed. Studies reveal that people tend to believe there is even a limited amount of good. People who seem happier than others "must have stolen happiness from others."[5] During the Middle Ages, even Europeans, reflected this world view.[6] By contrast, moderns view life as unlimited and open, and this extends to all aspects of life.

Social Identities

Fourth, traditional people are extremely communal. People are thought of, and think of themselves, as members of a particular group and not as individual in the modern or Western sense.[7]

Summary: Traditional Versus Modern World Views

Traditional world views make modernization a difficult pill to swallow. To enter the modern mythical world, one has to significantly reject one's past. One must believe the future can be shaped. Moderns are future shapers. By contrast, traditional people operate from a view of the world that is limited geographically and whose elements are imbued with a force or life of their own. Therefore, there is an absence of innovation, a belief that life is narrowly constrained, and a socially communal identity. The grasp of the cultural differences between traditional and modern peoples should help one to understand why American business people have such difficulty understanding and communicating cross-culturally.

A few of the newly industrialized nations, such as Japan, Singapore and Taiwan, among others, do not neatly fit such a sweeping categorization. Some nations share traditional culture's emphasis on communal social organization, and to a significant degree, the view that the future is controlled by metaphysical beings. At the same time, however, these nations have adapted to the modernist's idea that the future can be shaped through innovation. They have made the adjustments between the two mythical worlds in order to create highly productive states.

Some may argue that America can be characterized as traditional, because it has a definite conservative base. Without denying that many pockets of what has been described as "traditional culture views" exist in America, it takes much persuasion to effectively argue that we are a traditional culture when compared with the world's non-Western people. Comparatively and generally, the cultural orientation that drives America is modernity, even though not all have climbed aboard.

THE LURE OF MODERNISM

American technology and our relatively high standard of living are not what non-Western traditional peoples respect about us. Most view what they consider *our wanton materialism, its associated secular world view and lack of order, to be our key liabilities.* How does this match with the flood of immigrants, legal and illegal, that enter the United States?[8]

First, many factors *push* people to leave their own country. The most notorious of these are: (1) population growth that places undue strain on the environment; (2) famine or scarcity of basic food stock; (3) war and political violence; and (4) a feeling of being trapped in a social or economic class due to a lack of family capital or educational resources in their own village or region.

These forces have created a "brain drain" for many nations. Many immigrants would like to return to their homeland if conditions were more favorable. Many illegal immigrants from Mexico and Central America enter the United States for short periods to earn and save much needed capital and then return home. Most immigrants retain extremely strong ties to their native soil.

What *pulls* immigrants to the United States? What do we have that's impressive to others if not our technology and "wanton materialism?" It is our notion of individual freedom, the opportunity to work and provide for one's family, and the acquisition of material comforts in a free market economy. These virtues are driving factors in pulling immigrants from the former Soviet Union, Eastern Europe and other parts of the world. While appreciating and desiring some of our technological creature comforts, the world's people are, by and large, not anxious to copy Western culture.

In our own midst, Native Americans are an example of a people who have not fully embraced Western culture. They learn enough to work the system economically but retain their basic culture core. One thing is clear: America is not a melting-pot. We are a very culturally diverse nation which poses problems and challenges.

Most Americans are unaware that other cultures around the world do not have as wide a range of cultural diversity as we do. Nothing illustrates this more dramatically than listening to Americans touring, living or working in a foreign setting. As the honeymoon period wears off, they critically lash out at everything that appears to be an infringement on what they view to be individual and democratic rights. People in traditional cultures do not share our views of "rights". Deviation from traditional norms are taboo and those who stray can receive harsh penalties. Exile from one's group can be an ultimate punishment in many non-Western groups.

The more we know about cultures the more evident it is that no society can be held together unless its people's beliefs, feelings and actions are significantly shared. In the daily traffic of human, economic, social and political activity, most systems cannot stand too much diversity. While the Civil War put the issue of nationhood behind us, America is now faced with creating a viable nation out of literally hundreds of different cultures. How much cultural diversity is possible? The future will provide the answer.

While we Americans struggle, most of the rest of the world still generally operates out of traditional values and views. Most of these are admirable. Noted anthropologist Henry A. Selby refers to non-Western villagers as those who

> "...still have those elegantly tailored manners that we might aspire to, but never achieve; the soft-spoken manner, the ritual greetings, the enormous care not to offend, the specially groomed vocal inflections to indicate every shade of respect, the kissing of the hands, and, above all, the gravity of manner that marks a man of respect." [9]

SOME VALUED TRADITIONAL CULTURE TRAITS

Social relations among non-Western peoples is far more formal than our own. Those in Asia may be the most formal. All non-Western cultures attend to more complex social amenities than Americans. Generally, simple business events are wrapped in a multitude of rituals, which most often pose problems for American business people. We are impatient people. Time is paramount to us. We want to go to the contract issues, sign the contract and leave as quickly as possible. We are not so savage as to ignore a few pleasantries, such as "Good to meet you, thanks for your willingness to meet with us, you have a lovely country and we always enjoy coming." But after a few minutes of this, we are ready to get down to the business issues at hand.

Why are we less formal in our social relations? It may well go back to our frontier days when people shed their European formalities and adopted a quick and easy simplicity in their relations. We eschewed the Old World class structures and maintained that all were socially equal. Behavior which "smacks" of elitism became repugnant and was the butt of jokes. Even though all Americans recognize contemporary class differences, the fact that all polls show the vast majority claim membership in a middle class, indicates that our past clings tenaciously to us. As much as American business people value what they consider a simple, straightforward approach to business, the bulk of the rest of the world does not. But this fact should not deter us. Foreign business cultures should be exciting challenges. The fact that we need to learn from other cultures should not minimize our strengths.

Honor, or *face,* is another important aspect of human relationships in non-Western cultures. Honor and face are greatly valued in traditional societies. On the other hand in modern American society, sarcasm and blunt criticism seem to be an increasing part of our culture. We have come to idolize the tough-guy approach, while most non-American cultures value unwritten codes which make such behavior unacceptable.

Asian cultures are extremely sensitive to "face and honor." An American executive lost his temper in a meeting of Koreans and chastised, albeit gently, the Korean senior manager of the group. It was highly embarrassing to all concerned and resulted in a needless rupture between the American and Korean companies. One may get away with overt expressions of temper in the United States, but it is not acceptable behavior cross-culturally. One does not embarrass a leader in front of his associates in non-Western cultures, nor is it acceptable in Western culture.

Non-Western business relations should always be structured to maintain the foreign associates' dignity and honor (status). In Latin America, male honor *(machismo)* is a central feature of life. Profitable negotiations result from allegiance to a great many signals that communicate respect for the other person. There is a reported case in Latin America where an American company expected their new employees, who were all college graduates from upper-class families, to put on work clothes to do some plant work as part of the training program. They were not able to get the new group to comply with the training program until a senior level staffer suggested having them wear white laboratory gowns, which recognized their status as educated elite rather than of common labor.

The business world at large is becoming more of a place where softness, sincerity, honesty and personal respect are the operating norms. The era of the ugly American is vanishing.

While the preceding has presented some important differences between traditional and modern cultures on a broad scale, Americans must be aware of some features of their own culture that tend to impede cross-cultural relations, whether business, political or social. The most notorious of these are: our ethnocentricism, radical individualism, offensive body language, too loud talk, impatience and bluntness.

AMERICAN ETHNOCENTRICISM

A brief focus on Western colonialism provides a good example of how our ethnocentrism drives us. The idea of *manifest destiny*, or the belief that we have a mission to Westernize the world, fueled Western colonial impulses. Manifest destiny drove and still drives religious missions. Few intelligent Americans consciously maintain any of the old *colonial culture*. While the general idea of colonialism may be odious to us, we still carry a deep seated belief in the superiority of our culture and communicate this in many ways, consciously or unconsciously, to other peoples. A review of the print media in non-Western nations shows that our current economic, religious and political expressions are often viewed by foreign peoples as a continuing form of colonialism. A majority of Filippinos viewed the American military presence in colonial terms. We also have similar problems elsewhere.

We still try to export our religious beliefs, ideas on feminism, politics and about everything else. No matter how justifiable these may seem to us as Americans, we are often insensitive to the concept that other cultures have equally strong feelings about their cultural beliefs and social patterns.

The difficulty in defining the world through the propitious view of our American cultural lens can be exemplified by the problems encountered by a group of church workers in Guatemala in the late 1960s. Some church volunteers entered a small village in the lowlands to improve local life. As they hunted for something to improve, they noticed that clothes washing took place on the rocks in a river below the village. This led to the idea of building a cinder block washhouse. The final building had three walls with basins attached to the walls. Water was pumped up the hill from the river. There was an opening ceremony and all was well. The Americans went on to another village happy with their accomplishment. When they returned a few weeks later, the new facility was abandoned. The women were again washing in the river. Research revealed that the washhouse was like punishment to the women. Children stand facing a wall for punishment. The new washhouse had the women facing a wall even though a sink was attached. Equally significant, observation of the traditional wash activity showed it to be a very important social event. Women faced each other while they worked which provided the opportunity to socialize. The new structure had destroyed the more important social aspects of washing clothes.

The washhouse case is only one example where modern, Western efficiency does not transfer. Efficiency in one cultural setting may not be efficiency in another. Things are never as they seem.

AMERICAN INDIVIDUALISM:
OUR NAVEL FOCUS

"It is not easy for Westerners to realize that the ideas recently developed in the West of the individual, his rights, and his freedom, have no meaning whatsoever in the Orient. They had no meaning for primitive man. They would have meant nothing to the peoples of the early Mesopotamian, Egyptian, Chinese, or Indian civilizations. They are repugnant to the ideals, the aims and orders of life, of most peoples of this earth." [10]

Our focus on the individual is another critical impediment to smoother cross-cultural relations. This focus historically dominates our world view. We tend to measure political, economic and social issues according to the premise of the individual. This idea is rooted in the beliefs of a personal God, an individual's responsibility to work out his own salvation, and the priesthood of all believers – all basic tenets of Protestant Christian theological thought. Millions of dollars are spent annually on psychiatrists and self-help books in order to discover our individuality. Americans are the world's supreme *navel gazers*.

While our radical individualism is a source of cultural pride at home it can contribute social unease and conflict abroad. Our individualistic world view makes it difficult to understand traditional cultures whose personal identities are tied to communal meanings, such as a member of a tribe, clan, caste, family lineage or other groups. These identifications are internalized as intensely as our own individualism. Ultimately, we tend to be uneasy with such group emphasis, while some foreign cultures find it difficult to appreciate our emphasis on the individual.

Our Western emphasis on the *individual* recently clashed with the *societal* focus of Singapore over the punishment meted out to an 18-year old American from Ohio for numerous acts of vandalism. The Singapore court ruled that he serve four months in jail and be given six "caning strokes". The case received national media attention in the United States and an appeal for leniency from President William J. Clinton. Many Americans felt that the punishment was too harsh. It is interesting to note Singapore's Prime Minister Lee Kuan Yew's retort to those who argued for leniency. He reportedly stated in a TV interview on the evening of April 12, 1994, that people in the East value a harmonious society rather than individual freedoms as expressed in Western society.[11] He noted that although America may be the most prosperous nation in the world, it is a society in chaos because of its emphasis on the individual rather than society as a whole. To argue his point, he cited rampant drug use in the United States, murders of several

Japanese students and several notorious American murder cases where the perpetrators went unpunished.[12] This case demonstrated America's radical individualism before the world. It should be noted that Singapore's views are generally shared by most, if not all, non-Western societies.

Americans find it difficult to understand the over-arching significance of a Chinese family lineage, the Japan-*ness* of the Japanese or the importance of family in Latin America. Such collective orientation is not strongly identified with the American tradition and does affect the shaping of an American's world view.

A recent national news special focused on the rise of teen gangs in Los Angeles. The reporter chose to focus on the Latino groups, since this ethnic population seems to dominate the growing gang culture in that area. In spite of the increasing number of murders and the high probability of their own death, gang members constantly referred to their gangs as their *familias*, and the sense of self plays a subordinate role to the gang as a whole. Death was not a significant deterrent to their gang activity.

Familia does not make sense from the vantage of Western notions of individualism, but *familia* is the basis of the Latin American cultural context. The Latino *familia* provides one's identity, and the individual is subordinate to it. Tragically, the traditional family organization no longer works successfully for Latino male youth in a Western environment like Los Angeles. So, as a survival technique, youth extend the family by the creation of peer member gangs. The individual's identity is subservient in this extended-family structure.

As American business people travel the world and see signs of modernization as evidenced by the embrace of capitalism and the rise of democracy movements, there is an unquestioned assumption that American individualism is part of the package. This does not seem to be true, although it may develop as such in the future. The Japanese, for example, have proven how one can modernize, develop a capitalistic system and still maintain traditional *communal* ways, even if Japanese society is controlled by a select group of bureaucrats, politicians and top businessmen. Many of the older Japanese are concerned about the changes they see in their youth (*shinjinrui*: the new persons).

Indeed, as Peter Berger notes, Asia has successfully resisted Western individualism.[13] The fears reported by Japanese elders about their youth's assertion of individual rights may be predictable generational fears. Some are probably telling Westerners what they want to hear; some may reveal some degree of real changes. While there may be some truth to the rumors of change, only time will tell. The older Japanese have been reflecting this concern since occupation days. It is difficult for non-Japanese to understand the communal power the idea of race has on Japanese. Many Japanese analysts claim it is akin to a religion.

As further evidence of how deeply the notion of communalism permeates non-Western societies, the Japanese view with suspicion those who live outside the nation's womb for any length of time. Native Japanese rank foreign born Japanese (*nisei*) very low. Men whose firms keep them overseas too long will have a difficult time being accepted at the home office. While working in Japan my Japanese friends have often warned me about associating too closely with *nisei*. They are not to be trusted. The Japanese culture maintains hard and fast boundary lines between those who are truly Japanese and those who are not.

In the United States many American Indian tribes living on Reservations use a *purification ritual* for those returning from a time within the white man's culture. Many traditional cultures have similar processes for their returning members. One must remove the contamination of the profane Western culture.

Are Americans immune from this attitude ourselves? Only by degree. American companies often voice concern that their foreign staff is becoming too foreign. Ironically, an individual American's identity is also derived from communal associations, although the social construct is very different. We each have different family, regional, religious, educational, social and professional group associations. Each biography is a unique collage of traits composing one's self-concept, as well as the social self for others to assess. These inherited elements have a powerful ability to propel, or not propel, an individual in the pursuit of individual goals.

Compared to the non-Westerner's communal identity, ours is focused on *the Self*. This becomes clear when we realize that our social position and identities are derived from personal achievement, not family or tribe. When Americans meet, they do not ask one another about family, clan or tribe. Rather, they ask about each other's work. When strangers meet, they attempt to determine each other's social position by first assessing attire and grooming. On the streets, in office buildings, at airports, restaurants, shopping malls or other places, we all carry culturally derived sketches of how people should look, be they students, business people, blue collar workers and so forth. These are never precise enough. There is always a degree of caution exercised until relative positions are determined. Americans have difficulty relaxing until a person's work status is ascertained. Once this is known, a whole set of characteristics come together, creating the stranger's social profile in our mind. As a rule of thumb one learns that by understanding a person's position in the marketplace, one can deduce education, income, general basic value orientation and, most important, social status.

By contrast, when members of non-Western and more traditional cultures meet, they seek to identify one's group – whether family, tribe or clan or in the case of Japan, one's company. These are important cultural distinctions.

American business people would be wise to grasp the communal attributes of their foreign associates and understand the behaviors expected in response. It is important to remember how modernity has changed the world. William Manchester reminds the reader of our European roots. He presents medieval man's world view as devoid of modern man's ego perspective. He further expands on this idea by stating "even those with creative powers had no sense of self",[14] and then continues:

"...that Noblemen had surnames, but fewer than one percent of the souls in Christendom were wellborn. Typically, the rest–nearly 60 million Europeans–were known as Hans, Jacques, Sal, Carlos, Will or Will's wife, Will's son, or Will's daughter. If that was inadequate or confusing, a nickname would do. Because most peasants lived and died without leaving their birthplace, there was seldom need for any tag beyond One-Eye, or Roussie (Redhead), or Bionda (Blondie) or the like.

"Their villages were frequently innominate for the same reason. If war took a man even a short distance from a nameless hamlet, the chances of his returning to it were slight; he could not identify it, and finding his way back was virtually impossible. Each village was inbred, isolated, unaware of the world beyond the most familiar local landmark...Their anonymity approached absolute. So did their mute acceptance of it.

"...Among the implications of this lack of self-identity was an almost total indifference to privacy. In summertime peasants went about naked." [15]

The distinctions in the way American and traditional people have historically viewed strangers and outsiders are important for business men and women to understand. Today, even in what is considered the best of relationships, Americans are still outsiders in the social network of our foreign business associates. The basic issue facing our foreign associates is generally, "How can this *stranger* (outsider) help us?" Or, "Of what use are they?"

Another important difference between America's radical individual focus and non-Western collectivities is that it is believed that with native ability, initiative and determination, an individual can accomplish anything. Even a school teacher named Lyndon B. Johnson from Cotulla, Texas, became President of the United States! On reflection, most Americans understand there are reasonable boundaries to doing whatever one wants, but the emphasis is upon individual achievement as opposed to group achievement.

Americans also differ from traditional people in their view of ethics and morality. Americans believe an individual is responsible for his or her behavior. Schools and other social institutions encourage individual responsibility. Children are encouraged to think for themselves. Our fears of being told what to do and how to think are deeply rooted in our frontier history. This has been a liability as well as an asset over the years. Every American community struggles daily with the conflicts between the rights of the individual versus those of the majority.

By contrast, traditional cultures pass judgment on individual behavior every day. Even in Japan, which is typed as a modern, capitalist country, one's company provides an ethical orientation which is tuned to conform to a national ethical ideal. Ethical conflicts between groups are not supposed to exist in Japan.

This contrast between American individualism on the one hand, and other nations' communalism on the other, gives rise to certain foreign behavior that exasperates us, as in the case of Toshiba selling sensitive submarine technology to the Soviets, product dumping and other "unfair trade practices".

It is difficult to understand the collective orientation of other cultures. Americans believe that individualism is intrinsic to the nature of the universe and work hard to export our individualism. The idea of *manifest destiny*, coupled with our financial resources, provide the fuel for this task. Americans view individualism as an important element in religion, feminism, capitalism and everything else. It is most difficult to separate these elements, so they all work to propel our ethnocentrism.

OUR OFFENSIVE BODY LANGUAGE

In addition to the difficulty of coping with our individualism, many traditional people have trouble adjusting to our body behavior. Too often our animations stifle business relations. For example, we tend to overuse our hands. Business people must learn to sit on our hands, if necessary, and consciously control the rest of our body movements. Too much bodily animation can cripple communication. Even though this issue is generally confined to Asian relations, a more subdued body posture can only help relations throughout the non-Western world.

More and more articles are published on the topic of the cultural meanings of body language, such as the use of the "A-OK" sign where the forefinger and thumb join to form an "O" and the other three fingers flag.[16] In many countries this is an obscene sign. To this day the author still blushes with shame at his own gaffe in Brazil in the 1960s. When leaving a meeting, he had difficulty finding his rental car, so a man was kind enough to help him. As he drove away, he looked out the window and to let him know that all was all right, he waved and threw the "A-OK" sign. Instantaneously, he realized his dastardly deed and turned beet red! A stupid mental lapse!.

In Thailand one should never touch anyone on the head. The head is a very sacred part of the body. And, no back slapping, no playful punches to the upper arm or pointing. It is wise to keep your hands to your side and forego the American tradition of touching others.

Circling the ear with an index finger means "crazy" in America and most European countries, but in the Netherlands it means you have a telephone call waiting. Generally, cheek stroking means one is considering a tantalizing offer in America, while in Greece, Spain and some of the other Eastern European countries it means "attractive." Elsewhere it signals one is "ill" and "thin." One must be careful.

The stare is another American trait that can make many foreigners uncomfortable. My father taught me to look another person straight in the eyes when engaged in conversation. It was the *manly* thing to do. Among some cultures this habit can be very discomforting. Asians have a keen ability of sweeping the environment with quick furtive glances, while acting nonchalant. The "downcast eyes" pattern is especially strong in Japan as a sign of respect, while Koreans view another's eyes as the key to the soul. The practice of "eye reading" (munchi) is a central feature of all human relationships in Korea and reflects the importance of intuition when dealing with others, a general Asian cultural trait. Staring is not appropriate in Latin America, either.

Our cultural predicament extends to our body language. One's business relations are better served by a calm and studied demeanor. Do not assume the universality of body signs. The cultural variations of body language are enormous. One should review the literature and ask one's foreign hosts for help in understanding appropriate behavior. If your work takes you to many countries, it is a good rule to adapt a more stoic, humble and less animated posture. Watch the locals and pick up cues for such culturally proper behavior.

THE WAY AMERICANS TALK

Not only are Americans generally too animated, we are some of the loudest speaking people in the world.[17] It is very annoying to other people. We will give foreigners the last and most authoritative word on any subject. We will do so at the slightest hint of interest on their part, or without a hint of interest. Americans have an opinion on everything and are not bashful about expressing it! It comes in the package with our radical individualism. It is a source of annoyance to our foreign business associates and to many of our fellow Americans as well.

An associated feature of our talkativeness is a general discomfort with periods of silence. Many American businessmen have given away the store during periods when their hosts were quietly pondering the situation. Americans hate silent phases and feel the need to "fill-in-the-blanks". We misread our foreign associates' periods of silence and too often move to fill the void with further business concessions. All we needed is a "zipper-on-the-lip". Sales consultant Ben Schlain reportedly stated that "Samson slew ten thousand Philistines with the jawbone of an ass, and every day thousands of orders are killed in the same way."

We not only need to bridle our passion to preach to others and live with periods of silence, but American business people would be well advised to speak in softer, slower tones. The softer the voice, the more serious the issue.

As Mark Twain said,

"Noise proves nothing. Often a hen, who has merely laid an egg, cackles as if she had laid an asteroid." [18]

Lastly, one should seek one's foreign host's opinion on subjects and issues and learn to cultivate a talent for listening.

IMPATIENCE AND BLUNTNESS

American *impatience* and *bluntness* are other traits that prove extremely destructive in most non-Western cultures. It is easy to get upset when appointments are broken or constantly changed. Some of the frustrations which all business people have experienced are situations such as:

You stand in one long line after another, often surrounded by crying kids. You get to your hotel to find you do not have a reservation, and the hotel is full; they never heard of you– *and you are a big wheel back home.*

This is just the tip of the iceberg when it comes to enumerating all the frustrating issues that one faces working cross-culturally.

Most important are the frustrations of working out a solid business transaction:

Everyone you meet claims to know all the right people. Each claims to be on intimate terms with the right people, so "do not worry." A potential foreign business associate once told me he knew the former president of the country. I exclaimed, "But he has been dead for many years." The man retorted, "I know, we talk with him every week." Of course he does. Initially, you believe all these claims. You want to get the job done and get home. You want to deal with the right people. Then you find out, painfully, that the arrangement was a big mistake. Nothing happens. No sales. No activity–only talk.

Yet, you had a solid agreement which included an extensive legal contract drafted by the highly-paid home office legal staff. You went over it carefully with the foreign seller, buyer, representative or distributor. They seemed to understand the agreement. But, bad things happen. Your shipment was short. Or, on products you are exporting, your foreign agent keeps wanting more commission. You find your competitor's specifications and prices on bid-winning documents look like yours, and you surmise that your foreign agent is leaking your work to the competitors.

And on and on it goes. At this frustrating point, most Americans *cut and run*, labeling foreigners as crooks, liars, cheats or all of the above.

Usually, most problems are simple cross cultural misunderstandings. To non-Westerners legal contracts are not very important. Relationships are everything. The spoken word is more valued. Questions for non-Westerners are means of probing to determine areas of agreement so as to avoid conflict. Non-Western business people generally feel that it is rude to go directly to issues of disagreement.

Next, you came to make a deal. Your boss is expecting *results*. Your foreign hosts want to build a relationship, our usual American dilemma. If foreign relationships are not solidly built over many years, all the other bad things happen. However, you have to return and face the boss with something more substantial than "a relationship." Understandably, due to a different concept of time and a knowledge of American impatience, many contracts are signed as the American business person is being escorted to the airport to catch the return flight home. One cannot go home a failure.

In the midst of all the frustrations of working in another culture, it is important to bridle one's irritation and frustration. To show anger is to reveal a lack of maturity and social grace. It results in a loss of respect from those who observe the behavior. A lively sense of humor and the ability to laugh at oneself are perhaps two of the most important traits a good internationalist could have. Corporate executives who are greatly impressed with their position in life and take themselves too seriously have difficult times abroad.

Finally, let me offer an example of patience. (It also illustrates the degree of commitment one must have to do business cross-culturally.)

> A friend contracted to raise some funds in Asia for an American medical venture. Among the potential investors was one he had never met but had heard of his fabled wealth. He arrived in the particular country and called the man's office for an appointment. He waited several days but did not receive a reply. Finally, one morning he showed up at the office when it opened at 8:30. He waited all day. No meeting. He went back for six working days. He sat in the waiting room all day. On the afternoon of the sixth day, the executive secretary came out of the inner sanctum, looked at him for a few moments, then stated, "You are not going away, are you!" My friend replied, "No, Ma'am." She replied, "Then come on in, he is on a phone call from Hong Kong and will talk with you."

My friend got his appointment and carried out successful negotiations. That is the patience of Job, the kind that is needed to conduct profitable international business.

SUMMARY

In summary, this chapter first described, in a broad fashion, the essential differences between what has been labeled traditional and modern cultures which allows for a useful classification for the business person. Second, some traditional cultural features were noted for their superlative quality. Third, several American cultural features that inhibit good cross cultural relations were discussed. One can think of others, as well as nuances to those already put forth. Exceptions can always occur. It remains true that the traits mentioned not only impede the development of a useful cultural perspective, but they also cripple our international business relations and reduce profits. If these American cultural traits can be sufficiently muted or neutralized, then one can build more intimate, hence profitable, cross-cultural relations.

In the next chapter a useful cultural perspective will be set forth to expand on the idea of culture and to describe a set of cultural scenes as they comprise a useful instrument for viewing other cultures.

References Cited

1. Throughout this book modernism and capitalism are used interchangeably because they generally refer to the same Western industrial-technological tradition.

First: it should be noted that modernism and traditionalism have become repugnant to some anthropologists as a means of describing cultural distinctions in the belief that they are redolent of elitist ethnocentrism by Westerners. Any conceptual apparatus can be abused and/or lose its analytic function. These terms are used as I believe they can serve the purpose of showing what is admittedly a very high level generalization of differences. At the same time it is important to work at sanitizing these ideas from past abuses. If it means anything, I have a greater respect and appreciation for traditional social systems than those modern. If one were to be about the serious analytical business of seeking further anthropological insights, other terms could be used, but none are free from significant problems. None are utopian.

Second: Peter Berger, *Capitalist Revolution* (New York: Basic Books, 1986) has a good treatment of modernity versus traditionalist peoples in his discussion of the cultural aspects of Capitalism.

See also Joseph Campbell, *Myths To Live By* (New York: Bantam Books, 1973), p. 221f.

Third: some believe that the 1970s introduced a "post-modernist" era, although there is disagreement as to its meaning; as there is with the modernist label. Briefly, post-modernism challenges modernism's stress on absolute truth, the belief in linear progress, and other such ideas. Post-modernism emphasizes heterogeneity and differences. For the best treatment of this issue, see:

David Harvey, *The Condition of Post-Modernity* (Oxford: Basil Blackwell, Ltd., 1989). For example, Harvey sees post-modernism regarding flexible modes of capital accumulation, the demise of Fordist production (based on economies of scale) and the rise of current "just-in-time-production" (economies of scope), the dominance of "image-building" in all aspects of life, products, companies, and even American presidents and other politicians.

Dorothy S. Cobble, "Organizing the Post-industrial Work Force: Lessons from the History of Waitress Unionism", Industrial & Labor Relations Review, Vol. 44, Issue 3, April, 1991, pp. 419-436.

Wolf V. Heydebrand, "New Organizational Forms", Work & Occupations, Vol. 16, Issue 3, August, 1989, pp. 323-357.

Jorge R. Schement,"Porat, Bell, and the Information Society Reconsidered: The Growth of Information Work in the Early Twentieth Century", Information Processing & Management (UK), Vol. 26, Issue 4, 1990, pp. 449-465 tests post-industrial premise by analyzing United States work force during 20th century and finds the information sector started expanding in the 1920s.

Jack C. Stabler & Eric C. Howe, "Service Exports and Regional Growth in the Post-Industrial Era", Journal of Regional Sciences, Vol. 28, Issue 3, August, 1988, p. 303-315.

Lester Thurow, *Head to Head: The Coming Economic Battle Among Japan, Europe, and America* (New York: William Morrow and Company, Inc. 1992).

Lester Thurow, "The End of the Post-Industrial Era", in Business in the Contemporary World , Winter 1990, p. 21. Business people would be wise to familiarize themselves with this philosophical discourse.

2. Campbell, op. cit., p. 221f.

3. George Foster, *Tzintzuntzan: Mexican Peasants in a Changing World* (Boston: Little, Brown and Company. 1967), pp. 293-310.

4. Tortillas are a thin, round, unleavened bread prepared from ground corn.

5. Foster, op. cit., pp. 293-310.

6. J. Huizinga, *The Waning of the Middle Ages* (New York: Doubleday Anchor, 1956), pp. 9-55, especially pp. 37-38.

See also William Manchester, *A World Lit Only By Fire, The Medieval Mind and the Renaissance* (Boston: Little, Brown and Company, 1992).

7. Peter Berger, *Capitalist Revolution* (New York: Basic Books, 1986)

8. Our biggest wave of immigrants occurred between 1900-1910, with nine million Europeans. Europeans comprised the largest immigrant population during 1900-1960. Since the 1960s the move has been dominated by Latin America, especially Mexico (42%), with immigrants from Philippines, Korea, China and India gradually reaching approximately 41% in the 1980s. Source: Susan Weber, *USA by Number, A Statistical Portrait of the United States,* (Washington, D.C.: Zero Population Growth, Inc. 1988).

9. Henry A. Selby, *Zapotec Deviance* (Austin: University of Texas Press, 1974), p. 4.

10. Campbell, op. cit., p 61.

11. Robert Benjamin, "Singapore Official Lashes America for Opposing the Caning of U.S. Teen", <u>Houston Chronicle</u>, April 13, 1994, p. 2A.

12. Berger, loc. cit.

13. Ibid.

14. Manchester, op. cit., p. 21.

15. Ibid., pp. 21-23.

16. For a good compilation of cross-cultural behaviors, see:

Roger E. Axtell, *Do's and Taboos Around the World* (New York: Wiley and Sons, 1990);

Desmond Morris, *Body Talk: The Meaning of Human Gestures* (New York: Trade Paperbacks, 1994).

17. Edward T. Hall, *The Hidden Dimension* (Garden City, NY: Anchor, Doubleday & Company, 1969), p. 142.

18. Paul M. Zall, editor, *Mark Twain Laughing* (Knoxville, TN: University of Tennessee Press, 1985).

Chapter III:

The Cultural Perspective

"Culture is a discussion begun long before we arrived on the scene...we enter the conversation as best we can, add something to it if we can...and it continues after we die.

– Kenneth Burke

As Sophia, the delightfully saucy "gran'ma" on TV's Golden Girls would say, "Picture this...the year was 1961," and I was in Monterrey, Mexico. The nights serenaded me with a cacophony of barking dogs, braying burros, quarreling cats, snorting and coughing trucks, and now and then the soft whispers and giggles of couples as they walked past my bedroom window adjacent to the street. As daylight began to pierce the night, I was awakened by the melodic and rhythmic creaking of machines making tortillas next door, together with strange aromas! Thirty years have passed and I can still hear, smell, and see this scene. Memories such as these repeat themselves in dozens of countries. I also remember my feeling of ignorance about all that was happening around me, and of fighting waves of panic from time to time. *How does one make sense out of all this foreign stuff?*

BUILDING A USEFUL CULTURAL PERSPECTIVE: THE NEED FOR A SKEPTICAL MIND

The answer lies in having a useful conceptual tool or device by which to view and grasp all those strange sights, sounds, and smells. First, one must be extremely skeptical of information about others. *One must always check, validate, or legitimize other people's views about the common, everyday life of a people.* A healthy dose of skepticism has a critical leavening effect upon any final cultural portrait.

We have all found that what people say about others is often biased. What people say they do and what they really do are often very different. The scientific *debunking motif* is a critical part of any tool that attempts to sketch a portrait of another culture. One must be extremely careful in accepting common, taken-for-granted, everyday assumptions about what is "real," what a people are really like. Self interest or lack of verification characterize most reality statements. For example, colonial history reveals how gullibly new settlers or political appointees accepted their countrymen's ideas of the natives whether British, French, American or others. "Ah, the only good Indian is a dead Indian," or Chinese make good laundrymen, and so on.

There exists a general pattern of maintaining false ideas of others that can be captured in a story about a fictitious American firm, which we will call **RWB** (**R**ed, **W**hite and **B**lue) Inc. **RWB, Inc.**, has offices in many countries around the world. As new staff arrive in these countries, an old **RWB** country hand (to be referred to as "Old Hand") meets them at the airport and helps them get settled in an apartment and adjusted to the office. In the process "Old Hand" passes on all of his cross-cultural knowledge about the indigenous population derived, in turn, from a previous "Old Hand" who received it from a previous "Old Hand", and so on.

Our "Old Hand" too often passes false or inaccurate images from one group to another. These ideas take on a life of their own and become holy writ. Unfortunately, cultural analysis is not part of new staff's training at **RWB**. As the new **RWB** staff settle in the host country, they become encapsulated in an American community through office staff, community clubs, and various associations and such. "Old Hand" does not seek new views and, when offered, rarely accepts them. All an "Old Hand" needs to say to refute new views is: "I have been here for 100 years and that is just not true." The conversation is over.

While speaking of "Old Hand", note how the length of "time-in-country" creates a "nested hierarchy" of rank-relationships. The old timers can effectively suppress new views with a simple look of disapproval, a wave of the hand, a smirk, or condescending laughter.

A first-time contact between business people working internationally is also very predictable. After the usual amenities the next step is to determine how long each has been working in the particular country. Or, how many trips one has made to the country. Few enjoy being an outsider, so everyone swaps lies. On their second trip to a country a man might say, "Oh, I'm in and out of here all the time." They claim to have made dozens of trips. This pattern is repeated every day and in every country around the globe.

Now, let us challenge this by asking: what does the amount of time in a geographical locality have to do with cultural knowledge? *Is an accurate cultural portrait totally dependent on time spent in a country?* Not really. One can live a lifetime in a foreign country and not accurately understand the local culture.

THE CULTURE CONCEPT: THE MAIN FOCAL LENS

In addition to having a healthy sense of skepticism, the centerpiece of a good cultural perspective is a sharp concept of culture, the *main focal lens*. For our purpose, culture will be restricted to the shared internalized symbols, myths, meanings or codes that fashion reality for a particular people. It should be the concern of every business person to grasp the basic outlines of these symbolic webs, whether working in Russia, Nigeria or any other country.

Cultural anthropology emerged in the late 19th century with the aim of applying the scientific view and its methods to that elusive phenomenon referred to as culture. A dispassionate scientific view replaced historical ethnocentric ones. Humans were classed as animals characterized by two feet, two arms, a head and the use of complex tools. We communicate in a reasonably complex manner through a sound matrix called *language* and have a finite number of ways of organizing ourselves in order to fulfill such basic needs as acquiring food, clothing and shelter; caring for the new generation; passing on the culture and maintaining an orderly, consensual, conflict-free society where all strive for the common good.

It is easy to see why we find some basic similarities in all cultures. Humans are physically alike and have the same basic needs regardless of the physical environment. The cultural dissimilarities are due to a particular group's responses to variations in the physical environment, and even those variations are not infinite in number. All humans depend on land, water, plants and animals. All must cope with natural, seasonal and life cycles. All must contend with aging, the mysteries of birth and death, dreams, sickness and natural disasters. Here's the key: *we cope with all these things through our culture constructing ability and not through our genetic codes.* This fact is not appreciated by everyone. Here is how cartoon character, Calvin of "Calvin and Hobbes", sees it:

> Cartoon comic figure Calvin remarks to Hobbes, his stuffed tiger companion, that "When a kid grows up, he has to be something. He can't just stay the way he is. But a tiger grows up and stays a tiger. Why is that?" And Hobbes responds by noting there is "no room for improvement!" After considering this astonishing fact Calvin, quite exasperated, exclaims, "Of all the luck. My parents had to be humans!" And Hobbes tries to console Calvin by saying, "Don't take it too hard. Humans provide some important protein." [1]

Calvin reminds us that learning one's culture is often a painful experience. No people respond by constructing exactly the same cultural responses or there would be no difference between them. People use this cultural ability to adapt to their environment. People of different classes, work groups, gender and so forth, create unique variations to their general system of symbols or meanings.

The composition of what is called culture has the following characteristics:

1) Symbols, meanings, codes and rules that are learned from others and shared with others;

2) The functions of these symbols, meanings, codes and rules screen and organize all sensory data;

3) Of paramount importance in culture is language, the richest or most extensive expression of a culture;

4) The adaptability to various physical environments which has been the key to humankind's success and survivability as a species.

The fact that culture is comprised of a set of symbols, meanings, codes, rules or myths learned and shared from others is fairly elementary and needs no further comment. Nor does the issue of language. However, it is important to understand culture's *screening* and *adaptive roles.*

Not only does culture screen all the various sights, smells, tastes, sounds and feelings, but it also organizes and classifies all that data! This is critical to understanding human behavior wherever observed. The organization and storage of information takes place on a set of mental *pegs* or *hangers.* These "meaning pegs" are group possessions and act to select and sort everything one sees, feels, tastes, hears and experiences.

Some of these pegs around which we hang experiences are variously labeled good, bad, dangerous, ugly, beautiful, father, mother, boss, funny and so on. Culture even defines humor. Try telling a Japanese an American joke and watch his reaction! Thud! And vice versa. A Japanese friend told me the following joke:

> "A yakuza (Japanese mafia member) and his subordinate arrived at their office in their Mercedes Benz. The yakuza's subordinate was too nervous to get out of the car, however. His boss shouted, 'Hurry up and open the car door.' The subordinate replied, 'But boss, there is a guy standing in front of our office.' The boss proudly replied, 'he is a guard, and he is our new employee, you fool.' " [2]

When the author has related this story to Americans, he gets a stunned, confused look each time. Obviously, one must understand the social context of the joke. Japanese view *yakuza* members as uneducated, dumb-muscle types. Hence, the theme of stupidity. The *yakuza* is constantly trying to outsmart the government's attempts to put them out of business. In this case the *yakuza* are shown putting up a business front in order to put on a respectable face. The business front and stupidity are significant themes of humor to the Japanese. However, these themes may be the same in many cultures, but the social contexts differ.

One's culture not only provides a mechanism for screening and interpreting all one's experiences, but it also supplies a powerful tool for exploiting the environment. Humans have used culture to carve a living from most environments of this world. This includes the harsh conditions of the polar regions, deserts and even short periods in outer-space. How efficiently they adapt is a critical issue today.

To think of culture as an adaptive device allows one to speak of the differences between cultures without falling into the language of better and worse, good and bad. This should be of great importance to all, especially business people.

The *adaptive capability* of culture allows people to build on past experiences by testing solutions to new problems which lead to a more efficient culture or a more efficient adaptive strategy. Humans have been characterized by discovering, often accidentally, new products, processes and ideas that totally revolutionize existing patterns of thought. We see this as groups move from hunting and gathering to horticulture, thence to intensive agriculture, and finally to current "high-tech age" modern systems.

Given the fact that culture is fundamentally an adaptive device uniquely used by humans to exploit their environment, this feature can be used to measure the relative efficiency of cultures without using denigrating language. During most of the 20th century we were inclined to compare and rank cultures politically and ethnocentrically. At first, we described groups as savage, barbarian or civilized. Eventually, as society organized itself into identifiable economic behavioral patterns, the vices of Capitalism and Marxism were contrasted and debated as to their relative societal benefits,[3]

Now, experts are engaged in a debate as to which form of capitalism is most successful – the democratic, free-market type represented by the West or the state-managed model developing in Asia. It is more useful to measure historical human adaptation by looking at the relative efficiency of one technological mode versus another.

The difference between cultures that practice a simple hunting and gathering technology to harness energy and other vital resources and that of irrigation and mechanized plow agriculture is well documented in development studies. Let us focus on the various technologies in harnessing scarce energy (energy=caloric units).[4] Through the technology of simple plow agriculture, more energy per acre or hectare of land is harnessed than through hunting and gathering technology. Further, there are varieties of plow agriculture modes – man, four legged beasts and machines. A farmer, using a tractor-pulled plow technology, harnesses more energy than does a simple plow pulled by a horse or oxen. The same observations can be made to energy harnessed per geographical unit using irrigation technologies relative to fishing and other extraction strategies.

The more efficient the technology in harnessing energy, the more people are freed from the pursuit of food production or other basic necessities of life so as to allow them to specialize in other endeavors. People can work at shoe making, political administration, religious activities and other specialties.

The efficiency of plow agriculture on the Great Plains of Europe and America fed the industrial and agricultural revolutions. The efficiency of technology is seen by noting the small percentage of the population currently needed to meet the agricultural food requirements of nations. In many parts of the world, more efficient rice irrigation technology also is utilized and dramatically shows similar effects. It is more useful to rank cultures by the efficiency of their technology than by the usual ethnocentric ways.

Discussion about the degrees of technological efficiency of cultures should also include an awareness that technologies are tied to environmental factors. An efficient system in one place may not be efficient in another. The simple plow is not useful in the tropical forest areas of the world, nor in rugged mountain terrains nor in most other environments; thus, the plow did not evolve in those areas. Technology develops in response to a group's need to make an environment yield its productive resources. All human populations have the potential for developing needed technology. One group is not more intelligent than another. Through much trial and error, the West has become more sensitive to the need to transfer "appropriate technology."

A LOOK AT CULTURAL RELATIVITY

What is the ultimate value of any people replicating experiences? Do all these material things make a people's existence more meaningful? The idea of meaningful is a highly elusive judgment. Given the environment of the polar regions, the Inuit evolved a very efficient technology for harnessing energy. Likewise, the indigenous populations of the Amazon region have successfully adapted to meet their needs. Are we to assume these people, and others like them around the globe, have been devoid of happiness and spirituality? Have they been sitting around waiting for cars, TVs and other items to provide their lives with meaning? Obviously not. Anti-modernizing sentiments are increasingly heard from Third World peoples. It is important to view and treat another's culture with great respect and appreciation, and a good cultural perspective should accomplish this goal for business people.

Business persons generally have a narrow focus on culture. They tend to focus only on the marketplace. Other aspects are viewed as irrelevant mostly because of the highly segmented complexity of our own culture and the uncertain grasp of the nature of culture. The concept of culture is a mental system that includes all aspects of one's existence. *No custom, belief or behavior, not even all that takes place in the marketplace, can be rightly understood if detached from its broader, and more complex, cultural context.* The marketplace, regardless of time and space, is an integral part of its indigenous culture.

A STRATEGY FOR ACCESSING CULTURAL MEANINGS

To accurately understand another culture takes more than an inquiring mind and a sharp definition of culture. We must have a strategy enabling us to access those symbols, myths or codes that comprise culture. We see what people are doing as they buy, sell, trade, pray, dance, cry, laugh and so forth. We also view things they have made, such as houses, cars and so forth. But, most important, we can ask people to explain the "what, why, and wherefore" of their daily activity. All this external evidence comprises the products of a culture. Such action is a people's response to their symbolic networks and provides us with important pathways to those webs of cultural meanings. In summary, another important element in a useful cross-cultural perspective is a strategy for *accessing culture. This strategy is to observe what a people do and what they produce and ask them for their interpretation of events and things.*

THE SEVEN CULTURAL SCENES

In addition to having a skeptical and inquiring mind, a concise concept of culture and a strategy for accessing culture, it is useful to organize all that people do into *seven cultural scenes.* A sharp definition of culture alone will not provide business people with a useful grasp of another culture. It is one thing to know what a culture is by definition. It is quite another to access the symbols of culture and to organize them in such a way as to effectively sketch an accurate cultural portrait of a people.

These seven socio-cultural scenes serve as *a second focal lens to be attached to our first lens which defines a cultural focus*

54

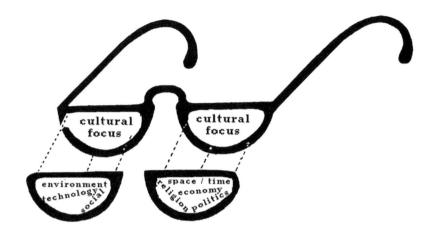

The Complete Cultural Reading Device

(see Chapter I, page 13). This is the second step in constructing our cross-cultural decoding device.

One can organize any group's *daily activities into seven scenes: social (kinship), economic, political, religious, environmental, technological and space/time.* If one carefully observes any people, a pattern or order to their daily activities will appear which, in turn, can be referenced to one of the seven cultural scenes. One can organize what one sees, hears and experiences into a meaningful picture, or portrait, that reflects the critical contours of a people's culture.

One must be careful not to prejudge the meaning of other people's activities because our assumptions are too often informed by our own cultural biases. It is essential to realize that any people's views of their society vary with their special social position, gender, race, ethnicity, class, age, and so forth. When a person is interpreting their culture, it is important to note their special position.

It is helpful to think of cultural codes existing in patterns. They are not randomly scattered about a cultural map. It is analogous to the way towns and cities cluster spatially on a map. Each cluster on a cultural map specifies ways of viewing and responding to the various scenic activities.

Life in the New Hebrides islands, for example, revolves around a "pig culture pattern". Families raise pigs, trade pigs, loan pigs (for interest, of course). Finally, when pigs are destroying the gardens and generally menacing the environment, the family gives a huge "pig feast" and destroys what may be the pig accumulation of a lifetime.[5] All social activity, for the most part, systemically revolves around pigs, thus creating a cultural cluster.

The more complex an economy, the more numerous the valued items. But all people rank objects in order of importance. The differences in valued objects, rules of access and distribution provide the substance for understanding different economic types of systems.

The cross-cultural perspective, our decoding device, consists of a specific notion of culture; a set of cultural scenes; a strategy for accessing cultural meanings which consists of observation; well-crafted questions and a healthy dose of skepticism. This mental device is the most useful way of viewing human activity. It allows one to paint an accurate and useful cultural portrait.

It is important to stress the idea of useful when talking of this cultural perspective. Business people do not need to have the same grasp of the contours of another culture as does an anthropologist. On the other hand, both are dependent upon accurately accessing a people's culture to do their respective work. The difference rests in the thickness of detail. Business persons need only sketch a group's basic cultural contours, while anthropologists seek intimate details that contribute to the body of knowledge in their discipline.

ASSOCIATED ISSUES

There are a number of issues that can impede accurate cross-cultural understanding. First, any portrait of another people is as accurate as one's social vantage points. The texture of a cultural portrait depends upon one's ability to sketch each scene from the various perspectives of class, gender, age, work unit and so forth. This may seem obvious, yet it is alarming how easily we make sweeping statements about another people when our experience has been with a small sample of elite foreign, middle-aged businessmen. This fact cannot be emphasized enough.

Second, one should always expect to find some degree of diversity and variance regarding rules and behavior. In his informative article, "Why a Perfect Knowledge of All the Rules One Must Know to Act Like a Native Cannot Lead to the Knowledge of How Natives Act", anthropologist Marvin Harris warns of the difficulty of easily determining a people's mental codes from observing behavior or, equally, of predicting behavior from a grasp of the mental codes.[6] This is true because every bit of culture, every *symbol*, has a great deal of variance. There are rules for breaking a rule and rules for breaking the rules that justify breaking the first rule. People in all cultures have a rationale, or rule, for every act, no matter how bizarre that act may be. These easily change as people innovate to cope with particular situations. Culture is not the neatly packaged and objectified thing we describe for others. One's commitment to a particular rule depends upon one's power relationship, the variance in age, gender, class, race, religious orientation and so on.

Harris' warning rightly underscores the difficulty of understanding another people, even our cultural selves. To glibly speak of knowing another people after a few visits or a brief sojourn is quite ludicrous. The author grew up along the Texas-Mexican border and has conducted research in the area relative to ethnic relations. Few Anglo-Americans raised along the border have a realistic cultural portrait of the Mexican culture. One South Texas rancher epitomized this dilemma when he explains the difference between Mexicans and Anglos by saying:

"If an Anglo and Mexican start digging a ditch together, the Anglo will outwork the Mexican the first few hours. After that, the Mexican will outwork the Anglo. Mexicans are born for such work."[7]

This is a cultural view easily labeled as an "inaccurate sterotype". An accurate cultural portrait is difficult, if not impossible, to sketch without spending time in a culture. But how much time is sufficient? One is always learning. Some are more perceptive than others, while some never learn much about their foreign associates. Others are just indifferent. Some business people just want to do their time and go back to the States. Others are driven by an insatiable curiosity and read everything they can get their hands on, talk with anyone who will talk with them, and generally end up painting a useful cultural portrait, and do so fairly quickly. Others work at it for years and cannot seem to sketch a very accurate cultural portrait of the local people. The amount of time needed to develop a useful cultural picture is difficult to specify and is dependent upon how well equipped one is.

The cultural perspective device offered in *Out Of The Mist* prevents a lot of confusion for those who would seek an accurate understanding of their foreign business associates. Too often business people land on foreign soil, see people in Western-style suits, operating out of Western-style offices, using what we consider to be Western gadgets and conclude that they are Westernized. It has often been said, "They are 'jest' like us." It happens around this world every day. This notion of being "like us" includes the assumption that they <u>think</u> "like us". This is a dangerous line of reasoning that results in the formation of an inaccurate cultural portrait. Inaccurate views of other cultures result in bad business.

There is the oft told story of the blind men who were asked to approach an elephant, touch it and define it. The first grabbed the elephant's tail and said elephants were like snakes. The second grabbed a foot and said elephants were like tree trunks. Other participants touched the elephant, each in different places, giving additional sketches of elephants, each accurate to the limited extent of what part of the elephant's anatomy was felt. Each one captured a piece of reality, not the whole. Similarly, for business purposes an accurate and useful understanding of another culture necessitates accounting for all its parts with all its scenes, systemically sketched from different social viewpoints.

This means that business people need to understand the basic codes that not only drive a group's economy but also its political, technological, religious, kinship, habitat and time/space dimensions.

Burke's conceptualization of culture observed in the epigraph that introduces this chapter probably came from Shakespeare's famous seven "Ages of Man".

> All the world's a stage,
> And all the men and women merely players:
> They have their exits and their entrances;
> And one man in his time plays many parts,
> His acts being seven ages. At first the infant,
> Mewling and puking in the nurse's arms.
> Then the whining schoolboy, with his satchel
> and shining morning face, creeping like snail
> Unwillingly to school. And then the lover,
> Sighing like furnace, with a woeful ballad.
> Made to his mistress' eyebrow. Then a soldier,
> Full of strange oaths and bearded like a bard,
> Jealous in honor, sudden and quick in quarrel,
> Seeking the bubble reputation
> Even in the cannon's mouth. And then the justice,
> In fair round belly with good capon lin'd,
> With eyes severe and beard of formal cut,
> Full of wise saws and modern instances;
> And so he plays his part. The sixth age shifts
> Into the lean and slipper'd pantaloon,
> With spectacles on nose and pouch on side,
> His youthful hose, well sav'd, a world too wide
> For his shrunk shank; and his big manly voice,
> Turning again toward childish treble, pipes
> And whistles in his sound. Last scene of all,
> That ends this strange eventful history,
> Is second childishness and mere oblivion,
> Sans teeth, sans eyes, sans taste, sans everything.[8]

References Cited

1. Watterson, Bill, "Calvin and Hobbes" cartoon, distributed by Universal Press Syndicate (Kansas City, MO: February 3, 1992).

2. Courtesy of Mr. H. Katayanagi, Tokyo, Japan.

3. Peter Berger, *Capitalist Revolution*, provides an excellent synopsis of this historical debate and its application.

4. Leslie A. White and Beth Dillingham, *The Concept of Culture* (Minneapolis, MN: Burgess Publishing Co., 1975); Leslie A. White, *The Concept of Cultural Systems* (New York: Columbus University Press, 1975).

5. Roy Rappoport, *Pigs for the Ancestors: Ritual in the Ecology of a New Guinea People* (New Haven: Yale University Press, 1968). Pigs have a wide range of functions on these islands.

6. Marvin Harris, "Why a Perfect Knowledge of All the Rules One Must Know to Act Like a Native Cannot Lead to the Knowledge of How Natives Act", in <u>Journal of Anthropological Research</u>, (Albuquerque: University of New Mexico), Volume 30, Winter, No. 4, pp. 242-251.

   In addition, Renato Rosaldo, *Culture and Truth: The Remaking of Social Analysis* (Boston: Beacon Press, 1989), p. 20; the author thinks of culture as "a more porous array of intersections where distint processes crisscross from within and beyond its borders," instead of some static system.

7. Don E. Post, *Ethnic Competition for Control of Schools in Two South Texas Towns?* (Las Cruces: New Mexico State University, Eric-Cress Press, 1975), p. 149.

8. Shakespeare, William, *As You Like It* (Act II, Scene 7).

Chapter IV:

The Social Scene

Society is immoral and immortal; it can afford to commit any kind of folly, and indulge in any kind of vice; it cannot be killed, and the fragments that survive can always laugh at the dead.

– Henry Adams

The headlines screamed:

"A woman in our nation's Capitol welcomed Queen Elizabeth II into her home in a warm and beautiful way. She gave her a hug."[1]

This simple American act turned to headlines around the world because British social etiquette forbids commoners from touching the Monarch. No one had explained to Alice Frazier, the "hugger," that common mortals do not hug Queens.

One of the most striking characteristic of humans, including queens, wherever found, is that they all are social creatures. We enter life via some type of social group and then are educated, married, rear children, play, laugh, work, dream, cry and die as members of social groups. We are all inextricably socially and culturally bound – embedded in a thick social web, as it were. People around the world have devised many ways to organize and codify their social relations in their own unique way so as to impart a unique characterization to themselves. That is what confuses us when trying to work cross-culturally.

Our task, whether business persons, travelers or diplomats, is to *decode* unfamiliar manners and use them for profitable business ends. We start from the basic premise that *every socio-cultural group organizes itself into a series of interlocking groups.* It helps to think of each group in this interlocking network as a *brick* in the total social structure.[2]

Second, society regulates group life through a series of *codes*, or *rules*, to ensure that relations of all members are conducted in a regular and predictable manner. We can think of these symbolic codes as the *mortar* cementing the bricks together to form a single social structure. Individuals cannot create their own rules. To do so leads to social anarchy! Most Americans can agree that our social landscape is increasingly chaotic. Our cultural diversity is so great that there is an increasing lack of cohesive, agreed-upon social norms and values unifying our citizens.

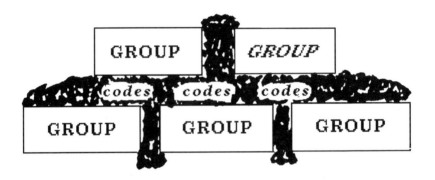

A Social Organization Structure

Third, there are some key organizational features that all groups in all cultures and at all times share: namely, *kinship*. Once basic kinship relations are understood, they can be used by American business people and other internationalists to *sketch the basic contours of extra-kin social relations features.* For our purposes it is only necessary to identify the social features that inform more productive cross-cultural relations.

Earlier chapters discussed ways that technical, economic and political constructions influence family and kinship structures. *The present task is to show how the culture of family and kin influ-*

ence technical, economic and political relations. Social relations are discussed as a measure of "intimacy," since our present concern is with the relative intensity of our cross-cultural relations. Of course, all people rank relationships as to the degree of intimacy. The Mexican kin system is used as the illustrative case later in the chapter.

In addition, since any treatment of social relations leads to questions regarding the myriad ways people define themselves and others, space is devoted to a brief disccusion of the universality of such phenomena. The fact that we Americans possess an historical predisposition to pretend the absence of such devices further drives the need for clarification of this aspect of group relations. This is followed by a discussion of some key non-kin groups in the marketplace that business people should identify and understand, and lastly included is a brief discussion of several key social tension-releasing mechanisms that can help enhance one's grasp of another culture's social scene.

BASIC SOCIO-CULTURAL
ORGANIZATIONAL BUILDING BLOCKS

One's birth group is a person's most basic social building block. The rules governing family and kin relations provide the mortar, or codes, defining all other social relations. Kin refers to all blood relations. *Extra-kin (fictive kin)* is the second social-relations building block. The lines between blood kin and extra-kin can often be difficult to discern.

A knowledge of the kin and extra-kin relationship codes, or rules are critical for understanding anyone's behavior. These social features determine self-identity and specify how one is to behave in a myriad of social circumstances.[3] A useful cultural sketch must show how such relations are structured and identify the basic rules defining proper behavior in and between groups. Any American, living in the midst of enormous cultural diversity, should be relatively aware that his or her basic family relations rules are not shared by all others. The patterns learned in the family and the extended kin network shape our attitudes with regard to gender roles, authority, class, religion, race and all other aspects of social life. This assemblage generally defines one's social personality.

The Intimacy Continuum

A diagram of another's social relations vis-a-vis kin and extra kin provides business persons and other internationalists excellent clues as to the composition of good business relations. The task is not difficult if one thinks of social relations as a continuum of intimacy or a "deed of trust" as it were.

Sketching family relations starts by asking what the members of a family call each other and what rules govern proper behavior between the various members. These rules not only define the *roles* each kin member should play, but reflect the various *statuses*. There is a delightful story that illustrates this fact:

> "...once upon a time a small boy burst into the great throne room of a medieval king. The boy was skipping and singing, as children often do. He was oblivious to the regal sobriety of the surroundings. He was suddenly scooped up by the nape of his neck by one of the armed guards, who gathered himself into a righteously indignant posture and hissed, 'Have you no respect, Lad? Don't you know that the man on yonder throne is your king?' The boy wriggled out of the soldier's grasp and, dancing away, laughed and said, 'He is your king, but he is my father.' The boy proceeded to skip to the throne where he leaped into the king's lap."[4]

A word of caution: Social behavioral rules are not ironclad. People are good at manipulating rules to suit daily needs. The kin system, like other cultural components, is very elastic and flexible. One must differentiate between the general rules and the exceptions; there are always exceptions to the general rules depending upon one's social perspective.

There are even exceptions to the exceptions! It does not take a lot of time to map family relations, but it is highly instructive. Most people love to talk about their culture and especially about their families. Encourage them to do so; it will prove an invaluable bank of information.

MEXICAN FAMILY AND KIN

A brief outline of key elements that comprise the majority of Mexicans will illustrate the importance that family and kin relations codes have on business and all other cross-cultural relations. A fictitious Mexican male named Jose Comacho will provide our pont of reference. His Mexican kinship organization can serve as an extremely generalized model for Latin American kinship, but one always has to look for nuances and variations.

First Tier Intimacy: Kinship

One should start the investigation by noting the basic kin types and list those rules people are expected to observe as they play out their assigned roles. There are usually big difference between *types* and *roles*, as noted by the acts of the king's son in the preceding story

Jose has a number of intimate kin relations to maintain which follows a universal pattern of concentric circle of relations whereby people are differentiated by the degrees of intimacy or closenss of social bonding as illustrated below:

GenerationLevel	Rules Governing	Added Feelings
1. First Ascending		
padre (father)	ultimate authority, task master	relationship of fear
madre (mother)	most important family role significant religious symbolism attached	basic socializer, deep love and respect bonds children
tios (uncles)	special respect bond	
tias (aunts)	special respect bond	

GenerationLevel	Rules Governing	Added Feelings
2. Second Ascending		
abuelos (gran-fa)	high respect, still somewhat aloof relative to grandmother	
abuelas (gran-mo)	high respect and more intimate bond than grandfather, carries religious symbolism	
3. Jose's Level		
hermanos (bros)	eldest has more authority in family; gradually forms strong bonds with male peers.	in late teens replaces father as protector of mother and family.
hermanas (sisters)	protected within home	responsible for household chores, chaperoned as they go outside home; respects household males, serves all; high level of modesty expected from all females in kin unit
primos hermanos (male cousins)	respect toward, responsibility to help	
primos hermanas (female cousins)	respect toward, responsibility to help	

GenerationLevel	Rules Governing	Added Feelings
esposa (wife)	key sexual partner, mother of children, homemaker	
4. First Descending		
hijos (sons)	to be obedient, serve family	
hijas (daughters)	obedient, serves family members, virginal until marriage	
sobrinos (nephew)	respect, assist in any way	
sobrinas (nieces)	respect, assist in any way	

Although the Spanish labels attached to the various biological relations have their English equivalencies, the *meanings,* or codes, defining these relationships differ significantly. The Mexican family is key to ordering all other social relations; which is a a feature shared by Latin American cultures generally. The *familia* acts as the basic norm for all of Jose's social relations. His family organizational life and the codes that specify how he relates to the various members is extended throughout the social system.

In other words, Jose relates to males outside the kin system much as he does within it, specifying different ways of responding as to age, status and so forth. His male age peers constitute his most trusted *fictive kin* social group. Female relations also tend to mimic the patterns learned within the kin unit. So it goes with the elderly and those in authority. Summarily, Jose's ego and social personality is a product of his kin relations – the bricks and mortar of his society.

Jose's Business Relations and Some Western Comparisons

Jose's business relations are extensions of his kin culture system. Business is fundamentally a family affair. Whereas it is common for Americans to work away from home, a Latin Americans' work is a family enterprise where, by and large, the home vs. work compartmentalization does not exist. This helps explain why Latin Americans differ from North Americans in their view of hiring family members or what would be referred to as nepotism. Nepotism is highly valued in Latin America, as it is in most non-Western cultures. Our anti-nepotism rules are seen as bizarre, if not barbaric, to Latinos. Kin, to the Mexicano, Latino, and most non-Westerners, are those who one can trust. Kin relations are one's most sacred obligation, and it is unthinkable not to hire relatives. Even the business of government is a family affair. Former President Luis Portillo is reported to have publicly stated that he was proud of his nepotism. No other relations are as intimate, none as emotionally tight, as *la familias*.

Relative to North-American kin relations, Mexican and non-Western relations generally are not only emotionally closer but more hierarchically structured. Gender is a major organizing factor. Males dominate. Jose looks to his mother and sisters to take care of his home needs. Males rule the household and other features of the system.

Age follows gender in importance. The older males have greater prestige and, therefore, command respect from their male juniors and all females. Jose's father has ultimate power and demands ultimate obedience from all members. Among the lower classes, which is the bulk of the population, a high degree of fear is reportedly attached to one's father. Jose and his brothers have power over the females with the eldest son having the most power.

Jose's mother is the strongest unifying and socializing force in the kin system. The mother role is strongly linked with the Virgin Mary and the idea of personal sacrifice. Mothers use this imagery to impose their will over their offspring, although it is generally subtle and unconscious. A mother's tears and pleadings trigger guilt and sympathy. If that does not work, she appeals to Jose's father – or other older males within the extended family –to intercede on her behalf.

Jose and all other Mexican males ideally relate to others in this hierarchical system through a set of status and role codes which are summed up in *machismo*, a term that has entered English usage. It is a label that tries to encapsulate the socially dominant power of the Latino male. Patrick Oster, in his book on Mexican culture, quotes the Mexican poet, Octavio Paz, as defining *machismo* as follows:

> "For other people the manly ideal consists in an open and aggressive fondness for combat, where we emphasize defensiveness, the readiness to repel any attack. The Mexican "macho", the male, is a hermetic being, closed up in himself, capable of guarding both himself and whatever has been confided to him. Manliness is judged according to one's invulnerability to enemy arms or the impact of the outside world. Stoicism is the most exalted of our military and political attitudes. We are taught from childhood to accept defeat with dignity..." [5]

Machismo is a set of codes that covers the whole gauntlet of male behaviors – wife beating, drinking, fighting, sexual promiscuity and so forth. It has its equivalent in most, if not all, Latin American cultures. It must also be stated that although representing the bulk of the peasant population, it should not be used to characterize the upper class. One should look carefully for variations on this theme when working in Latin America.

While the minority upper-class Latin American females are protected and pampered from a North American view, the lower-class females share what has been characterized as a servile existence. They are expected to be virginal until marriage, faithful in marriage, celibate as widows, good housekeepers, and loving mothers.[6] Formal education to learn basic skills is approved for Jose's sisters, but higher education is believed to be a waste of time. Jose's sisters and daughters are not supposed to go out in public unescorted and are expected to get permission for any and all such forays. Jose monitors his wife's comings and goings. By contrast to females, males represent the family's economic, social and political life. Formal education is Jose's right.

The preceding discussion of Jose's kinship network offers a brief and highly generalized orientation of Mexican culture's most intimate (first tier) set of human relation codes. It is the kind of task facing American business persons and other internationalists in seeking a more accurate understanding of those culturally different. We now move to sketch the way Jose and his male associates structure relationships beyond their family and kin: the second tier of social intimacy. The reader should remember that there are significant differences between classes that should be noted.

Second Tier Intimacy: Fictive Kin

The key relations in Jose's second tier intimate relations are those of his *compadres* and *patrons*. These intimate, but non-blood relations are best labeled fictive kin relations. Relations in this category are viewed as "like kin", but "not kin". These labels provide links, ties or bridging mechanisms between the kin group and others who start out in the broad category of strangers. As a population increases, so does relational complexity.

There comes a time in the life of most cultures where the kin group is stretched beyond its capacity to order social relations along blood lines. There are strangers in overwhelming numbers and their increasing importance for the family has to be dealt with. There are numerous cases, and not too long ago, when travelers, whether missionaries or explorers, were killed in rural regions because people in that region could not identity them as members of their kin group. The indigenous group lacked codes for relating with any degree of trust to non-kin or strangers. It has been said that the attitude of the majority of traditional peoples was "fete'em or eat'em."[7]

70

Compadrazgo

One of Jose's first strategies in building alliances beyond kin relations is the establishment of *compadres* (co-parenthood), a fictive-kin relation established through the Catholic ritual of a child's baptism.[8] The child and co-parents are bound in a fictive-kin relation. To the child these sponsors are his or her godparents (godfather is *padrino*; godmother is *madrina*). The child is to obey and respect his godparents and the godparents, conversely, are responsible for the welfare of their godsons (*ahijado*) and goddaughters (*ahijada*). Welfare support in this context runs the gauntlet from moral advice to financial assistance. In case god-children lose their parents, the *compadres* become responsible for raising the children.

Although the rite of baptism focuses on the infant, the primary importance of this new co-parentage relationship resides in the relationship established between the parents. It should be noted that though *compadrazgo* relations are historically rooted in the act of Christian baptism, throughout Latin America they are designed around all sorts of other events – marriage, dedication of a new home and so forth, but a child is still the primary focus. [9]

A few other rules, or reciprocal expectations attached to being compadres should be mentioned. Basically, *compadres* are included under one's umbrella of trust. One's *compadre* can be trusted "almost as much" as a blood kin; hence, the fictive kin nature of the relation. As Oster's investigation shows, trust is not easily given by Mexican males. Females within the family are off-limits to *compadres*. One jumps in to help a *compadre* caught in a fight, loans *compadres* money, learns news of the outside world, and so forth. One tries to find a *compadre* among those who are wealthier, more politically powerful and of greater social status. The resulting alliances of such fictive-kin relations serves to enhance a family's social and economic capability within the larger society.

It should be noted that North Americans mistakenly equate compadrazgo with their notion of friendship. Latin Americans rarely, if ever, refer to their male buddies as friends, which is a North American expression of significant individualism. Mexicans, to the contrary, use family terms that reflect a closeness beyond the control of any one individual.[10] When a Latino applies that term to a *Norte Americano*, it should be taken as a compliment denoting a degree of intimacy closer than stranger but not of the same intensity as reflected among his countrymen.

Patron

The second strategy Jose uses to build relations beyond his family and extended-kin system is that of the *patron*.[11] Ideally, Jose seeks to establish a patron relation with an older and more socially prominent, richer and more powerful political figure. This person will not be Jose's economic or social peer. Whereas the patron will sponsor Jose's social and economic well-being and related self-interests, Jose is obligated to serve the patron in whatever ways the patron deems necessary. This is a critical relationship. Since it is difficult to serve many masters, Jose has to restrict the number of patrons (usually one or two) he serves.

OTHER TIERS OF INTIMACY: EMPHASIS ON
THE OUTSIDER

Beyond the intimacy of kin and fictive-kin relations, Jose faces a number of options. There are those in his *colonia* (neighborhood or community), village, business, classmates and other who, althought not trusted as intimately as kin and fictive-kin, are nonetheless closer than *strangers* or what Selby found among the Zapotec of Southern Mexico as *outsiders*.[12]

People in every culture figure out ways to identify non-kin group relations. This may take the form of body decoration, totems (symbolic group association with objects), clothing, business cards or other such forms of identity. The purpose is not only to identify group membership, but to set group boundaries, which is a basic feature of human social life to be discussed later in this chapter.

The way people view outsiders, or strangers, is critical for American business people and other internationalists to grasp. All human groups have an outsider category into which they place certain persons. In China non-Chinese outsiders are referred to as *kwa lo* (foreign devils); in Japan, *gaijin,* and so forth. In Mexico, North Americans are generally categorized as *yankees* or *gringos*, and are observed with curiosity, with a high degree of mistrust and with a significant amount of fear. The category of *stranger* is the black box where all non-kin reside, and are ranked in descending order of intimacy to such as government officials, politicos, mestizo (businessmen from afar) or Norte Americanos.

The more intimate strangers are labeled *amigos* (male friends), *amigas* (female friends); *cuate, carnal* (Mexican-American usage), *mi compa,* and *companeros*; all associated group concepts. These are seen as casual, non-threatening relations with no obligation attached. An *amigo/companero* is an age and gender peer one has encountered numerous times in the neighborhood, at school or in business. It is a friendly, non-threatening relation but is not viewed as intimate. These are probably as close to our North American notion of friendship as can be found in the Mexican social relations landscape and is applied in a variety of ways. One must be careful assuming application of these terms, for they may be used to define a very close, non-kin relationship and have significant emotion attached.

By contrast, North Americans use the *friendship* label very glibly. We can meet another person, visit for a few minutes and later refer to each other as friends. Often the warm-fuzzy feelings of intimacy are only held by one party, leading to eventual disappointment later. A friend reported his European associates complained that Americans move almost immediately to first name familiarity, then forget to say good-by with the formality it deserves. In our defense it should be noted that our quick conversion of strangers to friends is probably a reflection of our frontier history. As a nation of immigrant strangers without deep kinship roots, it was in a person's self-interest to make quick alliances.[13] It is as important for strangers to understand Americans as it is for Americans to understand strangers.

Our often nonchalant manner of labeling others as *friends* is at the root of many of our problems in understanding foreign business relations. A recent book authored by Shintaro Ishihara, for example, shattered many people's illusions about Japanese friendships.[14] The book reflects a strong anti-American sentiment which led Beth Hughes, a San Francisco Examiner columnist, to write an article quoting a businessman with some experience working with the Japanese as saying:

> "It is unnerving when you discover that people you thought were your friends or who you've been trying to make your friends really don't like you, never did, never will and don't want to like you."[15]

Ms. Hughes discusses Mr. Isihara's book at some length and then adds:

> "...many Americans are only now realizing that a strong anti-America response is part of Japanese thinking underscores how ignorant many Americans, even policy makers, are about Japan...Hampered by cultural misunderstandings, bilateral communication is already stymied at the political and economic level, creating a sense of isolation on both sides.[16]

Americans can get pretty upset when they feel their intimacy is not reciprocated. We must learn to approach other cultures by shelving our own ideas of *friendship*. Profitable foreign relations must be worked out in the other's cultural context and appreciated by Americans thoughtfully and carefully. It takes years of constant interaction to develop close relationships with most non-Americans from our outsider/stranger position. Even if we develop a relatively intimate relationship, it is never comparable to those within our foreign friends' indigenous network.

This stranger category is not unique to non-Western peoples. It is played out every day in America's small towns and urban neighborhoods. Who amongst us has not been "the new kid on the block," or "the new kid in school"? All groups, large or small, have a special distrustful and suspicious black box labeled strangers. It even shows up in England. Writing, when England was contemplating joining the European Common Market, David Frost and Anthony Jay expressed English xenophobia thusly:

> "The blunt fact (is) that the English do not like foreigners. There have been many attempts to describe hell, but for the Englishman the best definition is that it is a place where the Germans are the police, the Swedish are the comedians, the Italians are the defense force, the Frenchmen dig the roads, the Spanish run the railways, the Turks cook the food, the Irish are the waiters, the Greeks run the government, and the prevailing language is Dutch."[17]

So it goes around the world.

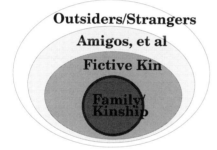

Summarily, a Mexican intimacy scale could be sketched as shown on the left which can also be used as a model for Latin America in general.

Mexican Itimacy Scale

THE UNIVERSALITY OF SOCIAL DISTINCTIONS

In sketching a people's social relations code, one should be aware that all people construct *insider/outsider*, or *we/they, us/them* social categories. All people use various devices to distinguish themselves from others. These various devices further serve as boundary-marking mechanisms. The inventory of possible choices includes *religion, race, ethnicitty, political beliefs, language, geography, economics, gender, kinship, and the modern idea of nationalism*, and this list is not exhaustive.[18] People are very creative when it comes to constructing these *we/they* mechanisms. These differences too often lead to great suffering and other ethnic conflict.

A good cultural portrait must include the knowledge of how the various groups in a particular region are differentiating each other and what rules and acts are used to highlight and maintain group boundaries. Social categories can be profoundly held and fiercely defended.

Relative to non-Westerners, Americans de-emphasize kinship while focusing on one's professional and voluntary associations, as discussed in Chapter II. We seem to have a schizophrenic approach to group relations because of our deeply-held notions of human equality. We tolerate contradictions. We eschew elitism, for example, and yet out-fawn the British over the Royal family. We have created a national presidency that is often viewed and related to and described as *regal* without the traditional verbiage. We are awed by old monied families, and adore, almost to the point of hysteria movie and TV stars as well as people who capture media attention. Our behavior belies the existence of a class system we ideologically abhor. Class in North America is a means of creating and maintaining social boundaries.

Similarly, we socially categorize people on the basis of such traits as age, gender, race and religion, and spend a great deal of energy denying it. All these sorting mechanisms are historically well documented. There are *boundary-maintaining views* that restrict territory, as it has to do with such things as *residence, dating, marriage, club membership* and *employment*, to name a few of the most notorious elements. Human creativity in establishing *we/they* boundary mechanisms seems endless.

Our history suggests we are trying to wed two contradictory social values. First, *we/they* constructions are intrinsic to all social groups. All groups wherever found define, defend and seek to enhance their identity. The stronger a group's identity, the more pronounced their exclusivity. The more exclusive, the more intolerant their activities are viewed by outsiders. Second, our egalitarian American value, backed by law, specifies that none can be discriminated against on the basis of race, creed, gender, age and religion as to employment, wages, use of public facilities, and so forth. These two factors clash as groups seek to find new ways to define and enhance their solidarity. Groups based on income, class, race, religion and gender still exist and continue to proliferate.

It is interesting to note that group discriminatory acts in North America often result from the good intentions of enhancing one's group. The late Barbara Jordan, an Afro-American and former Texas politician, was quoted at a woman's conference in 1991 to have said that "women have a capacity for understanding and compassion which a man structurally does not have, does not have it because he cannot have it. He's just incapable of it."[19] Many claimed that such statements are sexist and bigoted.

Jordan's speech to women was undoubtedly intended to enhance women's self-image and self-respect. It was a group promotion act whose effect was viewed by others as prejudicial. American life is replete with similar events. Unfortunately, group enhancement seems to be at the expense of other groups. Everywhere and in every conceivable way, people distinquish *insiders*, and view others through the social lens of the *we/they context* which, in turn, establishes social boundaries.

As for Mexico, Oster reports that the official Mexican government policy is to exalt the country's indigenous past, vis-a-vis the Maya, Aztec and others. Yet:

> "...most Mexicans have not bought the message. Pure-blooded Indians, as many as ten million Mexicans, are treated as social inferiors. They are generally among the poorest and least educated of the Mexican population. When a Mexican feels that someone has done something particularly stupid or ignorant, he or she is likely to exclaim: 'Indian!' Classified newspaper ads frequently ask for apariencia agradable ('agreeable appearance'). Translation: 'No Indians.'" [20]

Oster found that Mexicans get angry if you suggest that racism exists in Mexico. Those who have traveled and worked in Mexico for any significant period of time have also found this to be true. When Oster asked the publisher of a popular line of comic books that sketches the life of a boy who looks like Little Black Sambo, whose mother is the spitting image of Aunt Jemima, and who acts stupidly, about selling the comics in the United States. The man replied that it was not possible, since "people [in United States] would say it was racist." [21] When asked about Mexico's racim, the publisher is reported to have said, "But we have no racism in Mexico, so we can do it here." [22]

Meanwhile, Protestants and Catholics are at each other's throats in Northern Ireland; social relations in the Middle East and Africa are organized on religious and tribal lines; those in Eastern Europe and the former Soviet states are embroiled in ethnic and religious conflicts to varying degrees; Koreans, and all other non-pure-blood Japanese, born in Japan must register with the government annually because they are not viewed as citizens and are constantly abused;[23] Japan's lower class *burakumin* (outcasts) are discriminated against as an extreme form of "outsiders;" native Malaysians and Malaysian Chinese use religious, racial, and economic missiles in their historic struggle; Chinese in dispersion throughout Asia are engaged in similar social combat with native groups wherever they are; Indonesia's social landscape is not only marked by ethnic combat, such as that between the Chinese and local natives, but geographical. There is a clear distinction made between Javanese, Sumatrians, Achenese and those from hundreds of islands and of dozens of tribes; Burma's native population is currently driving out Muslims by the tens of thousands through a process of killing and abuse;[24] and, finally, African tribal conflict still continues.

Devices Creating Social Boundaries

GROUPS IN THE MARKETPLACE

Given the nature of social groups, *business persons and other internationalists should approach cross-cultural markets expecting to find an amalgam of competing groups.* The more complex the technology, the more layered and complex the group relations. Technical activity and economic orientation leads to distinct social groups, whether Arctic reindeer herdsmen, Latin American potters and weavers, or lawyers, doctors, rocket scientists, computer specialists and other such professional groups in modern societies.

At the beyond kin level of intimacy, these work groups seem to be increasingly important modes of social organization and relationships. American business people must grasp how different people uniquely organize these work groups in their market relations. These may look American, but they will not act American. They are not American.

One must be aware of the pervasive presence of governmental groups in non-Western markets and some such groups are not all happy to see American business people. Some do have a variety of ways to welcome you with one hand and dismiss you with the other. It is generally true that most non-Western nations want North American technology but not the Americans that come with it. It is therefore necessary for one to view goverment and ruling elites among those groups that reflect a people's social organization beyond the more intimate kinship level.

Commercial groups should also be noted. Their articulations with all other social organization categories must be understood, whether governmental, relgious, ethnic and racial, kin or other. It is the real group system network that must be sketched and grasped and not the one that appears on the surface. This exercise is important for aligning oneself most profitably.

It certainly is. One must always determine the costs that indigenous racial, ethnic and/or religious boundaries will have on one's business. What are the costs of aligning with one indigenous company versus another, where choosing sides is the only option? And then there are short and long term issues. Or, given a unique pattern of social organization in the country, how can I put on an indigenous face? Or, do I want to?

These are real concerns. Lastly, a discussion of social organization would not be complete without noting the ways that people have to deal with normal, everyday tensions arising in human relationships. Historically, non-Westerners solve their problems within the family while Americans use the courts. But, there are at least two further devices one should investigate: *avoidance* and *humor*.

SOCIAL TENSION-RELEASING
MECHANISMS

Avoidance is one of the most universally accepted means of coping with the stresses and tensions of social life. It is one way to prevent conflict, promote social equilibrium and reinforce a group's social structure. *Boundary-maintaining* devices can be seen as key *avoidance* tools.

There are universally acknowledged *avoidance taboos* against mother/son and father/daughter sexual relations. Here and there, now and again, there are mother-in-law avoidance taboos as well. Avoidance rules within kinship groups are usually easy to discover and of limited use to business people; but one should be aware of them. Others are not so obvious.

Some avoidance tactics can cause business persons grief. With few exceptions business persons will not encounter Guatemalan women running off into the fields to avoid approaching strangers. The author refers to this as the "avoidance with feet" rule. Although it is hard to predict that other Americans will not encounter this behavior in many parts of the world, few foreign business associates will run from you.

Gender avoidance is widespread throughout the non-Western world. In many Islamic cultures females are cloistered within the home and when allowed in public are clothed and veiled to avoid notice of non-kin males. We might refer to this activity as camouflaged avoidance. Latin American females are protected from male strangers outside the home but without the camouflage. Ideally, they are to be escorted at all times. This might be thought of as "custodial avoidance."

Avoidance strategies are well-worn universal means of reducing marital, friendship, work-related, religious and racial conflict. Avoidance is often a key business technique in many cultures. The failure to return a phone call or fax message seems to be increasingly popular way to avoid discomforting discussions in many cultures. It is hard for most Americans not to be hurt and angry when cross-cultural associates fail to return calls. It helps if we understand this tactic for what it is – avoidance of conflict.

The second most universal way of relieving social tensions is through *humor*. Little has been written to help us understand the cross-cultural differences in humor, but it represents a serious point of societal tension. Americans, like all others, find humor in those things that highlight taboos and conflicts: mother-in-laws, husband-wife, parent-child, and race relations are examples. Americans got a laugh out of Archie Bunker's working class malapropisms in *All in the Family.*

Laughter releases tension. We laugh at skits that treat obviously doltish behavior as acceptable, that run counter to prevailing role expectations and signify embarrassment. In addition to releasing tension, humor also serves to reinforce our group's values and behavior.

Understanding another group's humor codes helps business people understand their culture because such distinctions point to differences in world views. George Eliot noted that "a different taste in jokes is a great strain on the affections." [25]

Other ways of coping with social tensions and problems can be discovered as one seeks to sketch the social dimensions of another culture. Avoidance and humor are the two most universally dominant devices.

In summary, profitable foreign business is highly dependent upon one's ability to sketch the *brick and mortar of a people's social configuration. One must grasp a group's kin and extra-kin codes and behaviors and know how they interrelate.*

References Cited

1. Associated Press, Washington, DC, <u>Houston Chronicle,</u> May 16, 1991.

2. The author is indebted to Chad Oliver for the "brick analogy;" see Chad Oliver, op. cit. , pp. 225-226.

3. Research is ongoing to determine the precise genetic determinants to human behavior, but this is not relevant for the present discussion. Yet, it should be remembered that gene pools are familial possessions.

4. Courtesy of Ben Chamness, Kingwood, Texas.

5. Patrick Oster, *The Mexicans, A Personal Portrait of a People*, (New York: William Morrow and Company, Inc., 1989), p. 229.

6. Ibid, pp. 264-265.

7. Marion J. Levy, op. cit., page 59.

8. Mario Davila, "Compadrazgo: Fictive Kinship in Latin America", in Nelson Graburn, editor, *Readings in Kinship and Social Structure* (New York: Harper & Row, Publishers, 1971), pp. 396-406.

9. Ibid.

10. John C. Condon, *Good Neighbors: Communicating With the Mexicans* (Yarmouth, ME: Intercultural Press, Inc., 1985), p. 24.

11. Luis Rongier, "Institutionalized Inequalities, the Structure of Trust and Clientism in Modern Latin American", in Erik Cohen et al, editors, *Comparative Social Dynamics* (Boulder, CO: Westview Press, 1985), pages 148-163.

12. Henry Selby, *Zapotecs Deviance,* Ibid. See again the discussion of strangers and outsiders as applied to moderns in Chapter II of the present work, p. 12.

13. Francis Fukuyama, *The Social Virtues and the Creation of Prosperity* (New York: Free Press, 1995). This process is referred to as "spontaneous sociability.

14. Shintaro Ishihara, *The Japan That Can Say No,* translation by Frank Baldwin (New York: Simon & Schuster, 1991).

15. Beth Hughes, "Japan's America-bashing Book Stuns, Angers its United States Readers", <u>Houston Chronicle</u>, December 18, 1989, p. 4B.

16. Ibid.

17. David Frost and Anthony Jay, *The English* (New York: Stein, Day, 1968), pp. 201-202.

18. Fredrik Barth, *Ethnic Groups and Boundaries* (Boston: Little, Brown and Company, 1969) for a discussion of how boundaries are maintained by ethnic group. The author suggests that this process characterizes all group identities.

19. "Crossed by Jordan, Men Press Case", <u>Houston Chronicle</u>, February 4, 1992, p. 10A.

20. Oster, *Mexicans*, op. cit, page 249.

21. Ibid., p. 251.

22. Ibid., p. 251.

23. "Koreans Still on the Outside in Japan", <u>Mainichi Daily</u>, Tokyo, Japan, Aug. 23, 1988; "Japanese Discrimination Against Koreans Examined at Symposium", <u>Mainichi Daily</u>, Tokyo, Japan, Aug. 24, 1988.

24. "Muslims flee Burma's Campaign of Terror by Tens of Thousands", Associated Press, <u>Houston Chronicle</u>, January 28, 1992, p. 9A.

25. George Eliot, *Daniel Deronda* (New York: The Hovendon Company), 1876.

Chapter V:

The Religious Scene

*Each Nation knows it has the only true religion and
the only sane system of government, each despises all
the others, each an ass and not suspecting it.*

– Mark Twain

A friend spent days discussing Taiwan's political economy
with some of his new Chinese business associates in 1981. During
a tour of the City they visited one of Taipei's great Confucian temples. After viewing the temple with his Chinese partners, one
turned to him, moved in close, and with a note of great urgency in
his voice stated, "You may understand our politics, social and business ways, and other such things, but you will not truly understand
us unless you understand Confucius." So it is with most all non-
Western cultures. Religion may not have anything to do with business to the average American business man or woman, but this fact
is certainly not true in the non-Western world. Our emphasis on
the separation of Church and State, in tandem with the traditional
idea that a person's religion is highly personal, creates a secular
system. Good American business ethics suggests one should not
look at a business associate's religion – or politics, race, gender or
much of anything else except his or her ability to do the job. These
are formally taboo subjects, though we all know that they play a
significant covert role in business relations!

Although American business people carry on daily business
activities without a conscious nod to existing religious thought and
practice, their non-Western counterparts are quite the opposite.

Non-Western business persons do not compartmentalize their cultural lives as we do in America.

Failure to understand a foreign associate's religious orientation can make relationships difficult and communication awkward. In the non-Western world it can often be the most important piece of cultural knowledge one has. Americans are often ill-prepared to discuss religious values. Most find it very awkward, if not embarrassing. Many get downright hostile to the way other's beliefs fly counter to their own.

A culture cannot exist without clearly understandable and recurring rules for behavior. The rules are more compelling if vested with some metaphysical authority, whether the *God* of the Judeo-Christian tradition, Islam's *Allah*, spirits of departed ancestors, Shinto's *kami*, spirits residing in animals, lakes, mountains *(animism)* or other such phenomena. A group's religious rituals and other institutionalized paraphernalia serve to promote and maintain their most basic cultural interests in a highly symbolic manner. Religious *myths* are the most powerful in humankind's mythical arsenal. They claim absolute priority over their adherents, as demonstrated by the fanatic will of Iranian Muslim youth to fight and die in the recent war with Iraq or that of the youth who killed Israel's Yitzhak Rabin. Such beliefs often encapsulate and drive the political and economic scenes. Myths associated strictly with the family, kin, tribe, clan and/or nation have this same demanding potential, but even here they invariably rely upon the associated religious scene for ultimate support. In many cases the "ultimate claim" of religious beliefs supersedes that of State and leads to enormous conflict. Here and there, it has lead to the overthrow of the State. On some occasions the State has dumped the religion – as in the early *Mayan* case or in the continuing secularization of Europe. People must have confidence and assurance their way of life is right, good and of God. Every group going to war has to believe the gods are on their side.

There is no need to debate the relative intensity of religious beliefs and those that justify and support other cultural scenes. It is only important to understand the interrelationship between religious myths and those representing other parts of a culture. There must be mutual support between the various parts or scenes of a cultural system, with special emphasis on the religious support of the others. This is why it is so important for American business persons to understand a culture's religious scene.

The comic strip, "Calvin and Hobbes" may dramatize an increasingly secular view of the metaphysical by Westerners as he walked in the woods with Hobbes in early winter and mused,

> "Some November this is. The leaves are down, but there's no snow. Everything is just sitting around waiting for winter but nothing is happening. He then screams at the heavens, 'C'mon, what's the big holdup? Let go up there! Bring on the snow!' He and Hobbes spent some time watching the clouds, but nothing happened. He says, 'No efficiency...no accountability. I tell you, Hobbes, it is a lousy way to run a universe.' And Hobbes responds by wondering, 'Whatever happened to the work ethic?' "[1]

With this background the following sketches provide a brief orientation to some of the world's major religious mythic structures, a starting point, and only that. There is always the danger of losing the rich diversity of a religious form when generalizing in this manner. Nor is this the place to argue about the nature of religion. It should be noted for those who reduce the concept to belief in a personal God, as in Judaism, Christianity and Islam, most other forms are not religions. (Although certain forms of Buddhism developed the notion of the eternal Buddha who bestows grace, and in other ways meets the litmus test for religion.) If religion is expanded to include an other worldly or metaphysical dimension, the liberation of humans from worldly concerns and rebirth, then Shinto and the others certainly qualify.

It is assumed American business people are aware of the basic outline of their own Judeo-Christian tradition and there is no need to synthesize it here. The comments in this chapter only address some basic contemporary characteristics of Christianity that American business persons should consider.

The greatest concern is the failure to communicate the intensity of feeling, the ultimate concern, power, heart or passion that these religious myths generate in their adherents. Emotion, or feelings, are as important to grasp as are the codes in understanding another culture. Americans have a history of treating everything in a fairly abstract, dispassionate way. It is part of our scientific legacy, the benefits of which are well recorded. There are liabilities in trying to "simply understand with the top of our heads" another's religious commitments, or any other cultural aspect for that matter. The most important knowledge is derived by "getting inside the cultural skin" of another. This is the only way I can express the need for international business people to sense and feel the emotions impelled by a particular religious and cultural orientation.

SOME THOUGHTS ON CHRISTIANITY

It is important that Americans understand the relative importance of Christianity in the non-Western world. *Christianity* lays claim to a significant chunk of the world's people (close to one billion).[2] The Catholic Church is dominant in Latin America, the Philippines and many parts of Europe. Numbers are not important here, but cursory research will show that a majority of the populations in these areas specify Catholicism as their religion. Orthodoxy has a strong claim in Eastern Europe and the former Soviet states. Northern Europe, the United States, Canada and Australia comprise the Protestant tradition of Christianity. While South Africa has a Protestant history, the remainder of Africa cannot be described as either Catholic or Protestant. Sub-Saharan Africa reflects a religious mix resulting from centuries of missionary work by all Christian groups, but it is not a Christian population by any stretch of the imagination.

The missionary history of the Christian Church is not a pretty sight from the view at the end of the 20th century. Its exclusive and reductionistic message carried out a conscious, and sometimes unconscious, program of annihilating local cultures. Christians have had difficulty separating its *core* message (Gospel) from its own Western culture. It too often planted itself on foreign soil by force rather than appealing to the minds and hearts of the people. Even if, and when, it did appeal to non-Western minds and hearts, it had big problems.

While Western colonialism was striking in its radical ethnocentrism, missionaries and colonial administrators viewed the indigenous as ignorant, superstitious and barbaric. At best, they were children. The author found this pattern still being emulated by the local Spanish priests while living and working in a Guatemalan village in the late 1960s. Around the world Protestant groups have been forced to change their strategy, and most have turned over local work to indigenous converts.

Western culture is heavily endowed with Christian theology. The major Protestant groups reflect an industrial and post-industrial set of myths that have had relatively little impact on Third World cultures – if measured by the percent of religious populations. Islam, Buddhism and a mix of others, including native beliefs, tend to dominate the non-Western World. There is a significant evangelical Christian movement reportedly sweeping Latin America, Sub-Saharan Africa and East Africa that will be interesting to observe in the future.[3]

There are many reasons for the growth of evangelical Protestantism. *First*, rather than pushing a theology or creed on the front end, practitioners are appealing to myths that appeal to the emotions and are grafting a simple message onto the local indigenous folk religion. *Second*, the movement often feeds off a high degree of social dissatisfaction. Converts see the movement as a means of social mobility and/or are disenchanted with traditional Catholic or other indigenous structures. Islam is experiencing a similar growth for the same reasons.

Hinduism has deep roots in the cultural soil of India and claims approximately 648 million people throughout the world. The vast majority of its adherents are in India and Southeast Asia.

Hinduism manifests few, if any, of the usual traits associated with a formal notion of religion. There is no charismatic founder, and no formal creed or theology. There is no authoritative book of some kind or priestly class responsible for the operation, although there are writings and some people who wear the label as priests. The concept of God is not a pivotal feature. It is impossible to find any universally accepted belief that is common to all Hindus. The diversity in its unity is one of its most striking characteristics.

Hinduism is a culturally shared idea of a common tradition, an awareness of being Indian. Many discussions about Hinduism with Indians in order to find a clear set of features by which to determine the identity of a Hindu have led to a dead end. Usually, the only clear response was, "Because I say I am."

A few elements stand out in importance when Western minds try to grapple with Hinduism's slippery nature. *First,* the idea of *dharma* is important. There are various levels of meanings involved in *dharma*, such as accepting and obeying the rules of one's caste to eternal order, law, duty, righteousness or the right way of living. *Second*, there is the notion of *samsara*, the cycle of birth and rebirth. *Third, karma* means that every act builds on every other act from one life to another and defines one's progression, or lack of, in each life – in other words, a merit system.

These ideas are intimately linked. Following *dharma* adds merits (*punya*). This includes such acts as taking pilgrimage, bathing in the Ganges River and offering gifts to Brahman (impersonal Absolute, World Soul, Force and God). The idea of Brahman reflects the diversity of which the author spoke earlier. Some refer to Bbhagvan or Ishvara and those who worship Vishnu or Shiva talk about their chosen deity.   Each of these absolutes are firsts in a polytheistic system, although no Hindu will acknowledge polytheism as Westerners understand it. The universal Force is also conceived to be in certain animals (the famous sacred cow), people, rivers, mountains and other such.

Purification and cleansing rituals are very important to Hindus. They view the human body as dirty or polluting. All excrements, such as urine, saliva, semen and menstrual flow are included. Therefore, the morning bath is not just a bath in the Western sense but an act of purification. It reduces evil (*papa*) and increases merit (*punya*).

Hinduism reflects an adaptive system for coping with a difficult existence, as do all religions. Another key Hindu concept is that of liberation (*moksha, nirvana* to Buddhists) which is achieved through the various cycles of reincarnation. Once enough merit is stored up the person either becomes part of the universal Force or lives harmoniously with it.

To attain the ultimate union with the Force some reject everything in this life, family, jobs, money, sex and all other aspects of human life. They spend their monastic existence in a rhythm of ritual purification and meditation (*yoga*). There are others who seek to live in this life with an eye to bettering the world. There are several reference sources used by Hindus who opt for living-in-the-world: *dharma sutras, dharma shastras and the Bhagavadgita.* The first two codify Hindu society and Hindu behavior.

The *Bhagavadgita* is a poem which specifies the ways to attain Moksha, or liberation with the Force. First is the way of works (*kharma*), second, enlightenment (*jnana*) and third, loving devotion (*bhakti*).

The preceding discussion provides the essential elements of Hinduism in the midst of tremendous diversity. This sketch gives the international business person an orientation to guide observations and questions. There are multitudes of other elements one should investigate, such as astrology. Until recently, Hinduism was relatively unknown in the West. Since the 1960s there has been a significant flow of Americans to India in a quest to become more spiritual. A number of Indian *gurus* (teachers) have successfully developed a following in America.

BUDDHISM

Buddha

Although Buddhism originated in India, the Chinese assimulated it to Japan around the 6th century A.D. It is reported to have a following of very roughly 300 million. Buddhism's founder was an Indian prince, Siddhartha Gautama, who lived during the 6th and 5th centuries B.C. and was a member of a princely caste. Overwhelmed at age 29 with the idea that human life is an existence of suffering, he renounced his comfortable life, abandoned his wife and family, and set out in a search for truth that led to his enlightenment.

Guatama Buddha taught that an enlightened stage is acquired by overcoming such human deficiencies as greed and the associated desires that subvert the human community to conflict. The enlightened state (*nirvana*) is one of peace and tranquility. *Buddha* is a Sanskrit term meaning *"to become enlightened"* or wise.

Like other religions founded by charismatic persons, his teachings were later canonized by his disciples. A number of enlightened persons, or *Buddhas*, compose the historical landscape of Buddhism. Each Buddha embodies practical benefits as well as enlightenment. Siddharta Gautama did not assume himself to be the incarnation of *The Ultimate Absolute*. He was a role model. Emulate his experience and one attains the enlightened state. The various Buddhas that have emerged in history offer such specific specialties as healing, prosperity or other such benefits.

Gautama Buddha postulated *Four Noble Truths*: suffering is an important learning device; suffering is a result of man's emphasis on and desire for pleasure and things which prevent one from achieving enlightenment; rejection of pleasure frees one from suffering; and the Noble Eightfold Path (right beliefs, acts, aspirations, speech, livelihood, efforts, thoughts, meditation) leads to the ultimate enlightened state or *nirvana*, that is being at peace and in harmony with the universe.

The basic aim of Buddhism is to reveal the fundamental illusions of this life. Things are not as they seem. Truth is not evident, that which seems real is not, and those things people believe are of ultimate significance are not.

Buddhism moved out of India in many different versions as it spread across China and eventually through Southeast Asia to Japan and Korea. Early in its development it split into two schools, the *Hinayana*, the small vehicle, also known as *Theravada*, the "way of the elders," which represents the monastic form and still has many adherents in Southeast Asia, and *Mahayana* (the great vehicle), the more popular and eclectic form which spread to Japan. *Mahayana* freely incorporated existing folk religious thought and traditions as it spread throughout Asia. The enormous diversity is explained as variations to the central truths of the faith.

Hinayana, with its strict monastic observance dominates Buddhist life in Sri Lanka, Thailand and Burma. Only males can enter the monastic life and the minimum age is seven. Upon entering monastic life one takes a vow to seek refuge in the law, the community and Buddha. After having his head shaved the monk will spend his monastic life on very frugal terms. He is given a bowl to use as he begs for his one meal a day on the streets, which demonstrates his dependence on the community.

Mahayana Buddhism was founded by *Ashvaghosha*, an Indian who lived in the 2nd century A.D. He maintained that after the original Buddha attained nirvana people could no longer understand him, therefore there was a need for clarification of the message. The role of an intermediary, or *bodhisattva*, who postpones his own union with nirvana to remain and help others, becomes important in *Mahayana* Buddhism. This step lends itself to the idea of a personal saviour, clearly not the original intent.

When Buddhism moved into China, it underwent further transformations. Mahayana Buddhism accommodated to local Chinese culture fairly easily, especially the importance of Chinese ancestral lineage. Most of the prior acts of personal negation were discarded as it blended with Chinese culture. Probably the most important change is the emphasis on human life in this world, and not the Indian notion of freedom from worldly suffering and individuals therefore learn the moral agents of society as a whole.

As Buddhism moved out of China to Korea and Japan, it was no longer an Indian product. Its gradual assimilation into Japanese culture took many centuries, as the Japanese mentally massaged the entity to fit their folk traditions. The Chinese emphasis on the family and societal relations meant that the most difficult task had been done for the Japanese. The fact that Japanese leaders had great respect for Chinese culture also helped propel the implanting of Buddhism on Japanese soil.

Buddhism in Japan underwent some further changes. *First*, and the most important change, the practice gave people the opportunity of attaining the status of a Buddha in one lifetime, rather than the almost unattainable Indian pattern. *Second,* the roles between the intermediaries (bodhisattva) and the laity is diminished. Some priests, namely those of the Jodo-Shin sect are allowed to marry and women can reach buddhahood.

Wherever found, Buddhism is deeply embedded into the sociocultural fabric of a people. The ideas promoted through Buddhism need be understood by American business people.

TAOISM AND CONFUCIANISM

Taoist and Confucian religions are philosophical systems deeply rooted in Chinese tradition. Taoism, meaning the way, grew out of various legends and writings, now codified in a richly inspired work of eighty-one stanzas known as the *Tao Te Ching* or "Book of the Virtue of the Tao." Its impact beyond the Chinese borders is probably more visible by its calendar, which specifies lucky and unlucky days. The calendar specifies the festivals, appropriate wedding days, and all other such celebrations for much of Chinese, Japanese, and Korean life. Taoist thought emphasizes the harmony and order of the universe.Man's thoughts and acts should reflect this pattern of order and harmony. Man's ills are a result of living in a state of disharmony with the universe.

The *Tao Te Ching* emphasizes that Tao rules heaven, heaven rules earth, and earth rules man. The true state of existence is one of simplicity and humility; man must submit to the symmetry and forces of nature. One must be kind and good to all people and things must be humble and forego pretensions. It is evident that such teachings are universal and fit in neatly with many religions. Some say Taoism has developed streaks of magic and superstition, so one might watch for such characteristics and not be surprised to find them. The philosophy and rituals have dominated the lives of millions of people through the centuries. Taoism is reported to have 203 million adherents.

Lao-Tzu

YIN-YANG CREATION PRINCIPLES

The concepts of *yin* and *yang,* based on the principle of opposites, are rooted in Taoist thought and have become quite familiar to most Westerners. They play an important role in Chinese life. *Yang* is an active and masculine energy. It is light, heat, dynamic and related to Heaven – the Heavenly spirit. It is dominant in youth, summer, in the south and at noon times. *Yin*, as passive and feminine, is associated with yang's opposites: dark, cold, damp and associated with Earth. It is dominant in old age, winter, in the north and at night times. These two forces are responsible for the five elements: wood, fire, metal, water and earth. Tao gave birth to the One *(T'ai- chi)*, the One gave birth to the Two *yin-yang*) and the two to the five elements. The *yin-yang* five element theory is a key annual ritual in present Chinese life *(Su-ch'i)*. The *yin-yang* world view is essential to the Chinese and governs a great deal more than Taoist rituals. At death one's soul descends to the realm of *yin* (similar to Catholicism's purgatory) where it goes through a cleansing process before ascending to the heavens. During this period the soul can cause harm to living family members if they fail to provide prayers and food offerings. A key function of a *shaman* is to mediate between the living and the dead soul. A similar shamanistic role characterizes religious life in Korea, Japan and other parts of Asia. It is intertwined with Buddhist ritual as well.

FENG-SHUI

Closely associated with the yin-yang principles is the practice of *feng-shui*. It is a deeply steeped in Chinese folk religion and is the practice of placing buildings, homes and office buildings – even graves – in universally harmonious locations. A run of bad luck and misfortune, such as family health or business decline, are sure signs the home, the business, or a family grave is placed where universal forces are out of whack. Sharp 90° degree angles in buildings and homes, for example, are not conducive to "beneficial chi" which travel along curved and irregular pathways.

Feng-shui is currently practiced by the majority of Chinese, even though they may not understand its name and history. They will know that something is "not right" or "does not look right". A Chinese friend of the author recently returned to Hong Kong after living in Germany for many years. He had divested himself of a great deal of his Chinese culture while living in Germany. He candidly admitted that he quickly accepted the world view inherent in feng-shui and took up the practice of checking with a Geomancer regarding business decisions.

CONFUCIANISM

Confucianism has a more definite origin than Taoism. It is a system of thought developed by a man named *Confucius* (551-479 B.C.). There is an old saying that a man is not a prophet in his own house, so it was not until the unification of China during the *Han Dynasty* (478 B.C. - 202 B.C.) that Confucian thought was systematized.

Confucius

Confucian teaching emphasizes social harmony based on the virtue of obedience to proper relationships in human life. The family represents the basic model for all societal harmony and order. A son should obey his father and the father should respect and be benevolent to the son. The other primary relationship that occupied much of his thought revolved around a similar role relationship between ruler and ruled. It is necessary to understand that the principles set down were universal in type and enabled the Chinese to distinguish a difference between a moral and social order. Obedience and loyalty to the moral order (*the Way*) took precedence over obedience to a lord or the state. Chinese history is replete with speculations as to the legitimacy of rulers in the face of such signs as floods, earthquakes or other catastrophes. The most important facts to mention are several key concepts that communicate the basic impact of Confucian thought on human relationships.

First, an attitude of deep respect (Li) should characterize all relationships. The emphasis is on proper ceremony and etiquette. One's attention to correct forms of social relationships promotes harmony and peace. *Second,* love and affection (Hsiao) characterize family relations. *Third,* all friend and business relationships involve deep commitment and honor (Yi). *Fourth*, a posture of kindness and respect marks every human contact (Jen). *Fifth*, loyalty and respect should characterize citizens relations with their rulers (Chung).

SHINTO: A JAPANESE PHENOMENON

As in technology and some other areas, the Japanese have been efficient in absorbing various religious systems while maintaining their distinctive culture. Japanese religion and accompanying world view is a composite of Shinto, Buddhist, Confucian and Taoist thought and practice. The core of it all is traditional folk religion. Christianity and other religions claim very minor positions. In Japan it is difficult to unravel these various historical threads in the fabric of Japanese life, but a brief orientation to Shinto is important.

Let us join our Japanese business associate, as we would on our first visit to Japan. Our associate has led us to one of the many Tokyo Shinto shrines, where we notice a relatively austere environment or lack of statuary. As we glance around trying to make sense of this, we watch a woman approach a setting that is evidently the shrine. We watch her go through the motions of washing her hands and rinsing her mouth. Next, she approaches the shrine, claps her hands, seems to pray, leaves a few coins, rings a bell, claps her hands again and leaves. What is going on here?

Maybe we are fortunate enough to climb Mt. Fuji. As we climb, we notice a constant stream of people. We stop to rest. Three little old women, who must be in their eighties, trudge past and act as though they were out for a walk around the block! We feel a sense of embarrassment, so we get up and continue the arduous climb. As we proceed on our trek, we notice people of all ages doing the same. Some young men and women even carry their bikes to the top. Finally, we reach the top and lo, there is a Shinto shrine. Again, people are clapping, praying and meditating. Again, we wonder: What is going on?

Again, we attend a sumo wrestling match and notice that it all revolves around a Shinto ceremony. The Shinto priest pours water on the hands of the wrestlers, each rinses his mouth and tosses some salt around and claps his hands. We are told that all this is to purify him and to attract attention of the *kami* (spirits).

To understand what is to most Americans such strange behavior, it helps if we know that Shinto evolved within Japanese culture and means "the way of many *kami*". It is the most ancient of Japanese religious traditions. *Kami* are spirits, or creative and sustaining forces that can and do live in any object –trees, houses, temples, mountains, the Emperor and others. There is no need for statuary to symbolize the *kami* because they are assumed to be "in the medium"– rock, tree, mountain, whatever. The clapping is to get the attention of the *kami* and the bell ringing and clapping at the end of the ceremony tells the spirits the entreaty is over.

Early Japanese legends and myths speak of a time when many *kami* existed and the earth was just water and land. There came into being a divine *kami* couple: Izanagi and his mate, Izan-ami. The couple dipped their jeweled spear into the ocean and, presto, formed Japan. The divine couple produced other kami, among whom were Amaterasu, the sun goddess, and Ninigi, her grandson. Ninigi rules over the earth and symbols of his authority are a necklace, mirror and sword. These three objects continue to be symbols of Japanese imperial power and the Emperors are hereditary descendants of these divine parents.

The divine ruling family unified the populace, provided food harvests and took care of the people's needs. The Japanese people are a distinct sacred people. This organizing principle weaves its way through contemporary religious groups, villages and families. A person's identity is a Japanese communal identity. The group nature of Japanese life is so prevalent and pervasive that ethics are expressed in terms of national, village, company and family interests. This contrasts with America's set of individually held inner principles.

All Shinto rites, whether at the time of enthronement of a new emperor, by the emperor at harvest time, by priests at the start of the New Year or at other times, are to cleanse the group's ills and to restore peace and harmony to all. Neighborhoods and villages have their shrines, known as tutelary shrines, which are visited on festive occasions to cleanse and restore balance with the universe. Sometimes, especially during the major events of the New Year and mid-year festivals, people will rub a small paper doll against their bodies to transfer all the evil that has developed and leave these at the shrine. The doll festival celebrated on March 3, the flower festival on April 8 and the Boy's day, May 5, are especially noticeable to foreign visitors. These festivals are among a set borrowed from the Chinese and were originally part of the group cleansing process. These occasions have become more recreation than serious religious observances.

The Shinto shrine plays a key role from one's birth. It is usually a baby's first trip away from home. There is an observance on the first, fifth and seventh birthdays and on January 15th, when those who will be twenty-one during the year are honored. Daily and weekly crisis will also drive people to their local tutelary shrine. The dreaded exam period that determines university entrance drives many youth and their family members to the Shrine. The marriage ritual involves families of both partners and is often held in front of the *Kamidana*, home shrine, or *Butsudan*, a Buddhist home altar. Some of the larger shrines are increasingly used for the marriage ceremony.

The rites of death are an eclectic of Shinto and Buddhist practices. Death rites serve to cleanse the person and transform him or her into a spirit that in essence loses any individual identity as it joins an ancestral group or *kami*. If not cleansed, the dead will wander around and haunt others. Thus, Japan returns all their war dead to *Yasukuni Shrine* (resting place for war dead) in Tokyo. The process of transforming the dead to a healthy state of being with the *ancestral kami* is lengthy. If not done right, the living will be subjected to misfortune (to be haunted).

It is essential for Westerners to understand this latter point. Japanese families view their ancestors as existing kami (spirits). These spirits have the power to harm the living if not properly serviced in death. Ancestors are part of nature and all creation must live harmoniously. Japan's basic religion is very characteristic of the Japanese. Nothing is allowed to short circuit or replace this most fundamental historic fact.

It is necessary to realize that the person with whom one is trying to do business does not operate on the basis of some Christian or Western set of ethics. He, instead, conceives himself part of a group – nation, company, and family (ancestral corp as well). His loyalty and ethical orientations are extremely corporate. His primary loyalty is not to his foreign business associates, no matter how much business has been conducted. A foreigner is *gaijin* <u>and always will be</u>. There are exceptions to these general sociological strokes, lest some old Japan hands bristle at the author's generalizations. There always are.

One's Japanese business associates will act so as to create and maintain a harmonious state. The foreigner's needs will be seriously and honestly considered. The Japanese goal is to reach an agreement that serves his company as well as ours. If one focuses one short-term goals, it will often seem as though one's Japanese colleague has given in to American demands. He is always representing his company's long term goals. In order to create harmony he will often sacrifice short term goals or adjust them accordingly.

It is essential to understand the centuries of religious tradition that have shaped one's Japanese business associates, as these heavily influence his business activities. Even if he does not profess to being a "practicing Shinto or Buddhist," he is a product of what many describe as a highly controlled, tribally-corporate group system.

Japanese do not derive a moral code of conduct from their religious experiences that define good and evil or right from wrong in the Christian sense. Right behavior is defined by the various corporate groups, and all must be in step with the national precepts of the time. Right and wrong can be quickly redefined and even, at times, contradictory. The resulting Japanese moral malleability and relativity are of great concern to Westerners, both government and business. Whether by understanding religious traditions or secular formats, attempting to obtain a firm grip of understanding on Japanese business ethics, is difficult if filtered through our Western point of view.

ISLAM

About one-fifth of the world's people are *Muslim, or Moslem* (840 million people spread out in sixty countries). Americans became dramatically acquainted with Islam through what we called "The Iranian crisis", the overthrow of the Shah and the subsequent capture of United States Embassy personnel. The next exposure came with the oil pricing machinations of the oil producing states, (OPEC). The images created by Iran's fundamentalist Muslims were not the best public relations messages to send to the world-at-large. Among non-Muslims, the majority of whom were getting their first images of Islam, there is a tendency to remember the crazed and hysterical mobs, bearded men in robes and turbans, bloody floggings and executions.

This is not a good image to promote good business relationships. Lost in the media transmissions during the Iranian revolution were the *anti-modernization feelings* that fueled and drove the event. America symbolizes modernization and the threatened destruction of traditional Iranian life and values.

That a people anywhere would not want all the gifts modernization delivers is unbelievable to Americans. Islam's fundamentalist movement represents a significant rejection statement. It will be a challenge that will undoubtedly mark life on this planet for decades to come. Americans fail to understand that approximately seventy percent of this world's people still live outside urban areas and view the world from the perspective of age old, pre-capitalistic traditions. These people firmly believe tradi-

102

tional ways are far superior to what they see and hear in the modern West.

Islamic renaissance, as a force in social and political events, spread from Iran throughout the Middle East. It was triggered and driven by the believed failure of secular nationalist governments created out of colonial rule. To date, countries have exhibited this force differently. In Algeria the failure of the National Liberation Front to secure prosperity for the people led to the emergence of the militant, and largely underground, Islamic *Salvation Front*. In Syria, President Hafez Al-Assad's believed weakness has led to a very strong and active *Muslim Brotherhood*. Egypt's Muslim Brotherhood grew as a reaction to colonialism in 1928 and now has members in key political positions. Although Egypt's Muslims have generally been less violent than others in the region, they were responsible for the assassination of President Anwar Sadat in 1981 and have been reportedly killing tourists in the 1990s.

The dominance of Islam is so strong that it is constantly used as a political tool. President Saddam Hussein of Iraq constantly refers to Islam when appealing to his countrymen for support against the United States and the West in general. We are presently hearing Serb nationalists referring to the Ottoman Empire's occupation of what is now Bosnia and subsequent Muslim attempts to impose a fundamentalist rule over Christian Serbs as justification for their attempted eradication of the Bosnian Muslims. Yet, American business people must understand that the majority of Muslims do not condone violence.

Islamic History

Allah (Arabic for God) spoke to man through a line of prophets starting with Adam and culminating with Mohammed, or"*The Prophet of Islam*" (died 632 A.D.). He was the final messenger. The followers of *Islam*, an Arabic term meaning submission (to Allah) are called *Muslim*, Arabic for "one who submits to Allah".

Islam is a total way of life and the *Qur'an* or Koran specifies rules of order of all aspects of human life as well as the rituals for approaching Allah. The *five Pillars of Islam* are: *Shahada* (profession of faith), *Salat* (worship), *Zakat* (almsgiving), *Saum* (fasting), and *Hajj* (the pilgrimage). These became highly specified during the early centuries of Islam and differences of interpretation led to a schism. The schism resulted in two main schools, *Sunni* and *Shi'ite*.

The differences between the two schools, *Sunni* and *Shi'ite*, are somewhat elusive. In doctrinal terms, the Shi'ites claim the descendants of *The Prophet* are the only legitimate successors, while *Sunni* do not. There have been twelve of such legitimate *Imam* (leaders), vis-a-vis *Ayatullah Khomeini*, who shows the great power such leaders can accumulate (Ayatullah means "sign of God"). Sunni leaders have never been able to appropriate their Shi'ite counterpart's strong leadership status. The members of these two most popularly known schools view each other with a somewhat jaundiced eye.

The *Shahada*, or confession, is the essence of being a Muslim and is a simple creed: "There is no God but Allah and Muhammad is the messenger of Allah." The *Salat* (worship) consists of five daily prayers, morning, noon, afternoon, sunset and evening. In addition, all Muslims throughout the world attend their local mosque at noon on Fridays. The *mosque* contains a tower (*minaret*), from which the call to prayer is given, a pulpit, a recess in the wall indicating the direction of the holy city of Mecca to which people direct their prayers and a fountain for cleansing. The *Zakat* (alms) program has become institutionalized as a tax but this varies by country.

The fast consists of a twenty-eight day fast period called *Ramadan*. The Islamic calendar specifies the dates each year. Every Muslim is required to make the *pilgrimage* to Mecca if he can possibly afford it.

To Americans, with their Christian orientation, the world of Islam may seem fairly solidified, but it has many variations. Local cultures have forced their stamp on Islam whether in Africa, Indonesia, India or China. Islam constitutes a rapidly growing majority of the world's religious population. In India it has drawn millions from Hinduism.

What can the American business person expect when dealing with a Muslim counterpart? First, you must understand the Islamic world view, since Muslims comprise such a significant portion of the world's population. You can depend on a good Muslim to keep his word. Their ethical and moral beliefs are as honorable as those found in Christianity. There is no doubt that the system of Islamic law is more specific and justice is more swiftly delivered. Further, it is noteworthy to Americans that Islam is not compatible with Communism.

TRADITIONAL OR FOLK RELIGIONS

The preceding section seeks to encapsulate some of the most important characteristics of many key religious systems. A brief statement about folk religions is in order, since they have an important impact on business behavior throughout the non-Western world as well.

The idea of *folk religion* has to do with nativistic practices and world views held in a people's collective memory. They do not have the vast institutionalized baggage nor the mass following the aforementioned religious systems have. The author uses the term, *folk religion*, in an extremely broad fashion to include all remaining forms of metaphysical perceptions and practices, such as witchcraft, magic and animism (spirits in animate and inanimate objects). Some of these world views and their practices are evidently emerging in the United States, according to media reports, not only among middle-class Americans but from the heavy influx of immigrants from non-Western nations. For example: the actress Shirley MacLaine's report of spiritual experiences and views regarding past lives and channeling experiences certainly fall into this category. *New Ageism* that is starting to emerge falls into this same grouping. A recent news item reported that socialite, Marla Maples Trump, to be a New Ager.[4] The article tells us that her regimen includes "prayer (to whom we are not told), a strict dairy-free diet, anti-disease spinal adjustments, her quartz crystal which is supposed to 'exude warmth and love' and...the aromatic massage administered by...Meiread, who 'calls in the angels to bring us to our higher power.' "[5]

One must constantly keep in mind that *folk religion* forms the basis and provides important core features of all the major religious systems of this world. The Jewish and Christian systems are grounded in *folk* traditions, each starting as oral tradition.

SUMMARY

The religious sketches in this chapter account for most of the world's peoples. American business people have difficulty understanding and dealing with non-Christian religions for a number of reasons. First, the majority of Americans are products of a highly exclusive Judeo-Christian environment, but this tradition may be developing into something altogether different. Our comic strip friend, Calvin, and his tiger buddy, Hobbes, of "Calvin and Hobbes" may be harbingers of this fact as he was standing before the family's TV in a worshipful mood in one particular comic strip. Calvin ate his tapioca pudding in front of the TV as an offering. Then he bowed and uttered the following solemn entreaty:

> "Oh, greatest of the mass media. Thank you for elevating emotion, reducing thought and stifling imagination. Thank you for the artificiality of quick solutions and for the insidious manipulation of human desires for commercial purposes. This bowl of lukewarm tapioca represents my brain. I offer it in humble sacrifice. Bestow thy flickering light forever."[6]

This satirical comic strip may highlight a new America. Western Christianity is historically marked by strong feelings of hostility and open conflict, not only against non-Christian peoples but within the system itself. Scratch the surface of any small town or city in America and one can find the possibility of violence against those who differ religiously. Some sects carry on a constant tradition of feuding.

106

The chronicle of Christianity's reductionism and exclusivity is lengthy. The *first* and most basic theological tenets of the Christian faith have to do with love, compassion and all the other qualities that reconcile people. This is another part of the cultural baggage described in Chapter V that American business persons carry as they meet Muslim, Hindu, Shinto and practitioners of other religious views.

Second, not only do many Americans view these religions as strange, but as ignorant superstition. This not only results from Christianity's reductionistic posture but also from a scientific orientation that has led to a secularization or demystification of the universe.

Third, non-Western cultures have strong religious components, which are fused with politics, economy, social organization and technology. For example: General Douglas McArthur forced a decree on Japan that demystified the Emperor, but it did not basically alter the Japanese people's cultural myths or beliefs.

Fourth, belief in the spirit world, magic, sorcery, animism and a whole pantheon of gods, characterize most religious systems. Even the monotheistic fabric of Christianity, Judaism and Islam end up with significant threads of traditional religious thought and practices. For example, Islam in Indonesia, the world's most populous Muslim nation, is a blend of Hinduism and regional folk traditions.

It is safe to assume when dealing with one's Chinese, Thai, Indian, or other foreign business partners that his or her world view is heavily filled with a lively metaphysical pantheon whose inhabitants must be constantly placated. For example, Chinese doorways often have high doorsills. The reason rests in a view that since ghosts cannot lift their feet from the ground they cannot step over high doorsills and enter the house or office building to do harm to the living. Another example: notice how the entrances to many parks and bridges are often marked by a mazeway of right angle turns, similar to those cordoned stanchion barriers used in many United States banks or theaters to force people to line up.

Again, there is a belief that ghosts cannot turn right angle corners. Thus, these entrance mazeways protect the living from ghosts. The tendency of most of the world's people to view their lives as controlled by ghosts and spirits cannot fail to have a great effect on all their behavior. It would serve American business people well to grasp these issues. A Chinese sociologist visiting America reported his feelings as follows:

> "...the thing that felt most strange to me during almost a year of living in America was that no one told me any stories of ghosts. In a world without ghosts, life is free and easy. American eyes can gaze straight ahead. But I think they lack something, and I do not envy their lives."[7]

The brief sketches presented in this chapter are here to help business associates and other internationalists launch a more extensive investigation of a people's religious beliefs. *A useful cultural portrait must include a good grasp of a people's religion* and the way it is integrated into all other cultural scenes. Foreign profits often hang in the balance.

References Cited

1. Bill Watterson, "Calvin and Hobbes" cartoon, distributed by Universal Press Syndicate (Kansas City, MO: November 15, 1992).

2. Population figures for the various religious groups are from *World Book Encyclopedia,* 1989.

3. David Stoll, *Is Latin America Turning Protestant?* (Berkeley: University of California Press, 1990).

4. Houston Chronicle, Sunday, April 10, 1944, p. 2A.

5. Ibid.

6. Bill Watterson, "Calvin and Hobbes" cartoon, distributed by Universal Press Syndicate (Kansas City, MO: August 7, 1992).

7. "Speaker's Idea File", Ragan Communications, Chicago, Illinois, February, 1994, p. 3.

Chapter VI:
The Environmental Scene

"Nature! We are surrounded by her and locked in her clasp; powerless to leave her, powerless to come closer to her."

Goethe

As your head snaps back, your eyes narrow in amazement and your brow furrows in disbelief, you are wondering what a foreign group's environment has to do with your firm's ability to do business profitably! You are probably thinking, "My company makes computers and computer peripherals, not earth moving equipment, oil wells or agricultural products. Environmental features mean nothing to us." That is an understandable response, as the impact a group's physical habitat has in shaping their culture is not as evident as the social features we discussed in Chapter IV. Nor is it as powerful as kinship or technology, yet, its influence is often very significant and should be considered when sketching an accurate cultural portrait.

In cultural terms one's habitat or environment includes both the human populations and the terrain (tropical forest, desert and so forth). Every group's habitat has influenced the shape of their culture and continues to do so.[1] Since we, as moderns, seem to have screened off so many natural discomforts, all this may seem to touch on the absurd. We have managed to harness Mother Nature's binges of temperature extremes with air-conditioning and heating, some flooding by erecting dams and water control schemes, pests with pesticides and so on. Modern technology has certainly solved a lot of problems. No doubt about it.

Most of us arise each morning in the comfort of a climate-controlled home with all kinds of modern conveniences. None of us has to worry about re-thatching the roof after the latest storm or re-plastering the walls and floors with cow manure. Few of us have to worry about gathering fuel for cooking fires or whether food stored is safe from predators or of sufficient quantity to last until the next harvest.

As American business people, we leave our comfortable urban homes, composed of glass, plastic, metal, some wood and all sorts of composites, to crawl into climate-controlled cocoons called cars, listen to the weather, news and music from around the world on systems unimaginable a few decades ago, sip our hot coffee, perked on an electrical device that automatically clicked on before we awakened, and was ready for us as we headed out the door. We arrive at a climate-controlled workplace which is a cocoon of steel and glass. Although all Americans do not spend 100% of their time in such air-controlled cocoons, the description is broad enough to afford a characterization of the contemporary Western business environment. It is also true that such living has come to characterize urban life around the globe within a few short decades.

Even with our sophisticated technology, we are still intimately affected and shaped by our physical environment: our habitat. The mass media reminds us on a daily basis of Mother Nature's ability to wipe out the best of our constructions. The January, 1995 earthquake in Kobe, Japan, was certainly a painful reminder, as has been the flooding along the Mississippi River and her tributaries over the last few years. One could mention the litany of tornadoes, hurricanes and typhoons. We are presently forking over billions of dollars to reclaim that portion of our habitat that we have fouled through the years! America's farmers have known well this dependence on Mother Nature. Even Calvin, of the Calvin and Hobbes comic strip understands Mother Nature's dominance. On March 4, 1994, Calvin and Hobbes of "Calvin and Hobbes" were standing in a snow-covered field surveying the scene, when Calvin muses:

"It offends the human ego that nature is indifferent to us! Nature doesn't care if people live or die. It refuses to be tamed. It does whatever it wants and acts like people don't matter. It won't confirm our right to be here. That drives people crazy. We can't stand being ignored. It's insulting and... Hey!"

As Hobbes yawns broadly and walks away, Calvin, dejected at Hobbes' lack of interest, says:

"I think that's also why some people don't like cats."[2]

NATURE AND CULTURE

While it is easy to grasp nature's destructive effect on our physical creations, it is very difficult to see her influence on our culture building. The following describes some ways nature has shaped our own culture, then uses the *Inuit* (Eskimo) and *Japanese* cases to briefly illustrate this process. For obvious reasons there is no need to detail our own North American habitat, but some characteristics are needed.

OUR HISTORIC AMERICAN CULTURE

America's expansive temperate plains, so rich to the touch of the European plow, and our nation's wealth of other food sources, are greatly responsible for our emergence as a wealthy nation. The habitat was rich! The European technological advantages our forefathers introduced would have meant little if the physical environment had been narrowly restrictive. If, for example, our land was ninety-eight percent rugged, tropical mountains with the associated shallow fertile soils and narrow temperature and humidity ranges, our story would be entirely different.

Given these rich and expansive conditions, our European agrarian technology thrived in spite of the danger and toil. In fact, the milieu called forth a unique *radical individualism* and special notions of *self-sufficiency*, as well as *entrepreneurial and combative inclinations*. Although these cultural traits came to dominate our social institutions and personal behavior, they in no way minimize our European ancestor's peasant background.[3]

Further, the environment influenced our need to be *tinkerers, roamers,* and *optimists.* Our frontier ancestors had to fix whatever was broken and create new devices to solve new problems presented by the environment. We are, for the most part, still a nation of tinkerers, which feeds our entrepreneurial inclinations. When all the tinkering was done and problems still persisted, our ancestors packed up and moved to a more fruitful habitat. We do the same. Americans are one of the most mobile people in the world, without being tied to ancestral soils, homes or villages. We are a nation of roamers.

In the midst of our tinkering and roaming, our frontier ancestors quickly learned to organize beyond the family. Prior kin and social class ties gave way to a plethora of voluntary organizations, which were more adaptive in the new hostile environment. We are a nation of *joiners,* and an optimistic world-view came to be a critical survival motif during those settlement years. This positive attitude contrasts with the European's general pessimism and the non-Westerner's fatalism. Politically, we are one with our frontier parents in believing that a hero will come riding onto the stage atop his white horse. No problem is unsolvable. Someone in the group can come up with a solution. We continue to believe that problems can and should be solved personally – the old Emersonian view of self-reliance. If there is a problem one cannot solve, then the family can. If the family cannot solve it, we look to government – local, state and federal.

Summarily, our habitat has greatly influenced our culture and, hence, social institutions. Interestingly, many aspects of our agrarian life are still with us. We still want to get back to the soil. Contemporary Americans buy farms, ranches, or rural retreats as soon as they are financially able. Granted, the preceding traits are large brush strokes, but it is difficult for others to understand us, or for us to understand ourselves well without noting these historic features.

It is important to understand that all cultures are significantly influenced by their physical environment, though these features are easier to see in simpler and more exotic cultures that have not changed so dramatically over time. Research is continuing to determine the precise relation between culture and environment. There is no agreement on the precise correlations of these features. Nor does a habitat, even the polar, tropical or desert region, limit humankind's culture-creating ability. There are examples of groups occupying similar environments but developing much different responses to its resources.

There are, of course, some habitats that are more limiting than others, such as the extreme polar, desert, and high mountain environs. These do not provide the latitude of choices found in great plains or even tropical rain forests. Further, a group's size and relative isolation profoundly affects culture building. If a group's size grows beyond a habitat's ability to support it, there is an "out migration" force that can occur. And we are witnessing enormous out migration on a worldwide basis in our time. If there is nowhere to go, then wars, famine and disease arise to stabilize the situation.[4] Groups also try to reach into other areas for needed resources, a pattern that has characterized human history for centuries, as demonstrated by the Mesopotamians, Aztecs, Mayan, Inca, Chinese, and Romans. All nations now seek resources throughout the globe.

To further illustrate the influential relation between a habitat and a people's culture building process, the following will set forth the *Inuit* [5] and *Japanese* cases. While no culture is truly simple, the Inuit culture provides a contrast with the more complex Japanese system. It should be noted that the following is a brief summary of the two groups' key habitat/culture relationships. (A fuller treatment of both cases can be found in the *Appendix to Chapter VI* for those interested in greater detail.)

Studies reveal great complexity among the Inuit peoples. The following presentation examines the group as it existed prior to the impact of Western cultures. Although diversity has always existed, the Inuit population will be discussed "as though" it were a single entity for the sake of noting connections between their primary culture and environment. Sub-groups, such as the Lapps, Chuckchi and others, will be included as they relate to the study.

The Habitat

Temperatures in the Arctic winter average -30°F[6] but can dip to a low of -96°F[7]. A milder winter is experienced along the coastal regions of the Atlantic and Pacific Oceans with temperatures averaging close to -30°F[8]. Summer temperatures vary as well. Gale force winds are regular features of the landscape. The Arctic region is a harsh environment by anyone's calculations!

Soil conditions are marginal, at best. Most of the year the tundra is frozen with only the top few inches thawing during the short summer season. The small number of land animals – wolf, fox, caribou, reindeer, et al – depend equally on a small food chain, from plankton to fish, birds and sea animals; moss, lichen and an assortment of shrubs.

This means that human populations must create a culture that can maximize the use of snow, ice, rock and gravel, bones and skin from whales and other animals, fish, a few mammals and seasonal berries. Period.

Cultural Responses

The environmental effect on human cultural development in the Arctic is quite clear. *First, the environment did not allow heavy concentrations of people in any one area.* Small family bands of six to eighteen people were the norm. Neither did the harsh environs allow for rugged individualists.

Second, political control had to be vested in the kinship hunting unit, for decisions to move for the hunt had to be made quickly and independently of others. Authority resided in the male head of a family who kept the interests of the larger extended family in mind. Yet, it was important to keep a balance between the needs of one's family and the larger group.

Third, historic Arctic cultures were marketless economies driven by general reciprocity rules. Personal ownership of the small inventory of goods was, for the most part, nonexistent. Sharing was of primal importance. Everyone had to be able to carry their share of the work load for the group to survive. Only team players survived. Surplus females had to be distributed to productive hunting groups.

Fourth, the harsh and unforgiving environment and equalitarian social system called for complimentary personality traits.[9] Life was viewed fatalistically – a trait marking traditional peoples generally. The Inuit did not believe they controlled their own fate.

Therefore, the environment placed a high premium on personality traits that maintained group harmony. It was neither proper to point out another's faults nor to be one who was constantly complaining. One must not only be a team player but a positive and cheerful team player.

Fifth, although the technology is relatively simple, it is very efficient. Here, the use of the term "simple" refers only to the complexity of engineering. Inarguably, it takes a great deal of skill to use *Inuit* tools. Survival in such an unforgiving environment is a constant companion.

Sixth, Inuit religious beliefs were animistic, as is the case with most non-Westerners.[10] All animate and inanimate elements of their environment are alive, and imbued with a soul. The universe is full of forces that could kill, maim, prevent one from getting a kill, and so forth. There exists a whole mythology that rationalizes hunting activities. [11]

Implications For Doing Business

If one were trying to do business with the Inuit, it would certainly be worthwhile to grasp these preceding critical historic cultural developments. All Arctic peoples have now been affected to a significant degree by Western incursions. They now hunt with rifles, and herd reindeer and caribou from snowmobiles. Settlements have generous stores of Western goods, thereby eliminating the need for traditional migratory hunts and total dependence on Mother Nature. For the most part, the Western market economy has replaced the old share-and-barter system. Wooden homes have replaced those of stone and sod; Western clothing has replaced animal skins; Western-type schools have replaced parental lore; traditional myths have been replaced by Christianity taught by missionaries; and doctors and clinics have replaced traditional shaman and so on. But, most important, *the past is still in the present.*

An accurate portrait of another's culture cannot be sketched without knowing that just below the top layer of the cultural skin resides the cultural past – no matter who we are. For some that top layer may be thicker than others. In the case of the Inuit, the present Western layer is extremely thin by comparison with some others. The historic notions of fatalism; a preference for nonabrasive personality traits; a preference for sharing and trading; a relatively more mystical religious world view; a tilt toward family political autonomy; and the dominance of male heads of family; all are traits that should be taken into account in any business relation with the Inuit.

Nonetheless, American business persons are, for the most part, dealing with foreign business associates from more complex cultural configurations. The fact that their urban environments look like ours and they dress like we do complicates our task of understanding. All peoples have a distinct cultural past that informs the present.

The Japanese case provides another opportunity to see the impact of the environment on a more modern and complex culture.

A fuller treatment of this study can be found in the *Appendix to Chapter VI.*

Summary

The polar Arctic environment forced inhabitants to set fairly narrow limits on the size of hunting and settlement groups. Further, such a harsh environment favored an equalitarian collective organization, was intolerant of complex political organizations, minimized the number of tools needed for survival, accommodated a marketless economy of sharing and trading, encouraged a magical world-view and associated myths that focused on the habitat, and demanded positive outlooks from "team players."

THE JAPANESE CASE

The Habitat

Japan is an island nation, about the size of Montana. Only about fifteen percent of the land is cultivable.[12] The Japanese have had to maximize every nook and cranny of the environment. The large forests provide lumber for building and charcoal for fuel, although the Japanese have built a number of nuclear facilities over the last few decades and have for years been dependent on imported oil. Indeed, most minerals have to be imported. [13]

Since the islands lie in a northeasterly-southwesterly direction, the climate is extremely varied. The southern islands experience long hot summers and mild winters, while the north has cool summers and cold winters. Rainfall varies but is heaviest along the southeast coasts of the southern islands.

The islands are populated with 124 million people – a density of 860 per square mile which is one of the heaviest in the world.[14] Most of the people are crowded onto sixteen percent of the land in the non-mountainous area. This sixteen percent represents all the land available for cultivation, manufacturing, housing and all other human enterprises. This area is equal to that of West Virginia. Yet, the number of people per cultivated unit of land is the world's most efficient!

While the environment is not as physically harsh as the Arctic, nurturing a culture of such a large number of people in such a small, isolated space with such restricted resources is a significant challenge.

Cultural Responses

Sedentary farming practices seem to have been introduced by immigrants from Korea, the *Yayoi*, around B.C. 200.[15] Their rice irrigation system, the key to all future development and the mainstay of their culture, led to such surplus that specialities developed. Rice irrigation technology, for example, spawned a complex political apparatus and a significant technical capability along with the attendant social organization and craftsmen. It further exerted strong influence on all other aspects of culture.

Until reunification in the late 16th century, Japan's history had been marked by competition between feudal lords (*daimyo*) which in turn led to the emergence of a warrior group, the *samurai*. A class system developed that was similar to that in feudal Europe, but it operated on the basis of loyalty defined by Confucian ethics.

The feudal conflicts came to an end with the political reunification in the 16th century by the *Tokugawa* shoguns.[16] Exerting autocratic control, the nation was closed to the rest of the world. Travel outside the country was not permitted, and foreigners were prevented from entering Japan's borders. For the next two hundred and fifty years the system developed internally.[17] Urban centers began to develop. "Edo", now Tokyo, had a population of one million people; Kyoto and Osaka about five hundred thousand.[18]

A monetary system replaced rice as the basic medium of exchange. Swamps were drained as the government sought to increase food production to keep pace with a growing population; the merchant class expanded; the arts flourished; literacy grew; the old feudal estates gave way to autonomous villages; neighborhoods became extensions of the kinship system; and eventually *Tokugawa* control began to erode.[19]

In 1868, a year after the death of the emperor, a lad of fourteen was enthroned as the first emperor of the new *Meiji*, or "illustrious rule", restoration period.[20] But he did not in fact rule as such. An Imperial Council took power and issued what is known as "The Charter Oath," which stated that policy would be henceforth decided collegially. The Council's dream was, *first*, to create a wealthy country with a strong army.[21] *Second*, foreigners were no longer viewed as dangerous and new ideas from the outside world were welcomed. *Third*, the proposed army was to replace the *samurai*. *Fourth*, the Council eliminated class distinctions by emphasizing ability. Legally, all were equal.

Thus ensued a period of rapid industrialization. Japan transformed itself from a caterpillar to a butterfly, from a feudal peasantry to a modern state. Most importantly, for our purposes, this modern system was carefully grafted onto the traditional cultural configuration. Unless business people – or anyone else for that matter – understand this history, it is impossible to understand contemporary Japan.

Implications For Doing Business

Without knowing Japan's cultural history, it is impossible to understand the Japanese. It helps explain the intensity of the Japanese. The Japanese are characterized by the value placed on the past; the fascination tinged with varying degrees of fear of anything not appropriated and branded acceptable by the Japanese system; the dominance of the group and rejection of individualism; the strong control exerted by authority figures; the antagonism toward anything that divides the group; the dominant consciousness of being an island nation without needed resources; the predisposition to value traditional relationships as opposed to Western legalisms, and the special reverence for nature.

Summary

Japan's island environment, with its limited cultivable land, set very distinct limits on what could be done once the society moved beyond the fishing, hunting and gathering atage. If not for the immigrant *Yayoi* people, there is no reason to think that the original hunting and gathering system would have changed. The resulting rice irrigation system proved very effective in harvesting surpluses so as to free up major segments of the population so it could pursue other community interests.

It is in the nature of irrigation technology that a centralized governing authority is necessary because the productive elements of labor, land and water must be coordinated. This has led to Japan's highly stratified and autocratic management bureaucracy. In addition, irrigated rice technology, as a complex of activities, is not only labor intensive but requires a compliant labor force. It favors group-oriented personalities, not rugged individualists. This trait continues to characterize Japanese personalities to this day. Irrigated rice farming was a successful strategy, given the nature of the physical environment the Japanese faced. Although only about 9% of the population are involved in agriculture today, the historic culture produced by the irrigated rice process successfully continues to drive modern Japanese industry.

Japan's success can be explained by a number of historic features. *First*, rice farming required the productive organization of the population. Further, organized rice cultivation favored the development of strong political leaders' multiple specialties; and a highly stratified and hierarchically arranged society.

Second, the geographical isolation and lack of natural resources forced a heavy dependence by the Japanese on rice production whose labor intensive demands placed a high premium on group interests and solidarity. This, in turn, led to an eclectic religious focus which has served the interest in solidarity.[22]

Third, the organized cultivation of rice required hard physical labor, learning and an attention to detail rarely matched by other cultures. The confines of space and the total dependence on nature heightened the importance of space.

Fourth, the subsequent rise of a strong centralized autocracy, its rejection of outside influence and its internal social leveling, led to a more dramatic cultural homogenization. Although the doors were open to visitors and hence to outside influence, new ideas were reformulated so as to more seamlessly flow into traditional Japanese culture.

CHAPTER SUMMARY

There is so much more that could be said, but this should suffice to evidence the fact that a people's environment exerts strong influences over their culture-building efforts. Both the Inuit and Japanese cultures are products of significant environmental influence. It is extremely important for American business people to sketch the habitat's influence on a culture into a cultural portrait. Kroeber, an eminent anthropologist, while admitting that culture can be analyzed and understood on its own terms, insisted that none could be wholly intelligible outside its physical environment. [23]

References Cited

1. It is not the author's intent to sketch the arguments that exist in the anthropo-geography and cultural ecology literature about environment versus habitat, cultural areas, possibilism, functionalism, particularism and all the rest. The purpose is to provide foreign business persons with a perspective that "includes the relation of nature to culture development". The cultural ecology discussion is an interesting one and the literature is recommended to anyone wishing to pursue the details of the debate.See other suggested readings:

Roy Ellen, "Environment", *Subsistence and System* (Cambridge: Cambridge University Press, 1982).

C. Daryll Forde, *Habitat: Economy and Society* (London: Methuen & Company, 1934).

Marvin Harris, *Cannibals and Kings: The Origins of Cultures* (New York: Random House, 1977).

A.L. Kroeber, *Cultural and Natural Areas of Native North America* (Berkeley: University of California Press, 1939).

Ralph Linton, *The Study of Man* (New York, 1936).

Betty J. Meggers, "Environmental Limitation on the Development of Culture" in *Environment of Man* (Jack B. Presler, Editor), (Reading, MA: Addison Wesley Publishing Company, 1968), pp. 18-43.

S. G. Morley, *The Ancient Maya* (Stanford, CA: Stanford University Press, 1946).

Andrew Vayda, editor, *Environmental and Cultural Behavior: Ecological Studies in Cultural Anthropology* (Garden City, NY: Natural History Press, 1969).

2. Watterson, Bill, "Calvin and Hobbes" cartoon, distributed by Universal Press Syndicate (Kansas City, MO: March 4, 1994).

3. Marvin Harris, *Cannibals and Kings*. op.cit., pp. 168-189. The author reminds us of the human tragedy and cost of European peasantry.

4. T. R. Malthus, *An Essay on the Principles of Population* (London: McMillan Press, 1926).

5. Ernest S. Burch, Jr., *The Eskimos* (Norman: University of Oklahoma Press, 1988). p. 14.

Canadian Eskimos prefer the term, "Inuit", sometimes spelled "Innuit". Siberian Eskimos prefer to be called Yit and Alaskan Eskimos, "Inapuiq". These terms mean real or natural people, and another example of traditional ethnocentrism, discussed earlier. Also, when speaking of an individual member of the Inuit people, use the term "Inuk". Burch points out, however, that it is appropriate to use the term, Eskimo, due to the lack of unanimity on the label, and since Inuit "has never constituted more than sixty percent of the total Eskimo population", and that the term, Eskimo, "has been used consistently in the West for several hundred years."

6. *World Book Encyclopedia* (Chicago: World Book Inc., Volume 1, 1990), p. 637.

7. Ibid., p.637.

8. Ibid., p. 638.

9. Norman A. Chance, *The Eskimo of North Alaska* (New York: Holt, Rinehart & Winston, 1966) pp. 77-79.

10. Burch, op. cit., p. 89; Chance, op. cit., pp. 56-62.

11. Burch, op cit, p. 96.

12. Mikiso Hane, *Modern Japan: A Historical Survey* (Boulder, CO: Westview Press, 1986), p. 3; Peter Tasker, *The Japanese: A Major Exploration of Modern Japan* (New York: E.P. Dutton, 1987), p. 9.

13. Hane, op. cit., p. 5.

14. *Collier's Encyclopedia* (New York: MacMillan Educational Company, 1990), Volume 13, p. 454.

15. Hane, loc. cit.; Edwin O. Reischauer, *Japan: The Story of A Nation* (New York: Alfred A. Knopf, third edition, 1981), pp. 10-12.

16. Hane, op. cit., p. 21f; Reischauer, *The Japanese Today* (Cambridge, MA: Belknap Press, 1988), pp. 64-70.

17. Hane, op. cit., p. 81; Reischauer, op. cit., p. 68.

18. Reischauer, ibid, p. 70.

19. Ibid, p. 97f.

20. Ibid, p. 118.

21. Ibid, p. 119.

22. Frank Gibney, *Japan: The Fragile Superpower* (New York: W.W. Norton & Company, 1975), pp. 321-385.

23. Alfred L. Kroeber, "Relations of Environmental and Cultural Factors", in Environment and Cultural Behavior, Andrew P. Vayda, editor, (Garden City, NY: The Natural History Press, 1969), pp. 350-361.

Chapter VII:
The Technological Scene

*You will always find some Eskimos ready to instruct
the Congolese on how to cope with heat waves.*
> – *Stanilaw Lec*

Unlike the *habitat*, American business people have little difficulty understanding that a people's technology influences the
shape of their culture. A useful cultural portrait of another people
should include what views and acts American business persons can
generally expect to find among people with various technological
traditions. Chapter VII examines technologies devised by human
groups to solve their extraction needs and suggests ways that these
technologies influence one's culture. *Hunting and gathering
(includes fishing)* and *pastoralism* are briefly mentioned even
though their cultural patterns have diminished. It would be well to
remember that fishing and pastoral patterns still prevail among
people in this world.

The main focus of this chapter will be on *horticulture, irrigation, intensive* (simple to mechanized), and *modern (industrial,
post-industrial, hi-tech)* processes, since these technologies are glo-
bally predominant. This simple classification will suffice for our
purposes.

The goal of this exercise is to provide American business
people a set of technological categories that can be used in sketching cultural portraits and to provide some general ideas of what
they can expect to find among people who have been shaped by a
particular technology.

Technology refers to a people's set of tools, the muscular acts necessary to use the tools and the organization needed by the first two features.

Though most groups can be characterized by the *dominance of one technology,* most use multiple strategies. For example, the Inuit as discussed in Chapter VI are primarily hunters who also gather and fish. Some, such as the Lapps of Norway and the Chuckchi of Siberia, are mainly herders, who also fish, hunt, and gather. Each distinct extraction process necessitates a different cultural construction, although the more complex the technology, the more variations exist.

A problem that quickly arises when studying cultures is why various people, occupying the same physical habitat, develop different extraction strategies. Chapter VI emphasized that habitats vary. Some set fairly broad limits on what people can do. Others narrowly limit human potential. One cannot farm in the polar regions or herd camels – or any other animals – in a tropical rain forest. It seems that the more diverse the habitat, the greater the degree of diversity among human populations. Reasons vary as to why people sharing the same environment choose different technologies. There does not seem to be any reason which can be universally applied except human contrariness. It may be preferable to think of it as people's creative impulses. Someone tries something innovative, it works; others in the group imitate it and the innovation is established.

Improvisation and contrariness seem to be fairly universal human traits. Technologies are more than responses to the environment's broad limiting factors. They are *adaptive responses* to specific human needs and opportunities in specific localities. Individual impulses to try new ways of responding to their circumstances are the key to cultural adaptation. Technologies, historically, are developed within a group. These may be borrowed, imposed from outsiders or arrived at accidently.

While two contrasting cultures in Chapter VI, the Inuit and Japanese, provided the format for showing the relative impact of the environment on culture development, technological scenes will be used to shape the following presentation.

HISTORICAL TECHNOLOGIES

Hunting and Gathering (Includes Fishing)

Humans have spent most of their time hunting and gathering food resources.[1]

As noted in the case of the polar Inuit, hunting and gathering is a highly *nomadic, dispersive technology*. It has been strategically successful in almost all the world's environments: semiarid, forest, polar, plains and mountains. Hunting and gathering prohibits population density and large permanent settlements that characterize agricultural types. The tool inventory has to be small and resources shared. Hunters and gatherers must have keenly developed observation skill. They must know their environment, down to the most minute detail. A hunting-gathering society is highly egalitarian. Political authority resides in the family and kinship networks, and the economy is marked by simple sharing. Families consolidate to form *bands* and each band chooses a spokesman or *headman* who speaks for that band during contact with outsiders and who also settles internal disputes. These positions were quasi-formal. An individual remains headman as long as he maintains the confidence of others.

Religious and political relations are complex and make modern analysis difficult. The religious view is animistic which is the belief that rocks, mountains, trees, and such possess a life force. A *shaman* is a medium through which a society communicates with the spirit world. Death and interdiction rites[2] were often conducted by others.[3] The shaman represents a group's attempt to deal with the stress and anxieties brought on by an environment that seems to have a life of its own. The shaman further plays a key role in solidifying the group.

Although most Americans will not be doing business with today's hunters and gatherers, there are sufficient numbers of them that it is important to learn what to expect. This would include such geographically disparate peoples as the following: desert nomads, the Inuit, Lapps, Siberians, American Indians, Australian Aborigines as well as numerous Latin American, African and Asian groups from tropical forests – all of which comprises a large number of people.

In summary, one should be prepared for people whose mystical view of the world leads to a heightened sense of conservatism as reflected in a strong fatalistic mentality. Personal ownership is an alien notion. Land, water and all other natural resources belong to everyone. All have equal access. Kin relations are most trusted. Non-kin are strangers and, as such, they are to be feared. Elderly males and their respective kinship units are fiercely independent. These are ideas foreign to Western thinking and capitalism. Conducting business, as it is practiced in the West, is extremely difficult.

Pastoralism (Herding)

Pastoralism (animal husbandry) and horticulture are linked extraction strategies,[4] but, for present purposes, pastoralism will be treated as a separate issue.

Pastoralism refers specifically to the care, breeding and maintenance of herd animals. Whereas hunters only harvest animals, pastoralists protect their animals from other predators, disease and starvation. In return, the animals provide pastoralists with a form of currency with which to buy food and other products. Not all pastoralists are exclusively herders. Some may be only herders, but others may be herders as well as horticulturists.

Animals supplement garden crops and provide a form of protection in case the garden crops are wiped out. Pastoralism evolved as an adaptive strategy to the rigors of land cultivation and the intrusion of neighbors. As horticultural populations grew, they placed added demands on the environment. The tendency to settle on selected acreage reduced the time spent in the hunting and gathering process, putting greater reliance on hoe work and herding of small bands of animals. In turn, this meant that one could not easily pick up and move to a more promising locality when drought, disease, floods and other natural disasters destroyed the crops and ravaged the animals.

As herders became hoe cultivators and their populations increased, there was less tendency to move. With the increased population came the need to obtain more land to accomodate the greater numbers of people. In its simplest form this is how wars begin.[5]

When pastoralism is associated with horticulture, the herds are often small, although that depends on the grazing land available and pressures exerted from other landowners. Time is split between farming and herding. Those groups who largely depend on their herds are highly nomadic. It is essential to move herds from pasture to pasture to take advantage of grasslands, but no pastoralist is happy moving his herds.

Few groups rely solely on pastoralism, the most notable exception being the Bedouin camel herders of north Arabia.[6] A mixture of the two technologies has proven to be a far more adaptive strategy and is still the fundamental strategy in most parts of Africa, the Middle East and many parts of Europe.

While pure pastoralists, like their hunting and gathering forefathers, have few tools and implements, household inventory is transported by the animals themselves. All their implements have to be easily and quickly broken down, packed, unpacked, and put back up for brief periods of time.

Pure pastoralism places limits on the size of the population. It is not practical to have thousands of people tromping off across the plains, each herding hundreds of his own cattle. Chaos and environmental calamity would result. Not only must the numbers be kept relatively small, but the authority or political center has to be the head of the pastoral band, household or tenting unit.

The head of a pastoral band must be free to decide when and where to go. Pastoral people tend to be highly independent individuals who are quick to fight when their autonomy is challenged. But they operate in close proximity to more highly populated agricultural peoples, and they develop some fairly strong tribal political structures. The tribal affiliation serves as a protective association as well as a source for exchanging and bartering. It also serves as an exchange for information or providing news of environmental and land conditions.

Pastoral technology is not a totally sufficient system in and of itself. Herders have always had a symbiotic relationship with local sedentary peoples. Pastoral peoples tend to be found in those environments where farming is not entirely productive and where the grazing technique efficiently picks up scarce energy in the form of grasses and other plants. It also provides useful necessities for humans by providing meat, milk, blood, draft labor, dung for fuel, hides for clothing and houses.

The historical technologies, presented thus far, can be summarized as follows:

First, pastoralism varies in the degree to which it is dependent upon another extraction process. *Second*, it is a highly nomadic existence where kinship via the household or tenting unit is the basic social unit. *Third*, it is efficient for small groups that reside in harsh arid to semi-arid environments where conditions prohibit agriculture and dense populations.

Fourth, tribal affiliations are common and provide overall habitat coordination, group identity, protection and source of trade. *Fifth*, pastoralists are highly individualistic, emotionally volatile, and combative – traits prized by the technology. Pastoral people are hard to govern (e.g. Afghan resistance to the Soviets was led by pastoral and former pastoral peoples; also note the problem Saddam Hussein has had "governing" the Kurds).[7]

Sixth, pastoralism has few tools and those used require little muscular energy relative to those used by hunters and gatherers.

Seventh, pastoral economies generally provide a subsistence level life. They can be marketless, as in case of the African *Karimojong*,[8] or market related, like Turkey's *Yoruk*.[9] Yet, most are tied to some market. None rely solely on their animals for food. While animals determine one's status and prestige, vegetables, fruits, and other foods are acquired through barter and trade with regional sedentary farmers. Exchange relations may, and usually are, calculated on a market defined by agriculture and a broader national-market pricing system.

Eighth, pastoral religious world views vary from traditional *animistic-shamanism*, which typified circumpolar groups (reindeer and caribou herders), to *communal* (American Indian buffalo herders), to a highly philosophical *theism*.[10] While Mideastern pastoral groups are generally Islamic (monotheistic), their pre-Islamic history is polytheistic. The Judeo-Christian history is certainly characterized by pastoral polytheists.

American business people should approach pastoral peoples expecting to find people whose self-identities reflect clan and/or tribal affiliations, who prefer to carry out all cultural activities within their own group, whose world view ranges from animism to philosophical theism, and who have sophisticated trading skills.

CONTEMPORARY TECHNOLOGIES

Horticulture

Hoe agriculture technology evolved as hunters and gatherers discovered that preventing weeds from crowding and choking their edible plants led to a more dependable food supply. Using a simple hoe they began an elementary form of *horticulture*.[11]

It was discovered that the sowing of seeds, proper soil management and innovative planting methods produced fairly predictable harvests. Thus, *domestication of plants* began. These hoe cultivators were now able to reduce the uncertainty of food harvesting and increase the productivity per unit of land. This was a significant advance by humankind,[12] but increased the complexity for those hunters and gatherers who made the change.

Hoe technology shared with hunting and gathering the dependence on muscular energy. Hoe cultivators expended more energy to produce less of a harvest than their hunting counterparts. The technology did not immediately lead to consistently large surpluses. It was this subsistence economy that reduced the group's need to roam and led to the development of semi-sedentary villages. However, this did not mean that all hunters and gatherers wanted to settle down to a sedentary existence.

Hoe cultivation led to larger populations, significant independence from the former hunting-gathering kin units and greater demand on the environment's resources. These developments resulted in more complex forms of social organization, thus triggering associated changes in the rest of the culture which further demonstrates the systemic nature of culture.

The former hunting and gathering bands were replaced by households as the core of social organization. As households developed, a greater need for protection became apparent, thus kinship relations became more complex. Often there was a shift of control from males to females who owned and worked the gardens. This led, in many cases, to inheritance being determined by the female's blood line.

The early Western Pueblo Indians of North America provide a good example of female control.[13] Men worked the fields, hunted, spun and wove cotton and did many other similar chores. Females worked hard as well. Daughters usually stayed with their mother their entire life. Although sons moved to their wife's household, they constantly returned to their mother's house to participate in *clan* rituals.[14]

In such cases political control resides first in households, then in clans and tribal relations. Among the Western Pueblos a woman's clan owned the land, houses, and all other property used by the household. In severe times a clan could splinter off and seek a more productive farming site. As moving did not mean a break-up of the family, the clan provided all the cultural ingredients for a totally new village. In addition to clans the early Western Pueblo created religious societies which brought all clans together in a closely-knit tribal society. This effectively prevented clan competition from tearing the social fabric apart.

The early Eastern Pueblos provide an interesting contrast to their Western colleagues, however.[15] They utilized irrigation to stabilize their crop production,[16] but a price was paid for this change to irrigation. The strong clans, which were prone to follow their own interests, were replaced by centralized authority.

Although the harvest per land-unit was greater, the energy output (labor) was much greater than former technologies and not as efficient. Female dominance, as noted among the Western Pueblo, was replaced by male dominance in the Eastern group. It was soon realized that soils became nutritionally weak in a few years which led to a process called *shifting cultivation*.

One form of this shifting horticulture is *swidden*, or slash and burn. It was used extensively before the advent of the plow in Europe, by Indians and by early European settlers in America. The practice is still used in Southeast Asia, Africa and Latin America. Swidden is a form of shifting horticulture where fields are created by setting fire to the forest. After the fire is out and the ash has cooled, the soil is fertilized by the remaining ash, and the landowners use a digging stick or hoe to puncture the soil for bedding the seeds. Weeds are cleared with a hoe, as usual. A plot is used for a few years and then left to lie fallow. Sometimes it takes ten to fifteen years for a swidden plot to recover its nutrient capacity.

Hoe cultivators were gradually altering their habitat as they cut and burned the forests and brushlands. The more efficient the technology, the greater their reproductive capacity and denser the population. Thus, the larger the number of people, the greater the demand on the environment to produce greater amounts of energy and other resources.

Although more efficient than pure hunting and gathering, simple hoeing is the least efficient form of agriculture. It yields the lowest amount of energy and nutrients from a unit of land in relation to the amount of energy people have to expend than other forms of agriculture. Surplus is not generally produced. It is basically a *subsistence economy*.

While their tools are fairly few and simple, hoe cultivators generally know their environment as well as hunters and gatherers. They understand the different soils, topography and climate. They know how to burn a plot without destroying the whole forest and the basic needs of their plants. The tools still demand the use of human physical energy, but they do not have to maximize this energy in order to survive in a sedentary setting.

Gender continues to be the basis for a division of labor among hoe cultivators. Women generally tend the gardens and gather berries and other available foods. Men hunt and fish as well as help with the garden plots and gather foods now and then. While this technology does not produce a significant surplus, it does lead to greater population density and more complex social organization. The household, which usually included an extended kinship network, is the basic unit of horticultural social organization. Several households comprise a clan and a village which become important political units. As with hunters and gatherers, villages are governed by kinship, people's homogeneity of values and world views. Each village has a headman, but he continues to exert authority as long as he holds the confidence of the people.

The introduction of a hoe agricultural technology and the resulting increase in population density led to another change of view of the habitat. A village's interest in specific land and water sites, plus the need for women, led to greater group solidarity and more intense competition with other groups. Groups began to battle over scarce resources on a larger scale. The trade of women, scarce goods and the exchange of gifts and feasts became strategies for creating alliances and making peace. Balanced *reciprocity rules* are strong. A tooth for a tooth, an eye for an eye, a gift for a gift and a favor for a favor was the rule. Social life has not become easier or more peaceful!

The world view of hoe people takes what might be seen as a step toward greater complexity. While everything still seemed to have a life of its own, the dependency on rain and the need for protection from a plethora of natural forces suggested the need for greater help. This resulted in a *communal*[17] type religion marked by less individualism, by a growth in the belief in mythology, and by the practice of rituals according to seasons, individual life cycles and special events.

In summary, American business people should approach hoe cultivators and those with this cultural background as generally clannish or tribal. They tend to be suspicious of newcomers and are shy. They possess a tradition of trading and bartering as well as a strong commitment to balanced reciprocity in building their business relationships. The more intensive their farming tradition, the more the need to cultivate personality traits conducive to keeping peaceful neighborly relations. Aggression usually takes an indirect form. A provoked or embarrassed person will probably cut off the relationship completely, which means one is alienated from that household, village, tribe or company. Or, the wounded person may invoke evil spirits upon the culprit.

Westerners regularly find personal and group alienation prevalent in Latin America in various forms. One's failure to observe the reciprocal amenities, to deceive or fail to act will lead to quick loss of social affiliation. The casting of the evil eye (*mal ojo*) is an attempt to call down the demons on one in order to cause illness and harm.

Intensive Agriculture

Intensive agriculture originates with irrigation and extends to the plow, the use of draft animals to pull the plow and farm machines.[18] These activities differ from horticulture by their increased labor needs and productivity, or yield per land unit (hectare or acre).[19] Intensification not only increases the yield per acre of land but also allows more land to be worked more efficiently with more labor or energy input. Often one can realize two or three crops per year on the same plot, but to do so one has to have a reasonably dependable water source. It is the intent of this section to focus on the non-mechanized types of intensive agriculture, as most American business people will have knowledge of highly mechanized farming.

A study by Clifford Geertz in 1963 noted that the Indonesian island of Java comprises about nine percent of the country's total land area, two-thirds of its population, and the bulk of its food stuffs (86% of its peanuts, 60% of the rice, 70% of the manioc, 90% of the soybeans and other products).[20] Java's rice irrigation system is responsible for its high productivity per unit of land. The majority of Indonesians still practice traditional horticulture. This productive disparity eloquently displays the productive difference between horticulture and intensive agriculture while not taking into consideration the inefficiency of labor costs per calorie unit gathered.

Intensive agriculture is the result of introducing more intensive labor teams per unit of land and eventually substituting other, more efficient muscle or horse power. Animals yoked to simple plows provided the earliest form of this labor. Over the years we have added machines, coupled with more efficient strains of seed, man-made fertilizers and pesticides.

Intensive farming evolved out of irrigation technology. Historically, it looked like a reasonable upgrade from horticultural technology. It would not take many seasons of difficult hoe work and the continual loss of crops to drought to make one appreciate the importance of water. Couple this with increased population density, pressure to produce greater yields, encroachment by neighbors, attempts to keep the men home, and one has the ingredients that beget new solutions.

Greater production led to denser populations and increased specialties, which in turn led to the emergence of larger population centers. Some settlements were comprised of many hundreds of thousands of people.[21] The Spaniards were surprised by the size of Maya, Aztec and Inca cities at the time of the conquest. Many were larger than anything in Europe. The complexity of these early sites continues to amaze even contemporary humans.

Politically, headmen became big-men, chiefs, emperors, presidents or kings. There has always been an abundance of big-men throughout history willing to take on this coordinating and managerial activity. The big-men also expanded trade and territorial rights while defending their lands.[22]

Households and villages traded their independence to big-men in return for more productive and dependable crops and security. In other words, households, clans, tribes and peasant people lost control of their lands and their lives. An exploitative relationship continued to characterize relations between peoples and their leaders.

Although people changed over to intensive agriculture in order to increase yields by increasing their control of nature, the net effect in yield increase was not as beneficial as expected. It seems that the more people alter their environment, the more they labor to maintain the system. In the case of irrigation, the original source of the water must be watched; canals and terraces cleaned and repaired; weeds, insects and all type of pests must be removed; draft animals and/or machinery maintained; and good relations with neighbors constantly cultivated. Intensive agriculture is labor intensive and exhausting work.

Given the nature of intensive agriculture and its impact on culture, business people may expect to find people who are relatively subdued or acquiescent within their social and political units in comparison to hunters and gatherers and pastoralists. Their cultural homogeneity leads to suspicion and rejection of strangers. This does not mean traditional agricultural people are necessarily inhospitable to strangers, but the reception depends on a visitor's purpose. It means *strangers* are at the far end of a continuum of intimacy, a characteristic shared by all previously discussed premodern peoples. Berger notes that whereas Westerners live their lives amidst large numbers of strangers, non-Western people live their entire lives with intimates.[23]

If a *stranger / outsider* proves to be of racial or ethnic kin, he is viewed and treated as a more trusted stranger/outsider. Those of other races or ethnicities are strangers/outsiders, although there will be further classifications depending on the group. Given time, the *outsider* may move to a more intimate social position, either by marrying into the group or performing significant service to the group's welfare such as becoming a teacher or a doctor, or may tolerate the group's resistance to intimacy and exist in a socio-cultural isolation, or may depart by reason of the pressure.

There are many examples to illustrate the ways intensive agricultural people contend with strangers. Some of these were mentioned earlier in Chapter IV, but they are now repeated for emphasis. The culturally homogeneous Chinese place "overseas Chinese" in a special ethnic category that is significantly more intimate that non-Chinese. Non-Chinese are tolerated but never totally accepted. They are referred to as *kwa lo*, or foreign devils! Japanese raised somewhere other than Japan are labeled as *neisi*. When *neisi* return to Japan to work or live, they are looked upon and treated as *trusted outsiders*. Koreans and other non-Japanese born and raised in Japan are in a trusted-outsider category. It seems as though the whole Japanese population composes a single confined village. This *insider-outsider* pattern characterizes agricultural populations worldwide, regardless of modernism, with significant nuances.

Business people can expect to find a more complex religious world view among intensive agricultural people. This falls into what Wallace describes as *Olympian* or monotheistic.[24] *Olympian* refers to those early irrigation systems whose people found the forces of nature and their adaptive needs so great as to call forth a plethora of gods (polytheistic). The developing theology led to the construction of large temples, pyramids and associated religious paraphernalia. A copus of religious writing developed along with a formal priesthood. Rituals follow the change of seasons.

Olympian systems arose in Middle America (Maya, Aztec, et al), South America's Pacific coast region (Inca, et al), Africa (Daho-mey, Yoruba, Ashanti tribes in Uganda and Madagascar), the Middle East (Egypt, Sumer, et al), and Southeast Asia (Burma,

Thailand, Indonesia, China, et al). This established religious construct began to shape and govern the culture, which influence began to lead, in most cases, to a theocratic political system.

This sketches the basic and most general outlines of the relationship between intensive agriculture, religion and cultures. It does not account for the variety of differences in social, political, economic and religious constructions that are found between villages a few miles apart, as Pasternak's study of two Chinese villages reveals.[25] When we consider industrialism and its effect on these aforementioned traditional cultures, we face considerable complexity and a variation of responses.

INDUSTRIAL TO MODERN HIGH-TECHNOLOGY

Industrialism is characterized by the replacement of human and animal labor with machines and the rise of factories.[26] The use of machines, initiated by the invention of the steam engine, led to the development of a technology that greatly increased the amount of energy captured per capita far beyond any other technology.[27] This caused life to change dramatically.

Instead of tending herds, fields or plots of land, our most immediate ancestors tended machines. People became tinkerers and maintainers of machines and the associated gadgets produced by machine labor. Who has not experienced the exasperation that accompanies the maintenance of the family cars, air-conditioning and heating systems and other household machines or appliances which dominate our lives in this industrial, post-industrial and high technology society?

That great social philosopher, Calvin, of Calvin and Hobbes comic strip, often reflects our fears and frustrations. Calvin has been having a lot of trouble coping with his bicycle. The cycle keeps attacking him. On this occasion he rushes up to Hobbes, who is sitting under a nice shade tree, and reports:

> "I did it Hobbes! I did just what you said! I put a stick in the
> spokes of my killer bicycle! When it tried to chase me, it

flipped over! I wrestled it to exhaustion and then I let the air out of its tires! Ha! I guess that nasty ol' thing won't be coming after me anymore! We're too smart for it! Man triumphs over machine!"

The last frame shows Calvin's parents down on their knees trying to fix the cycle. His mother says:

"Training wheels! What a good idea!"

To which his father retorts:

"I pumped up his tires too. They were both flat."[28]

Has not the threat of our machines entered everyone's life? All can relate to Calvin's problem. Not only did machines geometrically heighten the amount of energy and other nutrients that could be drawn from a unit of land but gave humankind an ability to tap and use the world's resources far beyond our wildest dreams. This freed the majority of people from direct food production activity and resulted in a rapid proliferation of specialties. Moderns have now become a new breed of hunters: we have become *shoppers*.

For every industrial and/or hi-technology food producer, there are literally thousands of others in the service industry. Millions of industrial peoples are so far removed from their traditional rural agrarian roots that the only farm they see is on television or from the car window.

Urban insulation is a modern characteristic in the West. *Modernism* is a label that refers to the industrial and post-industrial cultural configuration[29]and to a people having the technical skills, attitudes and orientations needed for functioning in a post-agricultural technological system. This system includes the hi-technology ambience of the computer chip and the resulting transformation of communication and information management.

For our purposes there is little value in dissecting post-agricultural technology into conceptual parts in order to emphasize specific technical leaps, such as the smashing of the atom or the development of the computer chip. It is sufficient to recognize all post-agricultural technologies as *Western, modern or hi-technology.*

The following cites a number of the most obvious results of modern technology:

First, industrialization and post-industrialization technology has made the procurement of energy sources so productive that the world's population exploded far beyond anything imagined. The problem is no longer food production. Huge quantities of grains and other food stocks can be stored. Foods can be packaged, freeze-dried and concentrated for future use and world wide marketing.

Second, in this increasingly hi-technology sphere the activity of *work* has to do more with handling and managing information than operating and caring for machines or products. Management tasks now take precedence over manufacturing. Labor and the workplace have changed.

Due to the enormous ability of machines to extract energy, a relatively small number of people are directly involved with food and resource production or manufacturing. The latter is increasingly done by populations moving directly from horticulture or intensive agriculture and whose economies can handle what the more technologically advanced nations consider low-wage tasks. It is a known fact that a modern nation cannot prosper without possessing its own manufacturing base. This is an American dilemma.

The Western work place is a glass and steel, climate controlled cocoon where communications and the processing of information by electronic media is conducted. It is no longer conducted in factories or in fields but on the computer at home, in the car, plane or hotel room. We have moved beyond Fordism's economies of scale to economies of scope. There is a more dispersive batch-type production system that has compressed the world's space and time features.[30]

Third, the proliferation of specialties has accelerated beyond most people's ability to comprehend. Hi-technology tasks demand a high degree of literacy with the ability to think analytically and operate corporately, far beyond that which developed from earlier technological behavior. The old reliance on muscle, or masculine aggressiveness, is no longer useful. It is highly detrimental in

140

today's technological environment. The system demands technological specialization, not muscle power. This has led to the development of a vast educational apparatus, has increased time spent in formal training and has spawned the need for retraining to keep up with changes. Moderns must be lifelong students.

Fourth, probably no aspect of hi-technology provides Americans as much stress as does the need to adapt to *corporate dependency.* Modern technology no longer values rugged, radical individualists. This adaptability, or lack of it, demonstrates the ease or difficulty with which cultural change takes place. Time will tell whether modernization's historic emphasis on radical individualism can accommodate contemporary corporate demands. There may be room for both personality types, but the number of rugged individualists accommodating to the newer corporate individualism will increase over time. Hi-technology needs and rewards loyalty, team players and corporate members. It penalizes the individualist. Creativity, although historically linked to the notion of rugged individualism, is increasingly attached to the corporate or communal unit. While modernity is responsible for radical individualism and the freedoms we know so well in the West, it also made totalitarianism possible by the creation of large bureaucratic institutions.[31]

This new development may have produced the phenomena of corporate constrained individualism. Although modernity demands one's creativity, it must serve a communal interest. Individuals must be geographically mobile. One must be willing to leave the old neighborhood, hometown, and even family, to go where the corporate and communal needs exist.

Fifth, modernism has inherited the class, caste, religion, kinship and nationality features that marked social rankings of past intensive agricultural systems. They do not work well anymore. Modern technology cannot tolerate these outdated social configurations.[32] It creates new ones based on education and skill, not race, gender and family pedigree.

The old technological categories of race, gender, family or tribal pedigree impede modernization. Modern technology focuses on brain power and is blind to such distinctions. These old images cannot continue to dominate the social thought and behavior of any people seeking to either modernize or maximize their existing technologies. The continued existence of these social contructions is detrimental to all concerned.

Old colonial images continue to exist in global relations. People from former colonial nations have a tendency to relate paternally to non-Western peoples. Non-Western peoples tend to play their prior dependency roles. These tend to cling like old *shogun* mentalities in Japan. They no longer serve modern technology.

Sixth, hi-technology brings a whole new world view. In this critical sense traditional non-Western leaders are not mistaken. Modernism is a destroyer of past traditions. The advanced system that has now developed no longer supports traditional spiritual myths. The universe is comprised of chemicals and compounds to be mined, mixed and shaped into physical forms and not metaphysical beings.

Seventh, old political relations are no longer appropriate. Modernism has brought along with it a need for people to realize social bonds. Today's social integration patterns are much different from those prevailing in agrarian or even early manufacturing societies. Modernism liberates people from the former hierarchical socio-political relations of tribe, clan and village level organizations as it seeks to develop people's individualism. This is especially true of modernization's trend towards capitalism and democracy.[33] The urban environment, the region, the nation and even the world replace the village as a basic focus. Choice replaces fate, expectations rise and people dare to become more mobile.

This transformation leads to new socio-political realignments and triggers people's demand for greater control over their lives. Old race, gender, age and class subjugations attempt to cling on tenaciously.

Eighth, in relegating gender, race, nationality, religion and all their associated mental images to the outmoded past, modern technology seeks a globalization of these features. All people adopting modern technology move to establish educational and economic institutions that are so vital to serving the technological system.

The globalization of multinational corporations might be viewed as a first stage of the process. The emergence of companies that are, for practical purposes, global or *transnational* illustrates new ways to prosper. They can no longer be easily characterized as simply *multinationals*.

We traditionally looked at a multinational company as one developed and owned by the people in one nation that has branch or subsidiary operations in several other countries. Now the likelihood is great that a company will be owned by stockholders in many countries and will no longer be majority-owned by stockholders in the founding nation. The home office may be in a totally different country from either the founders or the majority shareholders. The company is no longer rooted to any particular national entity. It is a *global* establishment.

One can buy an American car and find the majority of its parts were manufactured in dozens of other countries. The final production company may be a joint venture between Japanese, German, Swiss and American firms. It is an entirely new cultural organization. Again, it is a *global* product.

Globalization seems to be culturally bringing large segments of people together as a unit, ignoring nationality, race, gender or any other category. Globalization may significantly level the technical and social inequities now existing, although we may see new ones emerging. The biggest question is how much of the old patterns, kinship, or religion will find compatibility in this emerging system? Only time or a great prophet will tell.

In summary, for our purpose modernization can be viewed as a totally new cultural construction. Great care must be taken in applying this idea as an accomplished fact to our foreign business associates or to all Westerners. Products do not a culture make. A camel herder in the Mideast can view a portable color television in his tent, but he is not Westernized; nor is there any reason why he would even want to be. The ideas and images conveyed through the television are selectively viewed and received. People are not Xerox copiers mimicking everything they see and hear.

Although Westerners live in what can be generally called a modern world, it is doubtful that all Westerners are modern. There are significant numbers who lack any number of modern cultural traits. Millions are still oriented to a horticultural type of system. Millions of others, living in rural areas, small towns and major cities are still significantly oriented to a plow culture. The cultural transformation is everywhere in process and is incomplete. American business people would be best served by assuming that their non-Western business associates are not completely modern.

It is certainly obvious that some things are directly responsible for triggering cultural transformations and others are not. It seems that those things most directly related to a group's extraction process, that necessitate supportive alignments from the other cultural components, should be thought of as strongly transforming. Once a change is underway other material developments can accelerate and drive the process.

There is no arguing that the hoe, plow and the cluster of activities surrounding herding, irrigation and the machine all triggered cultural transformations of great note. When new cultural alignments took place, newer and more efficient technology only increased the system's complexity. Irrigation technology radically transformed horticulture, while more efficient irrigation technology only increased complexity. Industrial technology was a dramatic change from farm culture, and the material goods produced from the industrialization has led to increased complexity.

For those who are interested in this issue, it is important to isolate those elements that are directly responsible for present-day modernization. Business people should not assume that the presence of television, western clothing, automobiles and McDonalds' hamburgers, to name a few, are direct transformations of traditional cultures. These items are but *global* products.

Cultural change may not come quickly or easily, but what we call Western hi-technology has certainly triggered the biggest cultural transformation the world has yet seen.

References Cited

1. There is a great deal of literature analyzing hunting-gathering peoples. See for example, any anthropology text and such works as:

R. Ardrey, *African Genesis* (London: Collins Pub., 1961);

D. Bates, *The Passing of the Aborigines: A Lifetime Spent Among the Natives of Australia* (New York: G. P. Putnum, 1938);

Marvin Harris, *Good To Eat* (London: Allen & Unwin, 1986);

Eleanor Leacock & Richard Lee, *Politics and History in Band Societies* (Cambridge: Cambridge University Press, 1982);

R. B. Lee, *The Dobe! Kung* (New York: Holt, Rinehart & Winston, 1984); and R. B. Lee and I. Devore, editors, *Man The Hunter* (New York: Aldine, 1968);

G.W. Stocking, *Race, Culture and Evolution: Essays in the History of Anthropology* (Chicago: University of Chicago Press, 1982);

Colin M. Turnbull, *Man in Africa* (Garden City, NY: Anchor Press, 1976); p. 1f; and Colin M. Turnbull, *The Forest People: A Study of the Pygmies of the Congo* (New York: Simon & Schuster, 1961).

Interesting and related are:

Marvin Harris, *Cannibals and Kings: The Origins of Cultures* (New York: Random House, 1977);

Robert Claiborne, *Climate, Man and History* (New York: W. W. Norton & Company, Inc., 1970).

2. Interdiction rites would be similar to Christian confessions and absolution. A rite was intended to restore universal balance.

3. Fred Plog and Daniel G. Bates, *Cultural Anthropology*, 2nd Edition (New York: Alfred A. Knopf, 1980), pp. 372-373.

4. Regarding pastoral systems, see:

Fredrik Barth, *Nomads of South Persia* (New York: Humanities Press, 1965);

Daniel G. Bates, "Nomads and Farmers: A Study of the Yoruk of Southeastern Turkey," *Anthropological Papers,* Vol. 52 (Ann Arbor: University of Michigan Museum of Anthropology, 1973);

B. Campbell, *Human Ecology* (London: Heinemann Press, 1983);

Dale F. Eickelman, *The Middle East: An Anthropological Approach* (Englewood Cliffs, NJ: Prentice Hall, 1981);

T. Ingold, *The Skolt Lapps Today* (Cambridge: Cambridge University Press, 1976);

Hunters Ingold, *Pastoralists and Ranchers: Reindeer Economics and Their Transformation* (Cambridge: Cambridge University Press, 1980);

A. M. Khazanov, *Nomads and the Outside World*, translated by J. Crookenden (Cambridge: Cambridge University Press, 1984);

Philip C. Salzman, editor,*When Nomads Settle: Processes of Sedentarization as Adaptation and Response* (New York: Praeger Publishing, 1980).

5. When people are geographically bound and population pressures squeeze limited resources even tighter, people develop rationales to justify driving others away. Regardless of stated "justifications", wars are generally waged over scarce resources.

6. Barth, loc. cit.

7. The literature supports this characteristic, but see especially Eickelman, op.cit., p. 63f; also Leacock & Lee, op.cit., Part III.

8. Plog and Bates, op. cit., pp. 136-140.

9. Modern ranchers are certainly market-dominated, as are the *Lapps* and numerous others who operate in a symbiotic relation with neighboring farmers.

10. Anthony F. C. Wallace, *Religion: An Anthropological View* (New York: Random House, 1966. Wallace also includes an intermediate religious type he calls Olympian that describes a step in complexity between communal and the theisms, but the author is unaware of any pastoral group that fits this model. The Olympian does fit the irrigation systems described later.

11. Regarding horticulture, see any anthropology text, also:

T. P. Bayliss-Smith, *The Ecology of Agricultural Systems* (Cambridge: Cambridge University Press, 1982);

H. C. Conklin, *Hanunoo Agriculture* (Rome: United Nations Food & Agricultural Organization, 1957);

E. K. Fisk, *The Adaptation of Traditional Agriculture* (Canberra: Australian National University Press, 1978);

Marvin Harris, *Cultural Materialism* (New York: Random House, 1979);

A. Kendall, *Everyday Life of the Incas* (London: Batsford Press, 1973);

M. Leahy, *The Land That Time Forgot,* (London: Hurst & Blackett, 1937);

Roy A. Rappaport, *Pigs for the Ancestors* (New Haven: Yale University Press, 1984);

Julian Steward, *Evolution and Ecology* (Urbana: University of Illinois Press, 1977);

Andrew Vayda, *War in Ecological Perspective* (New York: Plenum Press, 1976).

12. Leslie White, *The Evolution of Culture* (New York: McGraw-Hill Book Company, 1959), pp. 33-59.

13. Plog and Bates, op. cit., pp. 119-124.

14. Ibid, pp. 123-124.

15. Ibid.,

16. Wallace, op. cit.

17. Ibid.

18. Amongst the vast corpus of literature, some interesting sources are:

T. P. Bayliss-Smith, *The Ecology of Agricultural Systems* (Cambridge: Cambridge University Press), 1982;

K. Blaxter, *People, Food and Resources,* (Cambridge: Cambridge University Press, 1986);

B. Campbell, *Human Ecoology* (London: Heinemann Press, 1983);

Robert Claiborne, *Climate, Man and History* (New York: W. W. Morton & Company, Inc., 1970);

Marvin Harris, *Cannibals and Kings: The Orgins of Cultures* (New York: Random House, 1979);

Marvin Harris and Eric B. Ross, *Food and Evolution: Toward a Theory of Human Food Habits,* (Philadelphia: Temple University Press, 1987);

Sol Tax, editor, *The Civilizations of Ancient America,* (New York: Cooper Square Publishers, 1967).

19. White, op. cit., pp. 33-59.

20. Clifford Geertz, *Agricultural Involution* (Berkeley: University of California Press, 1963).

21. Several references will be helpful on this issue:

   George F. Andrews, *Maya Cities: Placemaking and Urbanization* (Norman: University of Oklahoma Press, 1977), p. 20;

   Jorge E. Hardoy, *Pre-Columbian Cities* (New York: Walker Company, 1964), pp. xxxi, 58;

   Leslie J. King and Reginald G. Golledge, *Cities, Space and Behavior: The Elements of Urban Geography* (Englewood Cliffs, NJ: Prentice-Hall, Inc., 1978), pp. 21, 23, 30;

   Ruth Whitehouse, *The First Cities* (New York: E.P. Dutton, 1977), p. 369.

22. Marvin Harris, *Cultural Materialism: The Struggle for a Science of Culture* (New York: Random House, 1979), p. 92f.

   See also Oliver, Douglas, *Islands, A Solomon Island Society: Kinship and Leadership Among the Siuai of Bougainville* (Cambridge: Harvard University Press, 1955).

23. Berger, op. cit., p. 32.

24. Wallace, op. cit., pp. 88-89.

25. Burton Pasternak, *Kinship and Community in Two Chinese Villages* (Stanford: Stanford University Press, 1972).

26. C. E. Black, *The Dynamics of Modernization: A Study in Comparative History* (New York: Harper & Row, 1966).

27. White, op. cit., pp. 33-59.

28. Watterson, Bill, "Calvin and Hobbes" cartoon, distributed by Universal Press Syndicate (Kansas City, MO: July 21, 1990.)

29. See footnote 1 in Chapter II. See also:

   Black, op. cit., p. 7;

   David E. Hunter and Phillip Whitten, editors, *Encyclopedia of Anthropology* (New York: Harper and Row, 1976), p. 272.

30. David Harvey, *The Conditions of Post-Modernity* (Cambridge: MA, Basil Blackwell, 1989).

31. Berger, op. cit., p. 86.

32. Berger, ibid., p. 50.

33. Berger, ibid., p. 49.

Chapter VIII:
The Economic Scene

Some men worship rank, some worship heroes, some worship power, some worship God, and over these ideals they dispute— but they all worship money.

– Mark Twain

Some of the ways habitats and technologies influence our views of the world and organize our lives, as reviewed in Chapters VI and VII, include the basic ways people have extracted food and other resources to meet biological and cultural needs. These are critical economic issues which were highlighted in the earlier chapter. It was noted that each habitat has a limited supply of resources available for human cultural development and that people craft their technology to meet these limitations.

On one hand, technology is restricted to a group's tools, the energy that is required to operate those tools, and the social organization that is needed to support their productive uses. *Economy, on the other hand, refers to how and why valued material goods are acquired and the rules of distribution.*

Several economic and allied issues, more directly related to understanding other cultures, are topics to be considered in this chapter. These issues are generally overlooked by American business people when working internationally and are critical to sketching an accurate portrait of a culture.

It cannot be overemphasized that one needs to grasp *how other "scenes," or aspects of a people's culture dramatically influence their economic culture.* It is important to understand some of the ways non-Western cultures have historically solved their economic problems and the possible effect these traditions can have on profitable business relations today.

THE ECONOMY AND THE REST OF CULTURE

All economic thought is not the same. Western business people tend to look for Western ways or elements to interpret a group's cultural influence on the marketplace, because Westerners analytically view and study Western economy as an independent, closed unit. Westerners need to be reminded that although our non-Western foreign business colleagues may have university degrees, live in urban environs, have traveled to other countries, and use products and ideas from around the world, they are still products of their traditional economic cultures. Their views and actions are based on non-Western cultural histories. The world is linked through currency exchange, letters of credit and other fundamental aspects of selling and buying, and even some notions of capitalism; *but all economic thought is not the same.* [1]

An example illustrates this circumstance. American friends stationed in the Middle East went shopping for antique, handcrafted, wooden doors. They found several they liked at a local bazaar and haggled over price with the first merchant without striking a bargain. They decided to visit some other merchants, only to decide hours later they wanted the doors they originally found in the first shop. They returned willing to accept his price, but he wouldn't sell the doors "at any price." He said he would rather burn his doors than sell to them! They were shocked at his anger. They had misunderstood the market "codes" and had offended the man's honor. He had engaged in laborious and sincere negotiations which they had too casually dismissed. They should have backed out of the situation by formally offering apologies for their lack of knowledge while praising the seller's kindness and truly honorable price. A bazaar functions on its own set of economic rules.

This is not an unusual case. Anyone who has dealt with non-Westerners can testify that just because people dress and speak in a Western manner does not mean that all parties are reading from the same cultural book! *It is very important to grasp how earlier, more traditional, pre-Western capitalistic economic meanings and habits contribute to non-Western business views and habit.* This understanding involves far more than how to pass one's business card, where to sit in a business meeting and all those other social rituals so necessary to conducting business abroad.

SOME ECONOMIC DIFFERENCES

Non-Westerners are often motivated by concerns other than monetary profits, and this can unnerve Westerners. The fact that a Japanese firm's primary interest is in market share, as opposed to our American insistence on a healthy net profit, is a good example.[2] The problem goes beyond the contrast between the United States and Japan.

Other examples include: the Indians of the Northern Rio Grande River Valley of New Mexico who rejected a new hybrid corn that would have given them a cash crop because it did not make traditional tortillas; or, how the attempts to change Navajo sheep-herders to farmers failed because the prestige of owning sheep was more important than cash crops; or, the case of the lady in a market stall in Panajachel, Guatemala, who refused to sell all her oranges, or even the bulk of them, to one buyer because she would not have anything else to sell for the remainder of the day.[3]

Similar examples can be cited in the high-technology areas of contemporary life. It is no surprise that many Americans working abroad have experienced a foreign buyer's preference for a locally manufactured item even though it costs more. Or, that local social relations often override what Americans would consider an economically rational act. We fail to grasp the social considerations that are being exchanged in these seemingly irrational acts.

At other times foreigners seem to jeopardize a good business arrangement by arguing over pennies, or by blatantly seeking too large a piece of the profits. They "just do not act as business people should";[4] they do not keep appointments; "they show up late and make life miserable" or they can operate in mysterious, indecent ways, as Texan T. Boone Pickens claims.[5]

Another practice that gives Americans difficulty abroad is the common practice of "buying influence." Although Americans are familiar with buying political influence when applied to business contracts, this practice is prohibited. We define the spreading of money for influence as bribery, payola, kickbacks or what Latin Americans call *mordida* and Mid-Easterners refer to as *bakshish*. The practice of paying money to elites in a business deal has been a prevalent mode of business throughout the non-Western world.

Americans have their own ways of spreading wealth. Calvin of Calvin and Hobbes cartoon reflects the American dilemma well in a recent comic strip, "Calvin and Hobbes". Speaking to Hobbes he states:

"If I've learned one thing in life, it's that everyone has his price. Raise the ante high enough and there's no such thing as scruples. People will do anything if the price is right."

Hobbes asks,

"What's your price?"

Calvin replies,

"Two bucks cold cash, up front."

Hobbes responds,

"I don't know which is worse, that everyone has his price, or that the price is always so low."

Calvin ends the discussion by musing,

"I'd make mine higher, but it's hard to find buyers as it is."[6]

Poor Calvin! As pervasive as the practice of influence peddling seems to be, we are constantly trying to figure out how to compete internationally while maintaining our own principles. No one wants to run afoul of the American prohibition against bribes or payola. Foreign cultures view business practices differently. In most non-Western countries payola is ranked with government subsidies and other economic development incentives as acceptable. Payola in most non-Western nations acts an an economic leveling device.

Non-Westerners tacitly understand the acceptable recognition to be given to the elites. When this limit is exceeded, those involved can receive adverse publicity. For example, Japan and South Korea have been rocked by revelations of extravagant payments to political elites. This is not newsworthy in most countries, although government control of the media makes publicizing the most blatant cases difficult or impossible.

Some locals see no wrong in taking advantage of foreigners, especially Americans. To do so is often accepted and is strongly related to prevailing social codes that differentiate *us* (outsiders) from *them*. Locals are not likely to accuse someone who shares the wealth with them of taking bribes. The Marcos family of the Philippines is an interesting example of this phenomenon, and similar cases can be found in most countries.

The payola issue highlights the kind of activities that make many American business persons nervous. Many American companies refuse to do business with foreign firms because Americans are deterred by the experiences of other firms regarding the need to pay off political elites to get contracts.

In the late 1980s a firm lost a contract in a Southeast Asian country because a competitor financed the American college education of a government official's lady friend. Such extra-business considerations walk a tight legal line, especially if you are the loser. This is a grave problem for American firms engaged in foreign business.

There are other differences between Western thinking and the rest of the world. *First,* Americans believe that all people try to maximize their assets. Some societies do have abundant resources from which they choose. Sometimes they try to get as much as they can from the little they have; at other times they economize by trying to get as much as they can at the lowest cost. These two strategies are not always and everywhere used, but these add to our Western dilemma when trying to understand other people's economic behavior.

Second, Americans believe that all people work to accumulate money and the things that money can buy. This profit motive idea has almost become a natural and immutable law to most Americans. Any doubts seemed to be demolished with the demise of the Berlin Wall and all it represented. Max Weber considered the idea of profit and capitalism to be a significant aspect of Protestantism, especially John Calvin's theological notion that wealth is a sign of God's election.[7] The secular version is most dramatically illustrated by a contemporary saying that "he who has the most toys at the end wins." Does this mean that such figures like Mahatma Ghandi and Mother Teresa are losers?

Profit, as we understand it, is not a paramount factor driving the economy in many non-Western cultures. To many non-Westerners our ideas about profit seem bizarre, if not evil, and this has spawned a genre of what is referred to as "treasure tales". There is the case of an elderly Mexican man who worked the hills adjacent to his village making charcoal for eighty years. He accumulated sufficient savings to buy other land and open a mill. The villagers account for his wealth by explaining that a large black car drove up to the old man's house one day and two men, dressed in black suits, got out and left two large bags of money. This accounts for the old man's wealth. But, it is added that the two black-suited strangers were the devil's agents. The money, therefore, is enchanted and will never be depleted.[8]

Taussig's study of peasant peoples in Bolivia and Colombia reveal similar views of capitalistic activity.[9] As peasant cultivators move into salaried positions in mines and large agri-business, they view the new economic exchanges as evil. There are reports that such newcomers to capitalism appeal to the devil in secret rites for protection as well as for increased wages. William Ellis of Pennsylvania State University at Hazelton, reports that even in America there is:

> "...an implicit belief that for anyone to become really economically powerful, there must be some implicit deal with the forces of evil." [10]

Latin America is replete with such "treasure tales" as traditional people encounter what they view as evil capitalistic behavior. Although it is true that a significant Western-educated upper-class is emerging in Latin America, the overwhelming majority of the people are still traditional peasants. Although one's business may be conducted solely with members of the upper-classes, it would be folly not to understand the underlying historic traditions. We need to ask if these views are really different from many of our own exotic assertions.

Third, although the foreigners that American business people will be dealing with have long lived with the concept of loans and interest rates, these have historically taken place within the kinship system as defined by extended lineage, clan, tribe or other. The kin system in pre-modern societies acts as a banking facility. The form of the loans has traditionally been non-monetary items, such as goats, pigs, cattle and crops. Although modern currency is now the preferred unit of exchange for most of the world's peoples, there are exceptions. The bulk of goods exchanged in most parts of the pre-capitalist world are bartered and not exchanged by means of hard currency. Interest rates and payback terms vary and are worked out through traditional personal relations which takes the place of national money markets.

This traditional trait plays a significant role in all contemporary non-Western business dealings and tends to make Americans uncomfortable. Foreign business associates often want to renegotiate contracts soon after signing and reportedly seek exceptions and favors on a regular basis. This trait is evident in the interest many non-Western nations exhibit in their preference for counter-trade business. They prefer to exchange large quantities of another nation's commodities for an item of equivalent value produced locally. Western companies which are willing and able to engage in counter-trade, especially for the large durable-good items, find most non-Western nations to be willing partners. It is the old barter strategy at large.

Fourth, although not specifically an economic trait, we differ greatly in the way we emphasize language in our business dealings. This difference has enormous impact on our economic relations with non-Westerners. Americans place great emphasis on words, especially those written in contract form. As Hall has stated, we see these words as valuable "in-and-of-themselves" – totally detached from who said them, when and how.[11] Non-Westerners, to the contrary, emphasize the speaker. The spoken word is more important than the written, for one must see who is speaking, note the inflection of the voice and observe the general body language.

Fifth, Americans' view of economic activity as a unique specialty significantly removed from other aspects of their culture sharply contrasts with non-Westerners. Non-Westerners view the world in an integrated manner. Their existence and productive labor as well as nature are all interrelated. To recall the Eskimo or Inuit case, animals and things are imbued with life.

*Sixth, i*n addition to the difficulties of the payment of wages and of the role of money, non-Westerners are also disturbed by the idea that Westerners should profit from the transfer of technology. Non-Westerners believe the West, the "haves", should share their good fortune with them, the "have-nots". It is part of the codes relating to social leveling that help maintain village harmony.

While working with a company in Southeast Asia, the Asians were mystified and angry to learn that Western firms insisted on making a profit on the transfer of certain agricultural technology. In their view, the American companies should give it without thought for a profit. An attempt was made to explain that profit drives capitalistic economic activities and that Western companies, being capitalistic, were in business solely to make money. The Asians were not impressed. The look in their eyes left no doubt that they thought Americans and American capitalistic attitudes quite evil.

REFLECTIONS AND ADDITIONAL NUANCES

Capitalistic and pre-capitalistic peoples have many different economic world views. Few, if any, Americans will be negotiating with Kalahari hunters and gatherers, Bantu tribesmen or other people from marketless economies. However, they will be dealing with people whose economic views and behaviors are variously informed by traditional economic views.

What is equally hard for us to grasp is that non-Western people do not accept many of our economic views even when they do understand them. Asian nations have invented a new form of capitalism based on their traditional cultural commitments to system-harmony, strong centralized control and associated features that have come to comprise "state-managed capitalism." If we could listen in on all our nation's international business negotiations, conducted in a given time span, it would be astoundingly clear that Americans are operating on the basis of a set of economic views that are not significantly shared by most of the world. For our part, we seem to be lagging in the move from the old system of mass production (economies of scale) to just-in-time production[12] (economies of scope). This also includes managing our markets. We can watch this process unfold before the glaring lights of the world's media as America painfully tries to maintain its old low-wage production habits and its idea of free-markets, while the Asians increase their global economic domination. It will be interesting to observe the development of the European Economic Union and watch the former Soviet states try to move from a peasant-type communist economic system to some type of capitalist market economy. Will we be able to figure out how to negotiate with the peasant leadership that is emerging in all these newly created nation-states, and can we compel the Japanese, Europeans and others to play by our rules? Economist Lester Thurow certainly articulates our American problem well.[13]

Regardless of the answer to America's problems, it is obvious that the change from traditional, pre-capitalistic, economic thinking and acting to some form of modern capitalism is painful. One has to accommodate a significant amount of modernist cultural baggage. Adopting modern technological forms has a transforming effect on all other cultural scenes – kinship, politics, religion and so forth; and most non-Western countries find that a difficult pill to swallow. Some have noted that this includes the idea and institutions of democracy.[14]

Most non-Western nations thought that they could bring in the West's technological infrastructures and instantly become a modern, industrial nation. The fact is, however, that modernism is a process that comes with a whole new way of thinking about the world. This re-thinking has created nightmares for many Third World leaders. The Shah of Iran's worst nightmares became reality, as did Gorbachev's.

In a real sense the world is caught in modernization's process-blender whether we like it or not. The technological revolution is already a reality. There is no conceivable way of avoiding its transforming consequences. In the past one could sail away to some unknown island and hide, but there is no place to hide today.

In summary, American business people need to recognize that their foreign business associates' modern economic language and behavior is informed, to some significant degree, by most of the generalized traditional economic views set forth above. Although they speak English and use Western economic terms, they will have their own unique cultural translation of the language. If these traditional patterns are not recognized, a business transaction can quickly turn bad and too many have done so already.

Thus far, this chapter has shown some of the key ways Western economic thought and behavior differ from most of the rest of the world. The chapters on politics (Chapter IX) and technology (Chapter VII) present ways pre-capitalistic systems regulate access to scarce resources and production processes.

This section outlines the historic ways that goods and services have been exchanged or distributed. These historic modes of exchange give Western business people more problems than the inherent meanings associated with resource access and production.

Since purely economic functions, according to non-Western thinking are so tightly embedded in other cultural components in pre-modern, pre-capitalist systems, there is no agreement on a classification system we can use to demonstrate differences. Westerners look and think in terms of "closed" economic functions or systems, and this fact illustrates how essential it is for international business people to grasp the nature of the non-Western family, as well as the interrelations and differences within all aspects of non-Western peoples, in order to more accurately understand the economic scene of a group.

Economic elements are such a part of other cultural components in pre-modern societies that it is almost impossible to separate them. Given this problem, George Dalton's classification of pre-modern economies can be an extremely helpful way of looking and thinking about traditional economies. He separates these pre-modern economies into marketless economies, peripheral markets only, and market-dominated economies.[15]

The overwhelming majority of American business relations are and will continue to be with those in market-dominated economies. It is well to be reminded that many different elements have served as *standards of exchange* for pre-modern peoples through the centuries. These modes of exchange differ from an American's concept of the role of money in affecting transactions to the extent to which they serve as the basic standard of exchange. In pre-modern economies money does not function in the all-encompassing, pervasive way it does in Western integrated market economies. Although a particular material may look and act like our money – whether cocoa beans, jade beads, cowrie shells or even contemporary paper and metals like reals, pesos, rupees, quetzales – they may not serve all exchange purposes. People may still acquire the bulk of their needs through non-monetary exchange relations at the local level. Money may not be the most important element driving the exchange process. It may be camels, fish, horses or any number of things. The previously reported "treasure tales" certainly tell us that although money may be used as a medium of exchange, it is not viewed in the mechanical, non-detached Western manner.

Marketless Economies

Goods, labor and land are tribal or kin unit possessions in marketless economies. Families, as an economic unit, are the smallest and most basic organizational unit. *Things are not sold or purchased; rather, they are given and exchanged through a system of rules called obligations and reciprocities.* These rules still dominate in non-Western societies. Pigs, goats and other animals and products are given as a due to a tribal chief, as gifts to the parents of potential bride, or to those who helped in a time of family need. In such marketless economies, it is difficult to analyze an economic system where goods and services are bartered and not bought or sold as commodities. Families are more interested in social reproduction rather than maximizing profits.[16]

Feast and party exchanges that so heavily characterize marketless economies still exist as one of the world's most pervasive mechanisms. Food and other valued commodities are distributed, and in return the giver receives respect, honor and great status – all highly valued social commodities.

The *fiesta*, so predominant in Latin America, is rooted in this tradition.[17] Selby says the Zapotec of southern Mexico,

"...will expend a year's earnings, a month of their time, and mortgage their lands in order to pay the expenses of the fiestas of the patron saint. Sponsorship of the fiesta has utility for them because it gains social power, (i.e., the respect of others in the community). It also prevents the possibility of being bewitched, seriously sickened, or injured; and, at the same time, it enables them to ask for the help of their kinfolk in other communal projects." [18]

There are the pig feasts of Oceania, Hawaiian luaus and other such extravagant celebrations.[19] We should not fail to mention the status accruing to Americans who indulge in elaborate party-giving (feasts) such as debutante balls and marriage parties.

The reciprocity rules that so clearly and powerfully mark non-Western cultures have their roots in the marketless economies. In marketless economies gift-giving is usually more frequent and in larger quantities, and is driven by stronger obligatory feelings. Even today, such gift-giving does not take place with the casualness that marks Western tradition because so much is at stake. In traditional societies, failure to follow the reciprocity rules can do irreparable harm to one's status.

It is important to introduce the different types of *reciprocity rules* as an important aspect of pre-modern economies.[20] Each reciprocity rule differs in the degree of formality and intimacy that exists between giver and receiver. *Generalized reciprocity* specifies gift-giving and the sharing of resources between kin members and what Americans call friends. Although a strict accounting is not maintained to the degree of the two types of reciprocity described below, life runs on the assumption of shared expectation which is the basis of total integrated economic dependency.

Balanced reciprocity means there is a clear accounting of gifts and favors, and the rigid expectation that all will be returned equally. This rule regulates relations between non-kin people of similar status who are socially distant from each other. It demands equal payment of similar value, especially labor transactions. Horticultural and plow agriculture groups operate on the basis of balanced reciprocity. The pattern still persists with varying degrees of intensity in all modern market systems. My father came off a

Nebraska farm. Until he died, he believed that all gifts and favors must be returned in equal or larger equivalency. He kept a strict accounting and when asked why we were helping Mr. Jones, he would list a series of acts by Mr. Jones to justify our help. I never understood why it was always "my labor" that was used for balancing the ledger.

Negative reciprocity accounts for economic exchanges between strangers and is largely impersonal. This is a view that cuts across most pre-modern and modern economic systems. Each party tries to maximize its benefits while minimizing the exchange.

We are all aware that many non-Westerners believe that it is acceptable to copy Western products, to ignore copyrights and patents, or to do whatever is useful to profit at the expense of distant strangers.

These reciprocity rules are critical economic devices. Selby's Mexico study illustrates the importance of reciprocity in maintaining village society.[21] He finds reciprocal exchange only possible in the context of humility, trust and respect – the value codes that underlie all cultural activities. People are always asking for favors because this favoring "is central to the value system of the community and is the act that creates the day-to-day system of social relations." [22] He writes that a "good man" is the "man who knows how to do you a favor," and a favor is the "unilateral act of exchange that carries with it the expectation of reciprocity."[23]

Reciprocity rules provide the fuel that not only drives exchange engines in pre-modern economies but also significantly affect America's business in contemporary non-Western nations. These are critical rules for American business people to understand and practice in their dealings with foreign business persons.

It should be noted in passing that some pre-capitalistic populations became large and complex: Mesopotamia, Inca (Peru), Maya and Aztec (Middle America), China, and Japan to name a few. In such cases significant political and social hierarchies developed which led to formal or politically enforceable *redistribution exchange systems* (taxes and tributes). European pre-industrial states and all modern states have adopted this form of exchange which further illustrates how old traditions continue in Western systems.

Peripheral Markets Only

Dalton views some pre-modern economies as peripheral markets.[24] *These operate much like marketless economies, but differ in having a linkage to a market-site where some items are bought and sold.* At these markets people may use some products as a standard of calculating value, such as blankets, furs, shells, beads and other such items.

Market Dominated Economies (*Peasantry*)

The bulk of the non-Western world operates on the basis of a market dominated economy. These economies share a number of features with pre-capitalistic market economies.[25] Our discussions follow Dalton's reference to market dominated peoples as *peasants* which is consistent with the bulk of anthropological literature. *Peasantry* is not a pejorative or demeaning label. It is only a characterization of a particular pre-modern, pre-capitalist type of socio-economy which shares the following characteristics:

First, in market dominated economies land and labor are exchanged along with other goods.

Second, peasant people become relatively more dependent on the markets in nearby towns or urban centers for selling their surplus and buying products for their own need. Since peasants have significant control over their production they differ from migrant farm workers or plantation slave laborers. They calculate their production of crops, animals and handiwork in terms of market sales.

Third, market prices begin to have an integrative function. Whatever is used as money regulates the value of most other things. Land and labor are often exchanged on this fungible basis. Traditional exchanges that take place within the kin unit and between friends as they settle obligations are still heavily emphasized. Reciprocity rules still influence exchange transactions. Eventually, as the marketplace becomes more complex, there is an increased reference to money as the standard of exchange. The meaning of land and all other resources also change, valued in monetary terms rather than tribal, clan or family terms.

Fourth, peasant reliance on market exchange differs from the more complex industrial, nationally integrated economies by the absence of a machine technology. Extraction and production processes are driven by human and animal energy.

Fifth, peasant people live in small population centers. Colonial conquest resulted in many peasant communities becoming closed to outsiders. Frequently, there was a prohibition on ownership of land. All members support and share the burdens of everyday life. This is especially true in many parts of Latin America, although Wolf found variations.[26] Yet, China's peasant communities have been relatively open. Outsiders were always able to buy and sell local land. Traditionally, there was significant inequality of wealth, but the Maoist Revolution destroyed much of Chinese cultural tradition.

European peasants, known historically as "serfs", were economically tied to land owned by the ruling Monarch who, in turn, granted land rights to lords or barons who, in turn, granted rights to work the land to area serfs. The system was held together by promises of protection and of economic and political exchanges.

Sixth, peasant communities, whether closed or open, are politically controlled by neighboring urban market elites. This control comes in the form of taxation, military conscription and the power of the country's administrative apparatus. Village level production increasingly flows to the urban market areas as centralization of control and exchange is exerted.

American business people should understand the critical importance of the peasant household. It is the most important social unit, and most daily issues are not thought of in market terms. Social coherency is of primal concern. Pure economic concerns, as we understand them in the West, are less important.

164

Some claim that peasant communities still exist in Appalachia and the Ozarks.[27] It is probable that all non-Western urban sites contain peasant neighborhoods or enclaves. There are large Amish communities in America whose life style might conceptually fit the peasant type model. The majority of people in Asia, Latin America, Africa, Eastern Europe and the former Soviet states are basically peasant people. This is critical to understand when conducting foreign business in those countries. It is difficult to see how Americans can conduct profitable business without relating to people with peasant traditions, even if they have become the elite class.

These early economic systems could be extremely complex. Even the contemporary bazaar's complexity is often hidden. The bazaar market is characterized in the following ways: by its small-scale size; worker relations based on kin or partnership agreements (not employee-employer); the primacy of negotiating skill (not technical or managerial); little or no government controls, usually no standardization of weights and measures; preference for a few selected buyers (as opposed to the general walk-in public); and contracts based on personal relations rather than legal documents.[28] Bazaar-type markets are found in most peasant societies, such as Mexico, Indonesia, China and the Middle East.

Implications

Most, if not all, of the foreign businessmen and women that American business persons encounter will have no memory, no matter how many generations deep, of marketless economies. There is a very slim chance one will encounter people with peripheral market memories. However, it is a historic fact that one will be dealing with people from market-dominated (peasant) economic backgrounds.

It is important to realize that people in peasant economies still maintain allegiance to traditional reciprocity rules with varying degrees of intensity. Negotiations always involve a high degree of personalizing followed by more favorable price considerations.

Business relations in the United States are also based on personal relations and trust but not to the degree found in the non-Western world. Those who have little experience in foreign business relations are always shocked by how different these relations really are. The Chinese call such relationships *guanxi*. This view is rooted in centuries of kin-dominated marketless economies. Dealing with "strangers/outsiders" is still a fundamental problem throughout the world. The role of American business people as strangers has been more fully treated in "Chapter IV: The Social Scene".

The haggling over price, even down to a difference in pennies, is a throwback to an earlier economic pattern where the margins were critical and one's self-esteem was dependent on cutting the sharpest bargain possible. Americans know that price is important, but we significantly differ to the degree in which this issue is pushed. Americans are always chagrined at the forceful and persistent manner in which foreign buyers negotiate pricing.

A group from the People's Republic of China requested assistance in purchasing some American agricultural commodities a number of years ago. I located a source of the products and relayed the prices "for that day," since prices of these products fluctuate daily. If you want to buy, you pay the market price. There is no haggling. Other buyers are standing in line for the existing inventory or production. In many cases agricultural commodities are similar to many chemicals in that the demand is often greater than production. In this case the seller had to first take care of his regular customers. After some discussion he was willing to sell my Chinese customers some of the next month's production.

I did not hear anything from the Chinese buyers for several weeks. When I did they wanted to know if the price could be negotiated lower, significantly lower! I called the supplier and told him what the Chinese wanted. He laughed. The "next month's production" he had earlier agreed to sell the Chinese was already sold. He held it as long as he could. On my next trip to China I tried to explain to the Chinese buyers that for many American commodities there is no time to negotiate. You have to know what you want, watch the market and put your money down. I further explained that American manufacturers will often negotiate a discount if the order is big enough and they see the development of a long-term customer relationship. These discounts are usually negotiated once and if the buyer keeps stalling, wanting more and more discounts, the American seller will withdraw with impatience. I could tell by the look in their eyes they could not understand any of this crazy American market behavior. Their economic reflexes are *peasant* in type, and they differ significantly from our own. Reciprocity rules continue to prevail.

MODERNISM[29] AND THE MARKET

In contrast to economic systems previously described, *Americans operate a democratic, individualistic-capitalist market economy.* With the exception of a small minority who maintain small farms or keep gardens for the production of vegetables for their own household consumption, we are totally dependent upon a nationally integrated market. All goods and services, land and labor are priced and exchanged in this market. A brief outline of some of the key attributes of our market views will further sharpen our understanding of the many ways we differ from most non-Western, pre-capitalistic peoples.

First, money plays the critical role. It is not one of several valued items that act as the standard of our exchange. It is the only one. Money basically drives our lives. It is the only medium by which everything is viewed and measured – labor, land, services, time, art, votes and too often love. Moderns place a money value on everything. We even rank each other relative to the amount of money earned and accumulated. A recent report by James Patterson and Peter Kim stated that

> "...for a fistful of dollars, we found that Americans would do almost anything: lie, cheat, steal, murder, abandon families and change their religion."[30]

Money to non-Westerners, as important as it has become in many places, is not the only driving force in their lives. Its pursuit is often overridden by family or religious meanings.

Second, and most important for American business persons, we de-emphasize social relations in market transactions and are generally devoid of the traditional reciprocity rules that controlled, and still largely control, pre-capitalist economies. Westerners do not care who the seller or buyer is, they just want to know the price. Transactions take place between buyers and anonymous clerks millions of times each day. Manufacturers and suppliers are faceless, impersonal entities who create self-images through media advertising. Public relations firms are a product of the transition from the personalized style of pre-capitalist economy to Western capitalist economy.

On the other hand, pre-modern life is very personalized. People live where their families have lived and worked for hundreds of years. The universe consists of their village and the surrounding area which may not be more than five to ten square miles. Moderns view continents, planets and wheeling galaxies but do not know their neighbors, nor do they really care to. Moderns are highly mobile.

Research shows that, although moderns find their most intimate associations in their work setting, this environ is still highly impersonal when it is compared with the social universe of pre-moderns. Lay offs, the constant threat of lay offs; job promotions that create jealousies and alienate people; the presence of ethnic and gender differences and conflict; the influx of new workers and the basic focus on the task for which one is being paid, all act to reduce the more intimate relationships that characterize pre-modern peoples.

Third, our capitalist economy is an integrated institution of its own, separate and independent of all other socio-cultural units. In contrast, pre-capitalist economies are deeply embedded and commingled with all the other parts of their respective village and regional culture. All this means is that when attempting to do business in foreign, non-Western economies, even though they may have a significant capitalistic posture, one should grasp the systemic nature of the culture.

Fourth, although non-Western systems possess many symbols of modernism, such as high-rise steel and glass office buildings, world-class restaurants, airports, computers, and television, they are significantly different from the West with respect to their management of the economy. One should not be misled by democratic and capitalistic images and talk. All such forms have been grafted onto the traditional organizational features of what is best described as *state-managed collective-capitalism.* Pre-modern traditions, most especially the political and kinship components, characterize the management of the market in most non-Western societies.

Non-Western capitalism did not arise historically through a peasant-based technological revolution, driven by Protestant theological principles, as it did in the West. It has been imposed by a ruling elite mimicking selected Western features. They took the technological forms and not the democratic philosophical underpinnings. Most non-Western leaders try to manage their nation's economy as their ancestors did within tribe, villages or pre-modern states. Rather than use "legal-rational" means, they resort to personalizations and patronage.

Singapore is a beautiful City-State of 2.5 million culturally pluralistic people, where business is conducted efficiently. One has to keep a wary eye on the government which manages the country with what many consider a heavy hand. Americans would view it as heavily paternalistic.[31] Fines have been levied against public littering, public spitting, urinating in elevators, smoking in restaurants and failing to flush public toilets, to name a few of the most famous cases. There was a real controversy in the 1980s when Prime Minister Lee Kuan Yew decreed that couples should limit their children, then later urged the development of a population produced by the most intelligent. The editorial policies of *Asian Wall Street Journal* irritated the government, so the newspaper was banned from Singapore. In January, 1992 the manufacture, sale and import of chewing gum was banned.[32] What prohibits such a strong government from deciding it is time to take over all foreign operations? Or to raise corporate taxes on American firms? Or add non-tariff restrictions to the importing of raw materials and exporting of products?

Such highly managed markets are not "free" in the Western sense of the term. They are not *democratic, individualistic capitalistic* types of operations.

Most non-Western governments play a relatively strong role in managing their economy. It is fairly safe to say that Japan and the four "Little Dragons of Asia" have invented *"a better mouse trap"*, a new form of capitalism. It involves a high degree of state planning and control. It has developed without mimicking all the trappings of our American-style democracy. Their success would certainly suggest that the traditional American belief that economic growth is only possible without state planning is open to question. Lester Thurow argues that we are observing the development of a new economic game.[33] At one point Thurow states:

> "America's problem is not winning – but forcing itself to notice that the game has changed – that it will have to play a new game by new rules with new strategies."[34]

America will play second fiddle unless we transform ourselves.

In summary, it is important to have good cross-cultural political skills when doing business with and in other nations. Non-Westerners either did not read Adam Smith with respect to his admonition that the state is best served when people are allowed to pursue their own unfettered interests,[35] or they just decided to ignore the advice. It is hard to argue with success, and this unique, strongly managed turn to democratic capitalism seems to be working well for many. The American business person must be prepared to deal with tightly-controlled market systems throughout the non-Western world.

SOME SUGGESTED STRATEGIES

The ability to profitably work in non-Western political economies certainly presents a challenge to American business people. The fact that these political economies are embedded in a plethora of other cultural elements further complicates the task. The following strategies are suggested in coping with this problem.

First, as it is usually the case that one's most profitable business relationships derive from personal relationships with one's counterparts, the business person should strive to develop such relationships at all levels. These relationships must be woven into the fabric of a business person's international commercial strategy.

This must start with grasping how a people define various types of relationships. The emphasis on relationships by non-Westerners is difficult for us to grasp because our own cultural views get in the way. It is clear that our own concept of friendship and the quick and casual manner in which we establish friends does not transfer to other cultures. It takes years to develop even a casual intimacy in non-Western societies because Westerners come as strangers.

Our domestic strategies fail as Americans endeavor to develop friends abroad. One or two annual business trips abroad are typically scheduled, each of a few weeks duration. A firm will often send different people on each trip which confuses foreign business associates who wonder why they cannot establish what they consider an intimate relationship with anybody from the Western firm.

Between trips, Westerners engage in a steady flow of telefax messages or phone calls. They are often unconcerned with whom the sender may be. The focus is on the *flow of information, not personal relations*. It is the way Americans do business. The foreign business associate is more focused on the sender and secondarily, on the information. Americans must realize that the most profitable business results from one person working many years with the same foreign business associates.

Second, it follows that it is vitally important to take extra care in picking one's foreign business associates. Companies in non-Western settings are deeply embedded in the local social fabric because the lines between economic functions and other cultural entities are blurred or nonexistent. Companies are subject to their culture's history. A foreign business associate's position can make a great deal of difference in an American company's profitable foreign commercial activities.

In many non-Western countries, the concept of advertising is not necessarily understood in the same way as in the West. The process of advertising for a business partner, a distributor or company president will bring forth people claiming to be socially and politically positioned, and each will claim to be intimates of their country's ruling elites and top industry leaders. One must have the skills to determine the reality of such claims. It is important to grasp how the various factions line up in the marketplace and who comprises what faction, especially those operating in your company's specific market sector. There is a great deal of indigenous ethnic and racial conflict in all nations. American business people are certainly in no position to play the social reformer role. One must be aware of the risks.

It is not always wise to choose one's foreign associates on the basis of *assumed intimacy* which generally means the person in question manifests a number of American traits that make us feel comfortable, but they are not criteria for good performance. The chances of being disappointed in their productivity are great.

There is no substitute for careful homework when choosing foreign associates at any level in any country. One must choose from a position of knowledge. Check, **check, RE-CHECK** and then verify the information. Put Western cultural preferences on the shelf and view the local scene from the perspective of the local culture.

Third, the second point suggests one choose American staff for foreign assignment in an un-American fashion. Seeking to find the key traits of overseas success, a recent study by Prudential

Insurance's Relocation Division polled seventy-two personnel managers working at multinational firms.[36] Nearly thirty-five percent said "cultural adaptability, patience, flexibility and tolerance for others' beliefs."[37] In America youth is highly regarded while the rest of the world reveres age and maturity for the knowledge and wisdom gained over a working lifetime. Age brings higher status and prestige. The young should keep silent, observe and learn until time comes for them to take the leadership. It may be true that American youth like to travel, enjoy foreign experiences and may be product specialists. Some may even be good managers by American standards, but to send youthful management staff abroad is an affront to many foreign people.

There are exceptions. In looking at this issue in numerous countries, there are many indigenous foreign business assosciate-who have adjusted to the embarrassment of having to work with our youth. Some adjusted because they needed what their American counterparts had to offer. Some were able to minimize the affront out of their own sense of courtesy and respect. What would one expect to hear from a foreign associate if told he is being sent a young man in his 20s or 30's to head up the operation? He wants the business, so he reluctantly accepts the youthful manager.

Senior American management must be able to access and develop good personal relationships with key foreign industry and government leaders. These people will be older and committed to the idea that maturity is the measure of one's worth. Such individuals' local status is high and derives from age and experience. While they may treat the young American manager cordially, they will not take him seriously.

The second feature is that one should not choose foreign senior staff primarily because they are product specialists. This is an almost heretical idea to put forth in America. *We consistently define management positions in terms of product experience.* The first qualification usually stressed has to do with a candidate's experience with a firm's products or process. Time and again, chief executive officers have narrowed their choice for overseas talent to a pool of company specialists. The same Prudential study, mentioned earlier, stated that twenty-two percent of multinational firms believe technical and management skills are the keys to overseas success. This suggests that we have a long way to go in retooling our perspective for success in foreign business.

As important as company culture may be, it should not be a firm's primary criteria for an overseas assignment. *Company culture usually battles with product knowledge* when company heads choose overseas managers. As one chief executive officer explained, "I picked Joe because he's young and needs the experience. He also came up through the ranks." Company culture was this man's top priority; a fraternity choice, which signals that "Joe is one of us." This is not the most effective way to think when foreign profits are in the balance.

Fourth, the more lucrative profits tend to come from those managers who have maturity and experience as well as a certain statesmen-like understanding. Foreign senior management of an American overseas subsidiary should possess a quiet self-assurance and be soft-spoken. Also, the following characteristics are helpful. The manager should have good listening skills, be of the highest moral character, reflect a compassion and caring for all people, have a strong curiosity, maintain a respect for other's cultural differences, possess a driving inquisitiveness about other cultures which leads eventually to understanding and have a sense of humor, good business skills and instincts. That profile fits a lot of American people.

If the person has product and technical skills, so much the better. If not, he or she can learn about the company's products and services. Even in America, senior staff lose much of their technical capability because they are dealing with management issues. Technical tasks, such as bid writing, presentations, and so forth, are assigned down the line to the appropriate product specialists or specialty work-groups. An American chief executive officer would be hard pressed to apply the product knowledge standard to his own upper management staff. It is much harder to transform a

174

product specialist into a productive international statesperson than to train a mature statesperson to be a product specialist.

In summary, a company's foreign profits in these critical times depends upon such *un-American* strategies as outlined above. One must acknowledge the existing cultural differences in world economic thinking and shape strategies that coincide with these historic patterns, even though the strategies may be contrary to those prevailing domestic traditions and company culture.

References Cited

1. Capitalism refers to socio-economic systems characterized by a class division between those whose ownership and control of production and its process for personal or private profit on the one hand, and the working class, whose members sell their labor to the prior group members on the other. Capitalism as an ideal type includes private property, money and markets and a significant differentiation and complexity in a group's productive processes. Although it is possible to point to capitalistic "elements" in the early Roman empire, China and the Near East, capitalism in the traditionally strict sense of that concept did not blossom until the last few hundred years. Analytically capitalism is described as having moved from 17th century mercantile capitalism to

18th and 19th century competitive industrial capitalism, to 20th century monopoly capitalism.

See David E. Hunter & Phillip Whitten, *Encyclopedia of Anthropology* (New York: Harper & Row Publishers, 1976), p. 67.

For a discussion of the debate about economic theories and the social sciences, see:

Henry Selby and Lucy Garretson, *Cultural Anthropology* (Dubuque, IA: William. C. Brown Company Publishers, 1981), p. 278f;

Harold K. Schneider, *Economic Man: The Anthropology of Economics* (New York: The Free Press, 1974).

2. Lester Thurow, *Head to Head: The Coming Economic Battle Among Japan, Europe and America,* op. cit., pp. 175-178.

3. Story relayed during a visit on December 12, 1991 by Henry Selby, Professor of Social Anthropology, University of Texas, Austin, TX.

4. See the classic study of Panajachel Guatemala, by Sol Tax, *Penny Capitalism: A Guatemalan Indian Economy* (New York: Octagon Books, 1972); this study describes an economy where a penny is the basic exchange feature.

5. Texas financier T. Boone Pickens bought 42.4 million shares of Koito Manufacturing Company of Japan and wanted a seat on the board. The Japanese claimed he was attempting to greenmail the shares, which means he would try to scare the company into buying back the shares at an above market value. Pickens maintained that he had a genuine interest in being an integral part of Kioto and was prevented from exercising what he believed to be a legal and legitimate role. The case received world wide publicity. In Japan the case was used to support the prevailing idea that Americans were racist. America generally viewed it as another dramatic case of Japanese protectionism. Obviously neither side understood the other's cultural orientation.

6. Watterson, Bill, "Calvin and Hobbes" cartoon, distributed by Universal Press Syndicate (Kansas City, MO: April 1, 1992).

7. Max Weber, *The Protestant Ethic and the Spirit of Capitalism,* translated by Talcott Parsons (New York; Charles Scribner's Sons, 1958), pp. 155-183.

8. Selby, conversation of December 12, 1991, see footnote 3.

9. Michael T. Taussig, *The Devil and Commodity Fetishism in South America* (Chapel Hill: University of North Carolina Press, 1980), p. 10.

10. Zachery Schiller, "P & G Is Still Having A Devil of a Time", Business Week, September 11, 1995, p. 48.

11. Edward T. Hall, *Beyond Culture* (Garden City, NY: Anchor Press, 1976).

12. "Just-in-time" production refers to the Japanese method of bringing parts to assembly/production process "just in time" for products to be assembled and out the door. No overhead and wasted space is required for warehousing parts. Production of parts can be quickly stopped for change-over as breakthroughs create new products.

13. Thurow, *Head to Head*, op. cit.

14. Berger, op. cit., pp.82-83.

 See also: Marion J. Levy, *Modernization: Latecomers and Survivors* (New York: Basic Books, 1972). The author emphasizes what he calls modernization's "solvent" effect.

15. George Dalton, "Primitive Money", in Jesse D. Jennings and E. Adamson Hobel, *Readings in Anthropology* (New York: McGraw-Hill Book Company, 3rd Ed., 1972), pp. 447-460.

16. Selby, conversation of December 12, 1991, see footnote 3.

17. Abraham Rosman and Paula G. Rubel, *The Tapestry of Culture* (Glencoe, IL: Scott Foresman & Company, 1981), pp. 108-113.

18. Selby and Garrison, op.cit., p. 263.

19. Rosman and Rubel, op.cit., pp. 118-124, 64, 102.

20. Marshall Sahlins, "On the Sociology of Primitive Exchange", M. Banton, editor, in *The Relevance of Models for Social Anthropology* (London: Tavistock, 1965); Marvin Harris supports the idea that reciprocity continues to significantly exist in capitalist societies, see Harris' *Our Kind* (New York: Harper Collins Publisher, 1989), pages 345.

21. Selby, Henry A., *Zapotec Deviance* (Austin: University of Texas Press, 1974).

22. Ibid., p. 59.

23. Ibid., p. 57.

24. Dalton, op.cit., pp. 447-460.

25. There is a large body of literature on *peasantry,*. See:

 Chayanov, A.V., *The Theory of the Peasant Economy* (Homewood, IL: Richard D. Owen, American Economic Association, 1966);

 Henry F. Dobyns, Paul L. Doughty and Harold Lasswell, editors, *Peasants, Power, and Applied Social Change* (Beverly Hills, CA: Sage Publications 1964);

 Oscar Lewis, *Five Families: Mexican Case Studies in the Culture of Poverty* (New York: Basic Books, 1959);

Jack K. Potter, May N. Diaz, and George Foster, editors, *Peasant Society, A Reader* (Boston: Little, Brown & Company, 1967);

Eric R. Wolf, *Peasants* (Englewood Cliffs, NJ: Prentice Hall, 1966).

26. Wolf, ibid.

27. A review of the urban anthropology supports this claim.

28. Geertz, op.cit.

29 Reader should refer to footnote 1, Chapter II, for a clarification of the use of *modernism* and *capitalism* and a brief introduction to the recent introduction of *Postmodernity*.

30. James Patterson and Peter Kim, *The Day Americans Told the Truth* (New York: Prentice Hall Press, 1991).

31. Joyce Barnathan et al, "Has Singapore Got What It Takes To Be A Finance Powerhouse?" Business Week, March 20, 1995, p. 54. The cover story describes Singapore's ruling regime as "restrictive".

32. Valerie Lee, "Chewing Gum Ban Sticks in Singaporeans' Craw", Houston Chronicle, January 10, 1992.

33. Thurow, *Head to Head*, op.cit. especially pp. 55, 57, 59, 82, 148, 176, 185, 257, 260, 294.

Unfortunately he borrows the idea of "communitarian" from George C. Lodge, *Prestroika for America*, (Boston: Harvard Business School Press, 1991), pp. 7-8, 15-16 to describe the new form of capitalism; see Thurow, op.cit., p. 32f. Communitarian refers to a member of a communistic community; see *Webster's Encyclopedic Unabridged Dictionary of the English Language* (New York: Portland House, 1989), p. 298.

I do not believe this is to be an appropriate label to be attached to the new forms of capitalism emerging in Asia. Certainly the new Asian types of capitalism are social "collectivities," in contrast to our "individualistic" type and they are highly "state-managed," but within a democratic type of framework.

34. Thurow, op.cit., p. 257.

35. Adam Smith, *The Wealth of Nations*, (Oxford, Clarendon Press, 1976), p. 423.

36. Sandra Dallas, "Rule No. 1: Don't Miss The Locals", Business Week, May 15, 1995, p. 8.

37. Ibid.

Chapter IX:

The Political Scene

Politics is the art of looking for trouble, finding it everywhere, diagnosing it incorrectly, and applying the wrong remedies.

– Groucho Marx

No sane person would argue that men or women are angels. Every group has to devise some rules to allow social interaction of its members in a predictable and orderly manner. *Order* is a requisite aspect of social control, and it is the social process by which the access to scarce resources is approached. When comparing pre-capitalistic groups with capitalistic groups, scarce resources may be game, fish, land, water, domesticated animals, labor, machines, metals, cowrie shells, jobs or even prestige. Rules for accessing such valued items become systemized and institutionalized. They define the social plan. In the United States the acquisition of money is governed by some rules, even though fairly broad ones, as Ivan Boesky and those of his kind can testify.

Order, in reverse, can represent repression. Over the years the world has seen what this type of order can generate in such places as Germany, the Soviet Union, South Africa, China, North and South Korea, Thailand, Ethiopia, Eastern Europe and even in the United States.

A close inspection of any nation will reveal what are considered human rights abuses. Men have been forever figuring ways to abuse their fellow human beings since they emerged out of the trees on the African savannahs many thousands of years ago.

Given our human predisposition to inflict pain on others, nation-building is a painful process. The purpose of this chapter is not to chronicle man's evil acts, to rehash political theory nor to review existing social science debates.[1] The purpose of this chapter is to describe some anthropological political models that provide a slightly different historical-political view than most hear. The early political systems will be omitted, as they have limited relevance for this presentation.

Chapter IX seeks to isolate those aspects of particular historic political modes that continue to characterize present political cultures. A people's political past dramatically explains their present. Cultural traditions are far more tenacious in pre-capitalistic, traditional cultures than in modern, capitalistic ones. This fact can be witnessed in European history, as the dominant political and social cultural modes of thinking persisted during the Middle Ages beyond their effective use. Huizinga notes that

> "long after nobility and feudalism had ceased to be really essential factors in the state and in society, they continued to impress the mind as dominant forms of life. The men of the 15th century could not understand that the real moving powers of political and social evolution might be looked for anywhere else than in the doings of a warlike or courtly nobility."[2]

Unless American business people confine their activities to Western Europe, they will inevitably be engaged with business people, government bureaucrats and politicians whose political codes and symbols are rooted in traditional, pre-democratic capitalist political modes. Business men and women must understand as fully as possible a group's political traditions in order to accommodate and ensure successful business results.

PRESSURES ON CURRENT
POLITICAL SYSTEMS

Since the end of World War II, some one hundred political entities have been created. Sixty-eight of these have emerged from colonial *cocoons*. Their initial charismatic leaders are now gone, and they are struggling with the somewhat amorphous task of building nations from a host of disparate nations within. They are referred to as pluralistic or multiple societies and composite or mosaic states. Sometimes the contrast is religious, as in India; sometimes it is tribal, as in Africa and sometimes it is racial, as in Malaysia.

The rising expectations of these masses suggests they are rushing toward modernization, but this tide often collides with out-raged traditionalists rejecting change. Such socio-political currents are yet aggravated by increasing economic disparity between and within nations. As if this is not enough cause for alarm, the dilemma is further complicated by an increased human population that has far outstripped the world's resources which support it.

This intensification of nationalism not only threatens world peace from time to time, but it is threatened by historic, ethnic, racial and religious differences within tribal loyalties. This situa-tion suggests important political risks for American business. The political crisis of the 1990s extends from Central Asia through the Middle East to the Balkans. Additionally, the former Soviet states' ability to transform themselves in an orderly fashion is still open to question.

Before examining the major historic political-culture types, the author has chosen to define the character of political cultures as well as some essential terms for viewing any group's political culture.

POLITICAL CULTURE

A political culture is most vividly reflected when asking these questions: *1) what constitutes the basis of power, 2) how is it used, 2) by whom and 4) for what reason.* These questions become a convenient formula for focusing attention on that aspect of the political culture that American business people must understand.

This formula can help one map *power relations* at all socio-political levels, from family to extended kinship in work settings, religious organizations, neighborhoods, villages, towns, cities and similar geopolitical divisions on national levels. It is not particularly important where one begins this mapping process, although business associates will undoubtedly start with their host country's business sector. A more accurate cultural portrait will necessitate understanding power relationships at various societal levels. By understanding power relations in the family, village and other levels, one will often discover critical nuances not easily detected by a single sector focus.

It is often evident that non-Western religious elites, for example, exert significant authority on power relations at all other levels. To grasp the way religious elites influence a particular people, it is more important to map the power relationships according to the preceding power-relations formula than it is to understand the theological issues. One must carefully differentiate between the reasons power elites give for their actions. Religious elites differ little in their exercise of power, and there are public and private reasons for their actions. One must isolate these differences in order to understand power relations in any society. Or again, as was pointed out in the Chapter IV, kinship power relations generally provide the basic model for all other societal power relations.

Power relations and the political rules of conduct are not always obvious. Westerners often make the mistake of expecting non-Western political systems to conform to the American system.

Thai government friends in Bangkok once asked if they might introduce me to the president of a major United States firm who was having some problems grasping the Thai political culture. They obviously felt this man would listen to me and provide them a tactful way of handling what was becoming an uncomfortable working relationship. We were brought together for lunch, but it was not a productive session. My American colleague blamed the Thai's paternal and personalistic politics for all his problems. A discussion revealed his ire over Thais' refusal to play the political game according to American rules. He refused to bow to local custom and insisted that they do not do things right. His attitude struck me as an extreme example of American ethnocentrism, but it is one that is replicated wherever Americans are engaged in activities in the non-Western world.

POWER AND ITS EXERCISE

It is important to clarify the use of the term, *power*, in the following discussion.[3] *Power refers to one's relative control over an environment* and is a function of things. Any thing can serve as the basis for *power* which could include an ideal as well as a gun. As people ascribe value to things in their environment, those who have the most are said to be power holders or wielders.

An elementary form of power can be the physical size of a man. In most social situations a man of great and imposing physical proportions can be said to control the immediate environment. Were even some youngster to pull a revolver, the gun would replace the giant's size and would exert greater control over that immediate environment. Every social event can be viewed in terms of what power things are being used to control the environment, by whom and for what reason.

The exercise of power also depends on whether the supposed power wielders have, in fact, the actual ability to control the environment and how effective they are in convincing those that they are controlling of the ability to hold control. *In this sense all human relationships can be said to be power relations, as every relation depends on what one controls and what is therefore useful to others.* A female may use her sexuality, family inheritance, income or other things to control her mate, friends and other family members. A man may use his size, income or other things to control his mate and family members. If we focus on national political entities, it is obvious to the most casual observer that political elites spend most of their time assessing their control over the groups in their environment and to what extent they may be able to control other groups. The assessments of power resources are what war is made of. Assumptions about a nation's power resources are a critical component of the political decision to wage war. Sadam Hussein moved on Kuwait because he believed his power resources were greater. He failed to assess Kuwait's ability to derive power from other nations and the willingness of other nations to allocate that power. This was a fatal mistake in the analysis of relative power relations, but human political history is made up of correct and incorrect evaluations.

Particularly in non-Western environments, individuals closely calculate their relative power positions. For example, Japanese businessmen study another's business card upon first meeting in order to place each other in the prestige hierarchy. One's language and bodily behavior (bowing, tone of voice and manners) must reflect a particular status position. In America, office politics is also about power and relative control of the environment. People defer to those who write their checks, even though those persons may not always be the brightest or the most capable members in the firm. They have power by virtue of controlling company funds. It is in the nature of people to reach out and use all sorts of things in an effort to control an environment.

People sometimes organize and pool their power in order to accumulate enough power to successfully compete with a more powerful group. This is why there are organizations, alliances, pacts and other such devices. Households unite to form community organizations, factory or office workers create a union or organize in some fashion. Youths organize gangs, and nations establish alliances. In this process the individual units, whether persons, households or nations willingly give up a certain amount of their resources and control of themselves to the larger group in a bid to create greater leverage. There is always a trade off.

Sometimes one miscalculates another's power and goes to jail, is beaten up, loses a job, is passed over for the company presidency, loses a war and so on. Worse still, my competitor wins the contract. My company loses; I lose. *Nonetheless, all human rela-*

tions revolve around the use of things as power sources. This is important for American business persons to understand as they seek to work in any political environment.

Authority usually refers to legitimate power, which can be a debatable issue in itself. Although more complex modern state systems refer to legitimate power in terms of a bureaucratic political system, in most cultures of this world these two phenomena, authority and legitimate power, are fairly synonymous. Those who exercise power are viewed as having the right to do so, whether fathers, clan leaders, headmen, tribal elders, chiefs or kings. Sometimes this is seen as a divine right, an interesting effect of religion on the political segment of a culture.

There are those who have no legitimate authority but whose exercise of power is often very substantial, such as shaman and ministers, healers, seers and other such types. Business persons must always probe around the social body, identify such individuals and calculate how their activity affects the marketplace.

HISTORIC POLITICAL SYSTEMS

It is important to identify power relations in any socio-cultural system. One's business dealings are critically dependent upon understanding the cultural contours of power which make up the politics of every scene.

Authority types are generally represented in kinship, bands, tribes, monarchies and nation-states.

The chart on the next page shows how these historic political systems generally differ in a number of key ways. The model serves a limited purpose of providing business people with an orientation to general political systems. Most important is an historical political perspective that the model offers. In other words, people moving from one political type to another do not sit down one day and have the following conversation:

	I	II	III	IV	V	VI	VII
			← Tribes →			— Nation/States —→	
	Kinship	**Headmen**	**Special Task Chiefs**	**Strong Chiefs**	**Monarchs**	**Elective/ Appointed**	**Despotic Heads**
GOVERNING STYLE	Consensus	Charisma	Charisma Clans Age Groups	Coercion Nobility	Coercion Tradition Nobility	Law/Popular Elections	Dictorial Coercion Coups
GOVERNING UNIT	Family bands	Family bands	Village	Nobility Specialists	Nobility Specialists	Bureaucrats	Bureaucrats
TECHNOLOGY	Hunting Gathering Pastoral	Hunting Gathering Pastoral	Hoe Agriculture Pastoral	Hoe & Intensive Agriculture	Intensive Agriculture Pastoral	Intensive Agriculture Industrial Post-Indust.	Instensive Agriculture Industrial
ECONOMY	Reciprocity	Reciprocity	Reciprocity	Peripheral Markets	Market-Dominated	1) Democratic Capitalism 2) State-man. Capitalism	Market-Dominated
INTEGRATIVE FEATURES	Common Culture	Common Culture	Shared Terr. Religion Warriors	Nobility Warriors	Nobility Army Tradition	Law/Army Police Nationalism	Army/Polic Nationalism
SOCIAL RANK (Stratification)	Egalitarian	Egalitarian	Emerging Classes	Classes	Classes	Classes	Classes

HISTORICAL POLITICAL SYSTEMS AND SYSTEM ATTRIBUTES

...we have been governed by village councils for hundreds of years. Now that we have a strong chief, we will abolish those and wait for word from our new nobility and their administrative specialists.

We also will have to quit our reciprocal trading and start using the Chief's new market system. Furthermore, we really need to develop our class system and quit this egalitarian system that has burdened us for all these years. If we don't do these things, somebody in the West is going to classify us as a special task-chief system—or even a headman.

And we can't have that!

The political types are guidelines only. With some adjustments they will provide American business people with a reasonably accurate political systems road map.

A glance at the chart will reveal that political systems are related to certain governing styles and units or functional administrative organs as well as certain technologies, economies, cultural integrative needs and social features. A group's technology seems to be the trigger that dramatically drives all the other components.

The concepts of *key integrative* and *social features* need some explanation. The key mechanisms that hold a group together are referred to as *integrative features*. A common culture as well as a common language, religion and general world view hold people together in the kinship and headmen types of political systems. As populations grow and power becomes more centralized, full-time police or military enforcers replace common culture features in maintaining order and integrating the masses. Sometimes it works, and sometimes it doesn't. The fact that millions have died in nation-building during the 20th century testifies to this.

Social difference (stratification) is inserted to signify the relationship of political cultures to the development of societal ranking of class and caste. Social ranking is not produced by any particular political style, however. It results from population increases and an unequal distribution of (and access to) scarce resources. Once populations grow beyond the intimacy of kinship boundaries, private property kicks into the technological and economic equation. Competition between various societal groups then becomes an increasingly dominant factor.

It is important to remember that organized bands, tribes, monarchies and such have developed through history as archetypical governing types. Like all other social models, they are merely classifications of governmental styles.

Tribes

Systems ruled by kinship, headmen and chiefs have faded from most of the Western world for all practical purposes. Although strong extended units exist throughout the non-Western world, these are all subordinate to nation/state political systems. Tribes continue to be significant actors on the political scene in many parts of the non-Western world. The *tribal* label is fairly broadly applied and generally refers to *a large group of people who share a common territory, some significant portion of a common culture, quite often the religion, may or may not have a developing warrior class, and, most important, thinks of itself as a big group.* The economic activity seems to be critical to the group thinking in determining tribal affiliation. Not all tribes have chiefs. Instead, the tribe coordinates tribal activities through a village council of elders or a similar structure.

Chiefs can become monarchs, presidents or prime ministers. Any formal head can become a despot or dictator. The human race has had more than its fair share of those types. When the President of the United States enters a formal event, a band plays "Hail to the Chief." Even in the United States, old traditions live on in many ways.

The idea of monarch is inserted to represent the strong autocratic political systems that characterize many pre-modern, pre-capitalistic states. The monarchial label is not used in general anthropological usage, but it provides a useful way of distinguishing early nation-state leadership from their modern heirs.. Monarchs were pre-industrial, pre-capitalistic despots in the formal sense of that term.

In addition to the pre-industrial monarchs of Europe with which American business people should be familiar, there were those of ancient Egypt, Mesopotamia, China, Africa, Peru and Meso-America whose hydraulic-irrigation technologies were presented in Chapter VII.

State political structures share a number of traits. *First,* they emerge with an efficient and intensive agriculture system with irrigation. *Second,* they set up and administer a market-dominated economy. *Third,* their leaders have a high degree of independent power that manifests itself through a warrior class, army, or other such unit. *Fourth,* loyalty of state members is significantly assured by armed force, although there is often a high degree of shared tradition that integrates the people; especially the shared origin myths, or sacred charter.[4] *Fifth,* heads of states rely upon administrative specialists to coordinate activities, which results in that bureaucratic disease with which the world is all too familiar.[5]

The preceding sketch of political systems is a useful and concise way for business people to view historic political behavior. As is true of other cultural cues, such as kinship, religion, etc., political attitudes and behaviors carry over, with varying degrees of intensity to new political systems. Pre-modern state specialists spawned today's governing bureaucrats, a system of written codified laws, and much of our political apparatus.

TODAY'S POLITICAL CULTURES

Although American business people do not need advice regarding how-to-do business in Western modern-state systems, profitable relations in newly emerging nation-states require a significant grasp of non-Western political history.

The persistence of earlier political culture codes can inhibit or enhance as a people seek to move to a new political system. Tradition's stabilizing influence is often an asset. When tradition collides with a people's rising expectations of sharing the good aspects of modernism, there can be enormous violence. Tradition often retards, or even prevents, needed change. We are witnessing the ascendancy of democracy, a form associated with democratic-capitalism, around the globe. The world's masses seem to be convinced that some form of democratic-capitalism is preferable to whatever they have had. In many cases it remains to be seen how prior political patterns serve the transformation. Can the former Soviet states make the change to some form of democratic-capitalism? Can other nations successfully mimic Asia's newly emerging state-managed capitalism? Latin American cultures, for example, are heavily invested with a system of patronage *(patronismo)*. Their political past is devoid of any Western democracy, where people are called on to participate in decisions that shape their communities. Traditional politics is marked by strong autocratic, and sometimes benevolent, leaders at all levels. African nations will undoubtedly continue to reflect historic tribal loyalties and former colonial patterns. It will be quite some time before nations in either region will play a significant role in world affairs, whether political or economic.

David Halberstam's characterization of Latin American societies as oligarchies should be noted.[6] To illustrate, he contrasts Latin American states with Japan's establishment, whose ruling elites understand their need to "sacrifice some of their own personal privilege and power and riches in order to make sure that the larger society works and is regenerative."[7] He sees Latin America's ruling elite as

> "...a very small handful of immensely privileged people who have it very good and who plan to continue to have it very good and don't care at all about the fact that the rest of the country is doing poorly. In effect, an oligarchy believes it can be successful even if the rest of the country is unsuccessful...Which is why those nations remain so unsuccessful." [8]

Unfortunately, he believes the United States increasingly reflects Latin American characteristics.

ON POLITICAL RISK ANALYSIS

It is unfair to leave the subject of politics without treating the subject of political risk. All American firms are concerned about the political risks of doing business in foreign countries. The assessment of such risks has spawned a significant industry. United States management wants to know the risks of profiting while having to deal with foreign labor relations, corruption, national economic management, regional political relations, religious conflict and ethnic unrest, and this is rightfully so. Of all the potentially damaging aspects that could be listed, ethnic conflict has become the most significant, and it will be increasingly so for the unforeseeable future. But it must be emphasized that the development of an accurate cultural portrait will help to provide companies with an accurate risk assessment in any country.

SUMMARY

An accurate and useful cultural portrait must include a sketch of a people's political codes and relationships wherever one is working or attempting to work. This will include the understanding of the following: what objects are valued and how they are ranked; who controls these resources (power elite); how the key resources are used (rules of access and distribution); and for what reasons (socio-political goals).

One should be able to discover the ways other cultural scenes impact a group's political patterns by sketching the preceding political symbols, codes and relationships. A people's current political traits will be rather confusing without a grasp of the past. Foreign business dealings very often depend upon a very clear comprehension of a people's political culture.

References Cited

1. As mentioned in Chapter VIII, Berger's *Capitalist Revolution*, loc. cit., provides a good discussion of the Marxist-Capitalist debate.

2. J. Huizinga, ibid.,p. 57.

3. The author is indebted to Richard N. Adams, University of Texas, Austin, Texas, for this conceptualizing of power.

4. *Oliver, The Discovery of Humanity: An Introduction to Anthropology* (New York: Harper & Row Publishers), p. 310f.

5. Ibid., p. 320.

6. David Halberstam,*The Next Century* (New York: Avon Books, 1992), p. 125.

7. Ibid.

8. Ibid.

Chapter X:

Time and Space

The wind blew and the crap flew, and I was only here for a day or two.

— Attributed to Pat Paulson

Paulson's reported expression of time's passage is certainly one that can be shared by most of us! But note that Paulson's reference to time is tied to an idea of *space: the "here." Time* and *space* are intimately linked in the human mind. There are some significant differences in the way people around the world view time and space. These differences cause American business people a great deal of discomfort.

Drifting around Mexico and Central America as a young man in the 1950s and 1960s, I received some jarring lessons about cross-cultural differences of space and time. Border crossings did not open on the stated hour. Appointments were often hours off the stated time. When someone said they would meet *after lunch*, they meant anywhere from seven to ten o'clock. I never knew how long to wait. Maybe they had forgotten our appointment. Maybe I was being snubbed. I was a typical impatient *gringo*!

People throughout Mexico and Central America did not govern their lives by the *tick of the clock* the way I believed people were supposed to. I still remember my feelings of frustration and anxiety. Since it is an insult to keep people waiting in my culture, the tardiness of *Latinos* certainly hurt my feelings as well as put a crimp in my travel schedule. I even had bouts of fear and depression over these time differences.

One of the important functions of *time's passage* is the gradual erosion of one's sense of self-importance. Age does have a way of putting life in a proper perspective. This is an important function of Western time for those lucky enough to get the message.

If that was not enough, everyone talked in my face – which was a very intimidating experience. My sense of personal space did not coincide with the Latinos sense of personal space. They would press within a foot of my face. Sometimes it felt like we were nose-to-nose. Sometimes their breath was terrible. At other times I am sure mine was. I probably covered more ground than all my travels combined in Mexico and Central America walking backwards rather than forward as I fought to keep a two to three feet minimum between the end of my nose and others. Sometimes more than three feet! There is no doubt that Mexicans, Guatemalans and others I met throughout the Central American region believed my behavior totally unfriendly. I am sure my youth and profound cultural naivete were the only qualities that saved me. I am also sure I confirmed their worst suspicion about the socially graceless characteristics of *Norte Americanos*. If I am not the butt of a lot of *Latino* folk humor after all these intervening years, it is only because other *gringos* have superseded me.

Since none of us like to be seen as uncouth, barbaric or lacking in good grace, to say nothing of experiencing intimidation and fear, it is essential for American business people to understand how their sense of time and space <u>differs</u> from others.

Time and space orientations are one of a people's most deeply embedded cultural codes. They are so embedded as to be unconsciously held–right along with a sense of humor, taste, love, hate and other such notable features.

We should be aware that people as intelligent as Albert Einstein warned us that time and space were not to be thought of separately. This fact is heavily emphasized as astronomers speak of vast spatial distances in terms of *light-years*.[1] To clarify these issues in the present business context, let us attempt to treat time and space separately, while acknowledging that these two phenomena are interrelated in the everyday, common life of the world.

Examples of exotic cultures such as the Nuer, Hopi and others used in this chapter illustrate the point that some people's concept of time and space vastly differ from our own and being aware of such differences adds to one's cross-cultural knowledge.

TIME

Much research is being conducted to help travelers adjust to the time warp that results from jet lag. As we move through time zones, our body needs time to reset its biological clock. All people, regardless of culture, experience the pain of time zone changes. Studies show that one's judgment is not at its best when out of sync with the local time zone. It is analogous to driving after a few drinks. One feels in control, but studies show that judgment and reactions are significantly impaired. Unfortunately, many business people insist on walking into critical negotiations while still in a time warp.

The essential fact is that we Americans have a notion of time that is often diametrically opposed to others which can warp our foreign business relations in serious ways. There are enormous differences in the underlying cultural codes that define a people's view of time. It is a universal fact that all humans, in all times, have wrestled with the inescapable experience of time. It did not take our ancestors long to note the cyclical rhythms of life as they experienced the daily, seasonal and life-to-death regularities of existence. All human groups create a symbolic way of reflecting nature's orderly rhythm.

The Nuer, a semi-nomadic tribe in the Sudan, studied by the anthropologist Evans-Pritchard, differentiated two types of time – seasonal and social.[2] The seasons were further classified as either wet or dry and related to the system of full moons. They have no concept of months or weeks in the Western sense. Using the movement of the moon, time segments relate to tribal activities. If it is time to break camp and move to another location for the wet period, then it must be "that time." Social events are viewed relative to the number of sleeps or moons, as per the Inuit, when discussing longer historical durations.

Neither the Hopi nor Sioux Indians have a word for time in their native vocabulary although sun priests kept accurate track of the solstices for ritual purposes. When referring to the Hopi, Benjamin Lee Worf reports that,

> "In particular, he has no general notion of intuition of time as a smooth flowing continuum in which everything in the universe proceeds at an equal rate, out of a future, through a present, into a past;..."[3]

No verb tenses exist to mark past, present or future. Instead, the tenses in Hopi verbs specify the speaker's experience or knowledge. International business personnel will not be dealing with Hopi or Navajo, but they do illustrate how differently some non-Western cultural traditions view time, and contemporary Hopi have significantly accommodated to a Western view of time.

Medieval Europeans shared this same non-industrial view of time. Manchester writes:

> "In the medieval mind there was also no awareness of time, which is even more   difficult to grasp...Medieval men were rarely aware of which century they were living in...There are great differences between everyday life in 1791 and 1991, but there were few between 1791 and 1991. Life then revolved around the passing of the seasons and such cyclical events as religious holidays, harvest time, and local fetes. In all Christendom there was no such thing as a watch, a clock, or, apart from a copy of the Easter tables in the nearest church or monastery, anything resembling a calendar. Generations succeeded one another in a meaningless, timeless blur."[4]

Time has definitely changed our view of time! Humans at all times and in all places have faced time as it relates to their own death; the time represented in our own life rhythm as we move through infancy to old age, life to death. As John Donne reminds us in his famous passage,

"Who casts not up his eye to the sun when it rises? But who takes off his eye from a comet when that breaks out? Who bends not his ear to any bell which upon any occasion rings? But who can remove it from that bell which is passing a piece of himself out of this world? No man is an island, entire upon itself; every man is a piece of the continent, a part of the main...any man's death diminishes me because I am involved in mankind; and therefore never send to know for whom the bell tolls; it tolls for thee." [5]

Over the centuries our ancestors invented many devices to symbolize and track the passage of time, such as clocks, calendars, chronologies and cosmologies.[6] The earliest known time-keeping device was developed by the Sumerians, ca. 3500 B.C., and was related to their emerging hoe agriculture technology as discussed in Chapter VII.[7] The Chinese developed a mechanical clockwork six centuries before clocks appeared in the European West.[8] Why should we be surprised! China, like the Sumerians, depended upon horticulture – not an inconsequential fact! Dependence upon seasonal rhythms and the associated rains, or lack of rain, turned our human ancestor's attention skyward where they noticed the cyclical movement of celestial bodies and their correlation with local seasons. Their keen observations led to the development of some very accurate, sophisticated clocks and calendars. The Maya and Inca were sophisticated astronomers and time technicians as well. Stonehenge, the Inca land sculptors, or any other such early constructions are not the result of alien visitation,[9] but are the creation of a people trying to either manage the unmanageable natural rhythms of time or synchronize their own activities.

Even today we are still trying to manage time. In America we talk of time as wasted, killed, lost, spent, used, bad, good, hot, short, long, flying, dull or boring. Companies hire time management experts and the general public spends millions on information designed to help use time more efficiently. Relative to the non-Western world, and possibly the rest of the West as well, we Americans seem to be obsessed with time. Lewis Mumford observed that the clock has so effectively detached time from human events that we see it as some type of mechanical and math-measured system independent of human life.[10]

It is as though time, as experienced through the tick of the clock, has a life of its own. As we find ourselves entering the 21st century on the Western, Gregorian calendar system, we find a significant number of the world's six billion people wearing Western time-keeping mechanisms strapped to their wrist. Inkles' survey of some six-thousand men in six different nations found an increased concern to have people "be on time and show interest in carefully planning their affairs in advance."[11] Inkles believes this need for time coordination to be a symbol of modernity.[12] But, this does not mean that Western clock time has superseded a group's own traditional view of time.

In some cases it means people have recognized the need to keep an eye on the watch as it effects their transactions with Western business people and technology (television, radio and other means of communication). It may also represent a status symbol and social decoration. We should be aware that the meaning of things change as they move from culture to culture. Things are never as they seem.

It is difficult for Westerners to believe that time can be thought of in any other way than by the tick-tock of a watch or clock, or that people can regulate their lives by other means. Briggs found sleep time still used in the 1960s, not an insignificant fact.[13] In the not too distant past, most people organized their life rhythms to that of the soltices of the sun, the movement of the moon and other celestial bodies. These celestial rhythms became *agrarian cyclical rhythms.*

Although it is true that the world's people are gradually adopting Western clock time and the associated Gregorian calendar (business time is synchronized to Western clock-time), the lives of most non-Westerners is still governed by different rhythms and views of time. However, as non-Westerners compose the large majority of the world's people, these differences can cause American business people problems.

198

When working in Islamic countries, one should pay close attention to the Islamic ritual calendar since it, and not the Western Gregorian calendar, regulates the rhythm of people's lives. During Ramadan American business persons should be careful not to smoke, eat or otherwise break the fast rules in public. Since locals understand that Americans are probably non-Muslims, they don't expect them to follow the rules. Neither do they expect non-Muslims to exhibit bad manners in public.

Muslims around the world are usually more familiar with Western time than we are with theirs, which is true for most of the world's cultures. They do pay attention to clock time, and they expect Westerners to be on time. That does not mean they will be; thus, it is best to leave some leeway. Make an appointment for "between ten and ten-thirty" in the morning rather than sharply at ten. If your Muslim business associate shows up on time, it means that he is too available, which may indicate that his business is not good which, in turn, may reflect badly on his business skills. It may also mean that he understands how Americans view time and is careful to meet our cultural needs, a situation which gives rise to a dilemma in knowing how to interpret his timeliness!

If late, your foreign business associate is trying to communicate his prestige. He is a very busy man. He will show up apologizing for being late but adding that he was on the phone to someone in London trying to close a big deal, then another call came through from his sister who is attending a major American University and so on. In each case he is communicating his prestige position while, at the same time, providing some conversational items that can drive the visit and the future relationship.

When working in most non-Western cultures, it seems prudent to view clock-time as a *general* and not a *specific* guide for activities. A nine o'clock meeting time should be interpreted as "nine-ish." This means the meeting will take place some time before the sun hovers directly overhead. Lunch will be anytime during midday. Daily events will follow this general pattern.

One must learn to relax when working in non-Western cultures. The second consideration when working in non-Western cultures is to change one's own cultural time rhythm to that of the locals whether ritual calendar, solar or seasonal time. That is not as easy as one may think.

American business people traditionally hit the international sphere with the same clock and calendar anxiety used at home. Trips are planned with daily and hourly schedules. Little or no flexibility to adjust to local rhythms is reflected. Any suggestion by foreign associates that one spend a few extra days without an hourly schedule to justify the time is interpreted as wasted time. It is tough for many Americans to re-program themselves to another time dimension. However, it is necessary to learn this for the benefits of one's business.

One must experience another people's time view in some degree to really understand it. Our inability to adjust to non-Western time orientations too often fouls good business relations. Non-Westerners place greater time value on personal relationships, the nurturing of which often supersedes business activities. People in non-Western cultures generally believe Americans to be less sociable and less intimate in personal relations. Non-Westerners will spontaneously visit and tend to family and friends in lieu of attending a business meeting, and Americans are left waiting at the hotel or office for that meeting; or, one's indigenous staff disappears with little warning for days on end in order to attend to family affairs.

In Southeast Asia time can be as fluid and as imprecise as it is in Latin America or the Middle East. Over the years the author has noticed that Western and Japanese business persons are increasingly picked up at the appointed clock time that characterizes Western rhythms. As the relationship becomes more familiar, there is a tendency to slip into local time rhythms.

Another generalized rule-of-thumb to remember is that non-Westerner's inactivity may not be as inactive as one may think. We Americans have a stereotyped notion of work and busy-ness. In the Western view – if you are having fun, you must not be working.

Inactivity is viewed as loafing or doing nothing. That is not the way time is viewed in most non-Western cultures. When a foreign business associate seems to be doing nothing, he may be trying to arrive at an important decision or reach a consensus.[14]

Edward T. Hall believes it useful to think of Western cultures in terms of monochromic time (*M-time*) because we schedule and handle tasks one-at-a-time and as isolated, independent units.[15] Conversely, he finds Mediterranean cultures (and it can be assumed other non-Western cultures as well) to be oriented in polychromatic time (*P-time*). Polychromatic timers are people-oriented, not task-oriented. They handle many issues and tasks at the same time. According to Hall,

> "...P-time stresses involvement of people and completion of transactions rather than adherence to preset schedules. Appointments are not taken as seriously and, as a consequence, are frequently broken. P-time is treated as less tangible than M-time. For polychromatic people, time is seldom experienced as 'wasted', and is apt to be considered a point rather than a ribbon or a road, but that point is often sacred." [16]

Using P-time and M-time, Hall specifies how this characterizes French and German business cultures. The chart that follows captures the key aspects of these differences in some key business sectors:[17]

P-TIME	*M-TIME*
FRENCH	GERMAN

Authority and Control

Bosses control employee's time; secretaries work overtime, even on holidays and weekends if needed. Coffee break cannot be disturbed, nor kept over for fear of missing P-time, plus centralized authority prevents scheduling like Germans.	Worker's time sacrosanct, limited hours when shops are open. Seems Germany is "one vast interlocked schedule".

FRENCH	GERMAN

Decision-Making

Agendas fluid, adjust to situations.	Information flow deep historically so all know where they are, memos to subordinates cover deep past of issue, agendas must be adhered to.

Information and Strategies

Centralized system, decisions move from higher to lower levels.	Stronger voices dominate at all levels.
P-time demand screening of info-flow, provided by secretaries and subordinates; don't like phones, prefer to see body language, but leaders prefer to be hidden.	Strong person can block or facilitate other's initiatives, both subordinate and bosses.

Image

More apt to reveal inner self than Germans or Americans, feel protected by group membership.	"Fronts" are very important. Mistakes o.k., but not revealed; never show incompetence.

Personal Relations

P-time brings people together, accentuates personal relations; yet, protects self by not putting name on door; protects either in a circle or out; so salesman owns his customers, this will not transfer.	Compartmentalizing M-time seals people off, so job defines relations. Care to protect privacy of others, while French are preoccupied protecting their own privacy. Communication stresses words and technical signs so detail and symbols of authority carry weight.

In thinking of cultures in terms of either *P-time* or *M-time*, Hall is quick to acknowledge that these are not so neatly applied. One can find both of these patterns existing in Western cultures and variations of both throughout the non-Western world. For example, there are many Americans who handle multiple tasks. Although it may be that our work is relatively impersonal in comparison to non-Westerners, it is a function of the technology and not time codes. Many Americans are very people-oriented. While Mid-Easterners are hanging out and smoking their "hubbly-bubblies" (pipes), their Western counterparts are having their coffee and tea clutches, breakfasts, lunches, dinners and parties of all sorts.

Hall's description of Mid-Eastern bureaucratic life as appearing to be noisy and chaotic to Westerners is supported by the author's experiences and can be justifiably applied throughout the non-Western world. There are exceptions, however. Generally, the fact that everyone seems to be talking at the same time in most public places throughout the non-Western world makes it difficult to figure out what is happening. One person may be shouting on the telephone while three or four conversations are taking place in the same room at the same time. In Mexico, amongst other countries, one can "sit in on" a friend's business meeting. In contrast, American business people tightly protect their business meetings and would be very angry to have anyone invade that most intimate of circles. It just is not done.

In non-Western cultures people often cope with waiting time differently. They do not form an orderly line, or *queue up*, as the British say, and wait their turn. Hall is quite right when he observes that most non-Western cultures use friendships to circumvent many time-consuming, bureaucratic rules and procedures.[18] Although he draws upon his Latin American experience in making this observation, it is basically true throughout the non-Western world. A Westerner waiting in line for service is never as important as a local's *friends* who get priority service. The author has often stood in lines, or more accurately in crowds, and watched those behind served first. Locals assume that if you are waiting you must not be well connected and probably are not very friendly, so you are not worth worrying about.

Not enough research has been done to build any precise models for the time differences of all the world's cultures. Business persons are able to produce a more honest and accurate portrait of another people by allowing the local people to direct the modeling. Although Hall's *P-time* and *M-time* are helpful, they should not bind one's observations.

People differ in their view of time. It is important for American business people to understand that the majority of the world's people do not act out their daily lives to the tick of the Western clock or the Gregorian calendar. The numbers who do are increasing because global business has been dominated by the West.

Many non-Westerners do not respect the tediousness of clock time. Appointments are easily broken or changed. One must grasp the local time rhythms and adjust mentally and emotionally to them.

SPACE

American business persons must not only adjust to *time* differences between cultures but also to *spatial dimensions* of many types and their interrelationships. Modern technology has obviously compressed the world's time and space.

MODERN TECHNOLOGIES:ANNIHILATION OF SPACE THROUGH TIME

Our contemporary communications and transportation technology is responsible for this global transformation. A condition most popularly heralded by Marshall McLuhan in the 1960s when he described the world as a "global village."[20]

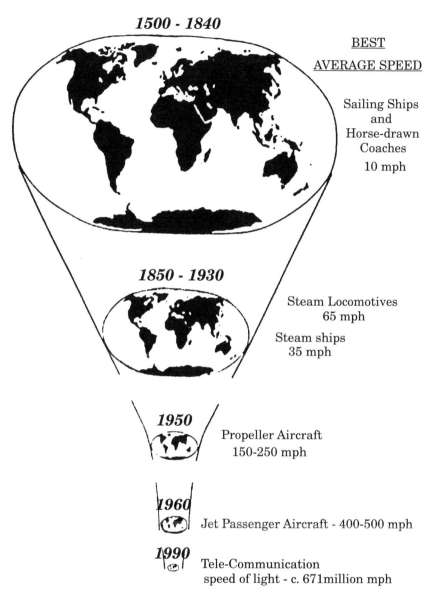

1500 - 1840

Sailing Ships
and
Horse-drawn
Coaches
10 mph

1850 - 1930

Steam Locomotives
65 mph

Steam ships
35 mph

1950

Propeller Aircraft
150-250 mph

1960

Jet Passenger Aircraft - 400-500 mph

1990

Tele-Communication
speed of light - c. 671million mph

The Globe Has Shrunk!

In Chapter II Manchester helped us understand medieval European man's lack of ego and his spatial limitations. There was a slight chance that one could find his way back if one strayed too far from his village. The changes over the last 500 years have been enormous. People distinguish themselves from others geographically[21] by using such landmarks as railroad tracks, the sunny and shady sides of mountains, direction points of south, east, north or west, designations indicating living on farms, in small towns, cities or nations. These are some of the spatial aspects shaping the contours of social relations throughout the world.

Spatial differences result in different urban designs which business people will encounter as they travel around this world. In Latin American cities, for example, inner-city space is traditionally more valued than suburban. There is a Spanish legacy that states: the closer one lives to the city's core, the higher one's economic and social status. The poor live in the surrounding suburbs. Their pasteboard, tin and cement-block shelters populate mountain view spaces for which North Americans pay large sums to possess in the United States. Conversely, North Americans favor suburban spaces, and let our inner-cities decay.

Hall characterizes European cultures' use of space as either "grid" or "star." [22] The grid design, which originated in Asia Minor, separates population centers along north/south, east/west points. It was borrowed by the Romans and implemented throughout most of Europe. The French and the Spanish use a radiating star design for similar human activity.[23] It is incredible how many facets of French life touch the radiating "star" pattern. As Hall observes, it is almost as though:

> "...the whole culture was set up on a model in which power, influence and control flowed in and out from a series of interlocking centers. There are sixteen major highways running into Paris, twelve into Caen...twelve into Amiens, eleven for La Mans, and ten for Rheims...for France is a series of radiating networks that build into larger and larger centers...the man in charge of a French office can often be found in the middle,–with his minions placed like satellites on strings radiating outward from him." [24]

Differences in spatial views have often been the cause for conflict between cultural groups. For example: European views of personal legal ownership of land clashed with North American Indian views of collective ownership. What our forefathers saw as vacant land, as it was not being farmed or ranched according to Western traditions, tribal peoples saw as collectively theirs. Whereas our European ancestors thought of private property in rational legal terms, non-capitalistic and non-industrial people thought in terms of non-legal tribal traditions. Here are two totally different spatial orientations. American business persons will often find non-Westerners who still cling to remnants of such traditional spatial orientations.

Spatial codes are as difficult to understand, accept and adjust to as those of time. It is necessary for business people to grasp how their foreign counterparts view various social spaces. *First*, in contrast to Americans, most non-Westerners tend to see space collectively, meaning it is an extension of the family, tribe/ clan, village. *Second*, whereas Americans think of space as empty or filled, relative to exploitation, many groups see an orderly design that includes nature. The Japanese epitomize this latter view, and these two views result in different approaches to the use of various spaces. *Third*, population density patterns of most non-Western nations has led to heightened spatial values that are in great contrast to the Western view.

These general spatial orientations create unique spatial patterns for individual interactions. For example: spatial patterns reflect the gender, age, social status and prestige of one's foreign counterpart. Unless the foreign culture's view of space is understood, our intended communication can be severely impaired. By and large, non-Western cultures share closer personal distance zones than Americans.

Latin American males embrace and generally touch in their relations. In most Mid-Eastern, African and some Southeast Asian cultures, males hold hands, put their arms around their friend's waist and generally exhibit intimate spatial relations that makes Westerners very uncomfortable. Whereas Americans feel comfortable talking at a distance of 18-20 inches, the Latin American and

Mid-Eastern pattern of 8-13 inches makes us very uneasy. In addition, Americans abhor touching and crowded conditions. The author has often witnessed Americans who refused to ride Japan's crowded subways for this reason. When they do, they are extremely ill-at-ease.

Hall's four "personal space zones," or what he calls informal spaces, helps to make sense of these variations. [25] The author has distilled the key elements from his models:

1. Intimate Distance

TYPE		CHARACTERISTICS
0 - 18 inches		Key senses; smell, feel of others
0-6 inches	Close phase	love-making, wrestling, comforting, protecting, body heat felt, smells
6-18 inches	Far phase	hand can reach other's body; head and face features distorted in size, body heat can be felt, smell still critical

2. Personal Distance

1 1/2 - 2 feet	Close phase	Can hold other, no further body feature distortion, noticeable eye-muscle feed-back, surface textures of other bold, limit of some body heat feeling, smell still critical
2 1/2 - 4 feet	Far phase	proverbial arms length stage, head size, other's features well defined and no body heat felt, smell important if strong perfumes and cologne used, breath can be detected.

3. Social Distance

4 - 7 feet	Close phase	Body size of other is normal, not distorted; more involved type of impersonal business distance, often people who work together.
7 - 12 feet	Far phase	More formal business posture; desks are large enough to keep people at this distance; most important to keep eye contact at this distance.

4. Public Distance

12 - 25 feet	Close phase	Easier for escape; Voice is loud, whole body can be seen and others in easy peripheral vision.
25+ feet	Far phase	30 feet usual for public figures; voice loses many subtle meanings; people seen as smaller, contact as humans fade.

Business associates working abroad should find Hall's spatial models a useful guide, but they should not be treated as an inflexible device. Observation of local behavior and discussion with locals will instruct one regarding proper spatial characteristics fairly quickly. It is also necessary to be aware of the variety of social characteristics that will effect Hall's spatial rules.

One must not forget that spatial codes generally differ with social class, age, gender, race and ethnicity, as well as the nature of the social event. It is important to remember Auden's warning:

> Some thirty inches from my nose
> The frontier of my Person goes,
> And all the untilled air between
> Is private pagus or demesne
> Stranger, unless with bedroom eyes
> I Beckon you to fraternize

Beware of rudely crossing it;
I have no gun, but I can spit.[26]

Be forewarned! In the interest of better relationships, it is more appropriate for American business people to adjust to their foreign business associates' spatial codes. This is true in spite of the fact that most foreign associates will do their utmost to adjust to American spatial codes. To observe Americans seeking to learn and adjust to their codes will have a stunning effect on foreign business associates.

In summary, the culture codes regulating a people's time and space patterns are critical features of any people's behavior, and their characteristics should be part of any good culture portrait.

References Cited

1. A light year is the distance light travels in a year. Scientists have determined that light travels at the speed of 186,282 miles a second.

2. E. E. Evans-Pritchard, *The Nuer* (Oxford: Oxford University Press, 1940).

3. Benjamin Lee Worf, *Language, Thought and Reality* (New York: jointly by Massachusetts Institute of Technology and John Wiley & Sons, 1956), p. 57.

4. Manchester, op.cit., pp. 22-23.

5. John Donne, *Devotions Upon Emergent Occasions,* (Ann Arbor: University of Michigan Press, 1959), pp. 108-109.

6. For an historical sketch of such devices, see:

   J.T. Fraser, *Time: The Familiar Stranger* (Amherst, Mass.: University of Massachusetts Press, l987); and

   Lloyd, H. Alan,"Timekeepers–An Historical Sketch", in J.T. Fraser, *The Voices of Time* (New York: George Braziller, 1966), pp. 388-400.

7. Lloyd, *Timekeepers,* Ibid.

8. Fraser, *Voices,* op.cit., p 106.

9. Erich von Daniken, *Chariots of the Gods* (New York: Putnam, 1970); von Daniken wrote a number of books on this theme.

10. Lewis Mumford, *Technics and Civilization* (New York: Harcourt Brace, 1934), p. 15.

11. Alex Inkeles, "Making Men Modern", in <u>American Journal of Sociology</u>, Volume 75, p.199.

12. Ibid.

13. Jean L. Briggs,, *Never In Anger* (Cambridge: Harvard University Press, 1970), p. 199.

14. Hall, *The Dance of Life: The Other Dimension of Time* (Garden City, NY, Anchor Press/Doubleday, 1983), p. 41f.

15. Ibid, p. 41f.

16. Ibid, p. 43.

17. Ibid, pp. 109-113.

18. Ibid., p. 71.

19. David Harvey, *Postmodernity,* Ibid., p. 241.

20.Marshall McLuhan, *Understanding Media: The Extensions of Man* (New York: McGraw, 1964; NAL, 1966).

21. See earlier reference to this subject in Chapter VI, pp. 76-79.

22. Hall, *Hidden Dimension*, Ibid.

23. Ibid, p. 147.

24. Ibid, p. 113.

25. Ibid, p.116f.

26. W.H. Auden, "Prologue: The Birth of Architecture", *About the House* (New York: Random House, 1965).

Chapter XI:
Completing the Cultural Portrait

We will never have true civilization until we have learned to recognize the rights of others.

— Will Rogers

It has become commonly known that knowledge is the key to higher profits in this information age. The need to know, to understand and respect the culture in which one attempts to do business cannot be overstated. It is the most fundamental prerequisite for maximizing profits! One may possess all of the business knowledge and skills available, be eminently successful in one's field — but *lack the ability to decode foreign cultures and thus fail to maximize foreign profits.* Cultural knowledge translates into greater profits, and American business persons should be equipped to decipher other cultures. However, there is no quick and easy path to cross-cultural literacy.

The most accurate cultural knowledge can only be derived from a veracious way of viewing something as slippery as a culture. One needs something that will provide a focus, like eye glasses or binoculars. An anthropological or cross-cultural perspective serves this purpose, as it is the most precise mental frame of reference or useful way of thinking for viewing other cultures.

Included in this cross-cultural perspective is, first, a *precise definition of culture* which is to be used as the perspective's focal lens, and second, a *set of scenes,* or clusters of human activities, which are themselves the results programmed by a people's mental codes defined as culture. Using this perspective as a decoding device, business people can successfully sketch the most basic contours of any culture. This process of sketching another culture is akin to creating a portrait.

We start any cross-cultural sketch by first recognizing that some of our own cultural features too often prevent us from grasping the most basic elements of any other's culture. Our over-inflated sense of our own culture's worth, radical individualism, some offensive body language, loud speech and a rude posture of impatience seems to be the most notorious impediments in comfortably relating cross-culturally. Once we are able to neutralize these features, we can productively focus on the contours of the six basic socio-cultural scenes common to all cultures and note the critical role a people's view of time and space plays in cross-cultural relations.

Each scene (habitat, economy, kinship-non-kin relations, religion, politics, technology) should be sketched with an eye to its cultural history and its relationship to the other scene. Present cultural phenomena can only be understood through reference to the past. The cultural past lies just below one's contemporary cultural skin. Many cultures around the world have not changed much over the centuries. Although we are not trained to view a people's religion, kinship relations, and environment as significant factors to international business, an accurate cultural portrait must account for these factors and show how they interrelate with all other cultural scenes. This provides the American business person with a new way of looking at international markets.

Accessing, or entering another's culture, demands a variety of tactics. Even with a good cultural perspective, it takes careful research and a significant amount of work. The first step is recognizing the danger of romanticizing another culture. There are a number of *pursuit strategies* we can then use in sketching an accurate cultural portrait:

1) Reading everything available about the culture;
2) Investing in home-stay time within the culture;
3) Sharpening our questioning skills; and
4) Honing our skills of observation.

First, Americans love to go places. We are great wanderers. That is good. *Second*, we have a deep-seated craving to be liked and appreciated–if not loved–by everyone. That also is good...sometimes. We spend a lot of time and money trying to make ourselves better, more lovable. That, too, can be good, if it works. It usually does not–unfortunately. *Third*, we carry with us a notion of sociocultural preeminence among peoples of the world. We strongly believe we have historically acted beneficently toward the world's peoples. Though we believe a presidential administration might have erred from time to time, we argue that the hearts of the American people have always been, and still are, in the right place. It is from that standpoint that we expect foreign peoples to respect and like us personally. We want to be accepted. That is often the big problem!

In the late 1960s the daughter of a good friend was one of many young adults in this country looking for a social and cultural *Garden of Eden*, minus the serpent. She was a soft-spoken, unpretentious and kind person. Her search took her to many parts of the United States, Latin America, Europe and finally Asia. Each time she settled into a foreign site, she believed she had found that perfect place where everyone loved each other and her, of course. After some months she became aware that these people were no more righteous than those she left behind in the States. Finally, she found her *Eden* in Japan! For many months she spoke in glowing and romantic terms of how kind and wonderful the Japanese people were. She worked at learning the language, tea ceremony, flower arranging and so forth. Alas, the serpent emerged in *Eden* the second year. Local Japanese drove her out of their neighborhood. Rocks were thrown through the windows of her apartment. So much for Eden! She returned to the United States, and the last I heard was doing well in the midst of her own culture's evil.

This case may seem slightly exceptional. But, it is not. One should not romanticize other cultures.[1] Although I have never kept count, I suspect most Americans working abroad report some degree of pain associated with being an outsider. The degree to which one is shut out varies from culture to culture, person to person. The effect is similarly depressing. Americans desperately want to be an accepted member of any group whether at school, in local community organizations, at the work place or within another culture. Sometimes this need is further exacerbated by our insistence that the relations be defined on our own cultural terms.

Our culture's radical individualism heavily accounts for this characteristic. We do not have the intimate historical family roots so characteristic of non-Westerners. We seek and derive personal psychological security (trust) through intimate friendships developed at school, work group or any number of voluntary associations. These are quickly and easily exchanged as we move around the landscape from town to town, city to city, work group to work group.[2] We have a craving for intimacy and, thus, create it relatively quickly.

Intimacy seekers we surely are. Our need for quick intimacy is not shared by non-Americans. Non-Americans seek intimacy in their business relations with Americans, but it is certainly not quick. Good relations with foreign business associates begin slowly, taking years to develop. American business people need to understand this process. While patiently developing relationships, one can pursue the greater cultural knowledge: sketching the culture. One does this by reading, home-stays, asking questions and listening (two different skills), and observing foreign scenes. Some of these pursuit strategies seem fairly obvious, but each has some notable twists.

READING THE LITERATURE: PURSUIT STRATEGY ONE

One must read. One can attain a fairly accurate grasp of another culture by reading the literature. It is important to remember that few works can be accepted as the definitive picture of a people. The more one burrows into the literature, the more pronounced the profile becomes.

216

One must read. There is always someone who asks if you have read a certain new book, and you hate to admit you have not. To do so may imply disinterest. Read as much as possible on the culture of your choice even though it is hard to keep up with the new material. To be productive at any endeavor takes commitment and hard work. Your business profits depend on the accuracy of your cultural portrait, and a knowledge of the literature is a key ingredient in that product.

As outsiders in a foreign setting, one must always assume an unfeigned posture of ignorance. We must always be learners.

HOME-STAYS: PURSUIT STRATEGY TWO

As a fond memory of childhood, we all grew up spending the night with our childhood friends. That was one of the most exciting events as children. We not only had fun, but we also had an opportunity to see how other people lived and that their lives were somewhat different from our own. It raised as many questions as it answered, but it was very educational.

The same experience awaits American business persons who take advantage of home visits: *spending the night.* The dark-suit, white-shirt-and-tie crowd that populates every first-class hotel in non-Western cities, is significantly challenged. The challenge is to get out of the first-class cocoon and into the local culture. It is extremely difficult to develop a good cultural portrait from the sanctuary of first-class accommodations. There are some notable exceptions to this general rule. Field engineers, for one, usually have to get out into the rural areas. They have an opportunity to sketch that cultural portrait more rapidly than others–if they have a good cultural perspective and if they will take advantage of their situation. Unfortunately, most engineers share the tendency to congregate amongst themselves and party with the rest of America's international business contingent.

Most foreign business associates are happy to help their American business associate experience a traditional home setting. Although a traditional home setting of an urban area will suffice, one should also get to the village or small town level. Spend as much time as possible. Weekend periods are especially helpful.

Re-entering the first-class western cocoon after a stint in a village or traditional home setting is to experience a dramatic shock. One will emotionally and intellectually know what all the writing and talking world cannot communicate! One will better understand how much difference actually does exist between local culture and one's first-class womb. One's cross-cultural life will never be the same. Such experiences put modernity into proper perspective. Some say it is easier to see the insignificant aspects of modern life as opposed to basic human elements. A cultural portrait painted from an experience in the culture will be more vivid, accurate and lasting. One will be a better cross-cultural business partner, and therefore a more profitable one.

This is also important for expatriates to understand. American business associates living in a foreign site for an extended period of time, cocooned in the usual American world that characterizes foreign assignments, can develop a fairly slanted portrait. They live in a Westernized home or apartment. Many have a driver, housekeepers, cooks, yardmen, private clubs and all other Western, first class accoutrements that build barriers and prevent direct contact with the local culture on an even footing. Hired staff are very guarded about what they reveal of local culture to such moneyed outsiders. Little useful knowledge results from this type of working condition.

The author certainly would not argue against comfortable, healthy and safe living conditions, but such things should be understood in context. When one needs to understand the culture – to paint an accurate cultural portrait – the expatriate living environment tends to inhibit the authentic process. As a businessman I am extremely wary of what my colleagues say about the local culture. I listen – warily. Therefore, it is wise to cautiously entertain stories and explanations about the local culture spun by Americans until they can be validated by the indigenous people. One must learn to double-check, or validate viewpoints expressed by non-indigenous persons.

American military personnel's overseas experiences are plagued by similar problems. Military personnel experience the local culture from the vantage point of the military base and its mission. They share a military point of view. It is difficult to gain an accurate understanding from this perspective. Sometimes, however, a person is able to stand outside his military posture and paint a fairly accurate portrait of the local culture, but is still a difficult task.

Tourists are also significantly screened from the local culture. While it is true their focus is not diffused by business issues or wrenched through a military culture, the time spent in a country is limited. It can be argued, of course, that most foreign business trips are little more than tourist jaunts. That they tend to be.

It is also true that many tourists go seeking a good time – some fun-in-the-sun – and care little about learning the local culture. This is understandable. However, the problems arise when tourists claim to understand a particular culture after a brief sojourn. We all wish it were that easy.

Peace Corp volunteers provide an excellent example of cultural immersion. The majority return with a good understanding of another culture and the complexity involved when trying to compare, change or do business cross-culturally. The author does not advocate that all American business people should have a Peace Corp stint, although that may not be a bad idea. The fact that Americans of all ages have lived in non-Western environments via the Peace Corp is proof that business men and women can do the same from time to time. A short stint of three or four months at the village, or small-town level of life in any country would certainly be a great training program for any American company's present or future foreign staff. It certainly should be recommended. If the CEOs of America's top 500 companies would spend a month or so in a non-Western village, it would most certainly change the way America does international business.

There is no guarantee that living in another culture will automatically generate an accurate cultural portrait. Not every Peace Corp volunteer returns with an accurate cultural portrait of the people with whom they worked. Although staying with a people for some extended period of time offers the best opportunity for accomplishing this task, one still has to know what to look for and how to organize all the diverse sounds, sights, and experiences into a meaningful portrait. This can most efficiently be done by entering the local environment.

SENSITIVE QUESTIONING: PURSUIT STRATEGY THREE

In addition to reading about a culture and experiencing the culture through home visits, one should sharpen the ability to ask penetrating questions. Although all of us have eyes to see, ears to hear, and minds to create questions, it is a well known fact that we do not all use this equipment efficiently. There is also a skill to asking questions. Unfortunately, there is no magical formula.

The *cultural perspective* provides the tools for crafting insightful questions. The *scenes* provide basic categories for shaping the direction of the questioning. The skeletal cultural history pegs provide organizational points from which to craft proper questions. There is a *what* and *why* to all cross-cultural phenomena. The preceding cultural perspective makes it fairly easy to find significant cultural facts that comprise the *what* of one's investigation. The purpose or reason for that fact is not always obvious, the *why* factor. India's cultural view of cattle provides a good example.

India's taboo on killing beef cattle, the sacred cow tradition, in the midst of enormous hunger and abject poverty has always bewildered Westerners. Studies show that the cow serves a variety of important functions in Indian life that makes its killing hazardous for life in general. For example, the cow grazes freely, "harvesting energy" (grass, weeds etc.) around the edges of buildings and other such places unavailable to man in any other form; cow dung is a critical source of fuel and housing plaster; and the milk and by-products are staples.

The benefits of putting the cow in a sacred category are many and outweigh the short term benefits of butchering the animals for beef. Most cross-cultural behavior that seems irrational to Western eyes has a similar adaptive reason for existing. Every technical element, social pattern and cultural code has a systemic reason for existing. One must be skeptical and keep probing until the value or act makes sense in the context of the general cultural portrait emerging. Each fact should be validated by a significant number of locals.

There are always a few things that defy imagination. We have a few cultural irrationalities of our own, at least when we are honest. A cultural trait can become so habitualized that it loses its original reason for being. In most cases people just act without question. In other cases a new justification emerges to support and maintain it. American business people will discover that most marketplaces reflect some of these hangovers. This leads to the issue of socio-cultural change.

The area of cultural change is itself a topic for a great deal of research. Culture is very tenacious. Change is usually very painful. Most people will go to extravagant ends to resist culture change. This is somewhat disconcerting to many Americans since our own culture seems to be in constant flux. In fact, we have come to identify change with progress. Not so within the non-Western world. It is somewhat unnerving to most of us to find that the majority of the world's cultures tend to resist change. There's an old Spanish saying, *"Vale mas lo viejo conocido que lo nuevo par conocer,"* : "that which is old and known is more valuable than the new yet to be understood". We must learn to accept and appreciate people as they are and not as we would wish them to be.

One must be prepared to discover that not everyone can explain their culture well. A persistent search will eventually lead to people who are articulate. They will be your best guides. They will be able to take generalized questions such as how a local family is organized or what racial and ethnic divisions exist, and fill in the blanks. It is still necessary to check and double-check statements of fact until a consensual picture emerges. One's posture of ignorance results in a lot of "who, what where, when, how and why, and explain that"– and so forth.

It is essential to remember that a people's view of reality differs with gender, age, social status and education. One must never assume an accurate sketch of another people's culture without exploring each of these major perspectives.

In summary, an accurate portrait results from constant questioning and the ability to listen carefully.

OBSERVATION: PURSUIT STRATEGY FOUR

In addition to reading, home-stays, and asking a lot of questions, one must be observant. This seems to be an easy task. We tend to be keen observers having arrived in the midst of a strange environment. New images crash in upon the mind, day after day creating a heightened consciousness. A cultural newcomer's eyes are always moving, flitting here and there like a rapid firing uzi. But our eyes filter these sights through a pre-programmed set of cultural codes that distort such new images. We see what our cultural perspective allows us to see, and even that is highly suspect. People do not function as copy machines, objectively picking up everything in their path.

We are all aware of the difficulty of getting two or more people who witness an accident or crime to agree on what really happened. This selective perception was highlighted in the case of the hunter, who every time he shot a duck, his dog would retrieve it by running along the top of the water. After accomplishing this feat a number of times, the hunter turned to an onlooker and asked: "Did you notice anything unusual about my dog?" The onlooker replied: "Sure did – he can't swim."

So what we observe others doing should be subjected to the same skepticism as all other sensory data we receive about another person. Given the crippling effect of our own cultural tools, we have to invent a new way to see, hear and experience if we are to understand how other people put their world together. We face great difficulty understanding another culture "on its own terms." We need to substitute a device that helps us see things and events previously hidden. To see and understand the way indigenous people see and understand: the refusal to allow one's American cultural filter to interpret what is seen in a foreign culture is critically important.

In summary, all *pursuit strategies* work together in helping one grasp how another people see and interpret the world. One must use all possible means to crack a cultural code and pursue every available strategy to sketch an accurate cultural portrait. This ability is a prerequisite to maximizing all the business skills one may possess. The more accurate the cultural portrait, the more profitable one's business.

Don Shula, former coach of the Miami Dolphins football team, reportedly said: "Sure, luck means a lot in football. Not having a good quarterback is bad luck." American companies seeking foreign profits without the most efficient cross-culturally capable sales and marketing personnel face similar bad luck. Let us train our people to decode other cultures, thereby increasing our foreign profits.

References Cited

1. Shapiro, Michael, *Japan: In the Land of the Brokenhearted* (New York: H. Holt, 1989). Details are given of the painful experiences of four different people as they sought to integrate into Japanese society.
2. Francis Fukayama, op.cit.

Appendixes

Appendix to Chapter VI

Bibliography

Index

Appendix to Chapter VI

THE INUITS

The polar regions include the Arctic and the Antarctic regions. The Antarctic is one of the coldest and most desolate area on earth. No animal life exists inland, and the only human habitation is in the form of modern scientific stations which are environmental cocoons fed from outside the region.

The Arctic climate has been more hospitable to plants and animals, which attracted migratory populations from northern Asia on the heels of the last glacial age some 2,000 to 10,000 years ago. Historically, populations do not mass migrate like tour groups. Small hunting bands drift across the landscape as they leisurely follow game. As the ice sheets pushed south, they drove the wooly mammoth, rhinoceros and other game south as well. As the ice retreated north, those human populations who had become dependent on the large animals followed and became the ancestors of present-day Arctic dwellers. This diverse group of early Asian hunters brought cultures capable of coping with the Arctic's harsh conditions and an ability to take advantage of its relatively restricted resources. Of course, they amended their cultures over time to become more "adapted."

As noted in the main text, Arctic temperatures are cold, and hurricane force winds are common. They regularly blow fifty to eighty miles per hour. Penguins and other egg layers have been observed exerting all their might trying to keep winds from blowing away their eggs.

The tundra soil only thaws a few weeks each summer and is extremely soggy and thin, an inch or so at best. During the summer this soggy mess breeds mosquitoes, flies, mites, and other pests which annoy man and beast. Below this soggy quag lies the permafrost, or permanently frozen ground, reaching depths of 1,640 to 1,970 feet.[1] This permafrost tundra can be greatly damaged by a herd of reindeer or human exploratory and exploitative activities.

The summer Arctic tundra is able to provide nourishment to some 900 species of flowering plants and many types of moss and lichens.[2] Near the sub-Arctic tree line one can find willows, birches, alders, and pine; but all are of shrub or bush size.

Meanwhile, the chain of life in the Arctic follows the rising of the sun. The sunlight shining on the polar seas creates a nutrient condition which allows for an abundant growth of plankton, a major source of food for sea crustaceans, especially krill, and these provide food for large fish. The seas, bays, and fjords teem with fish of all sizes during the summer. The fish, in turn, attract birds and animals such as the walrus, seal and whale. At the same time, numerous species of water foul return from their winter sojourn in the south. All this activity attracts and feeds such land animals as the wolf, fox, ermine, bear, and herds of caribou, musk ox, and reindeer. Finally, there are the various human groups trying to sustain an existence on all of the above.

In a twinkling of an eye, it is all over. The sun disappears for nine to ten months, the birds and caribou head south, others go into hibernation, and some "batton down the hatch" and prepare for the long and lonely winter. All the creeks, ponds, fjords, and the soggy tundra freeze. Snow and ice reclaim the total environment. Man is one of those who battons down the hatch and prepares for a lonely, howling, dark and extremely cold period.

The resource options available to the Inuit are few. One is surrounded by ice, snow, rock, and at times gravel. Dwellings are of rock, whalebone and sod in the north, and wood, whalebone and sod in the south. The familiar ice block igloo serves as a temporary shelter during hunting expeditions.[3] Clothing comes from animal skins. Food is sought chiefly by hunting and supplemented by fishing and gathering a few roots and berries available during the summer. The inland Inuit of North America were an exception, as they organized around the herds of caribou that migrated through their area during the year.[4] The *Lapps* of northern Scandinavia and the Siberian *Chuckchi, Euenks, Yakuts*, and others, developed a very efficient form of reindeer herding.[5] The resource recovery of herding allowed all of these groups to be relatively sedentary.

The environmental effect on the cultural development of Arctic populations is quite clear and pronounced. *First,* the groups had to be small, as explained in the main text. Even during the less active winter period, settlements probably held no more than thirty to fifty families and they constantly shifted as some moved out to hunt and others returned. In summer the families scatter to hunt full time. The environment is highly restrictive in this regard.

Second, political control had to be vested in the kin hunting unit. Much like desert nomads, such as the Kung Bushmen of the South African Kalahari Desert, polar hunting units had to be politically independent to make decisions quickly. No formal chiefs existed. As stated earlier, authority rested in the male head of a family unit. Yet, decisions were made with the rest of the group in mind. A tenacious balance existed between family units and the larger society. The fragile environment set clear signals of how indispensable the total group was to everyone's survival. Members could display their displeasure and quickly bring another to heel or drive them from the group. Being banned from the group was an ultimate and shameful sentence, and given the harsh environment, it was almost a sure death sentence.

Third, Arctic cultures were marketless economies driven by general reciprocity rules. Personal ownership was almost nonexistent. Sharing of tools, dogs, sleds, food, lodging, and even females, was normal practice. Surplus food was left across the tundra in stone caches for use by anyone who needed it. And everyone had to work. If a man's wife was too ill to help with the hunting, he would leave her with another man and take his wife. The environment and the technology necessary to harvest the resources for survival did not allow individual preferences that made one stand out from others in the group. When one became too old to keep up with the hunting migrations, they were left to die. It was a tough life.

So, everyone had to be attached to a hunting group, which was the basic economic unit. The environment did not allow for rugged individualists. Surplus women had to be distributed to families and sometimes a man had more than one wife. There were also times when females were scarce and unmarried men had a tough time. Shortages accrued because of female infanticide, which was itself a response to a severe lack of game and reserve food stocks.

Fourth, the harsh polar environment and equalitarian social system rewarded complimentary personality traits.[6] Life was viewed fatalistically, as mentioned in the main text. And although physically tough and courageous, men were socially gracious and helpful to all. A great deal of merit was placed on personal restraint. Demonstrations of emotion were frowned on, especially anger. This does not mean there was an absence of murders or fights, but that the total dependency upon each other demanded by the environment put a higher premium on those traits that maintained group harmony and solidarity. Personal problems were not discussed, nor was it tactful to point out one's own or others.

Those who stepped out of line, by taking too big a share of the kill, for example, were publicly ridiculed, chastised and sometimes driven from the group. Women who were hard to get along with found it difficult to find a husband and, therefore, an economic unit.

Anthropologist Jean Briggs lived among an Intuit group in the Canadian Northwest Territories and found the deprivation to be so overwhelming that she often expressed her anger and frustration in front of others.[7] As they puzzled over this strange behavior, Briggs says,

"It is possible that in the early period they were watching, weighing, not yet confirming unpleasant judgments but puzzling how to interpret my strange behavior, just as I puzzled how to interpret theirs."[7]

She finally suffered the ultimate punishment. She was banned. One Inuit stated in a letter that "she is so annoying, we wish more and more that she would leave." [8] Many have undoubtedly had the urge from time to time to expel and ban Westerners from their midst!

Inuit children were quickly integrated into family work and taught the social amenities necessary for survival in such a hostile environment. They played with Husky pups, harpoons and all other implements necessary for survival. Girls were usually married off by the time they reached thirteen or so, and boys were considered men and looked upon as mature hunters when they reached early teens. Culture was passed on orally from one generation to another which was the form that formal education took. One knew all that was needed by the early teens.

Fifth, although simple by engineering design standards, the technology was highly efficient and developed as a response to the environment. The tools were simple, but complex in use.[9] The technology served the Inuit's ability to act and react quickly, to understand the intricate and subtle behavior of all forms of arctic life, and to accurately read the weather. The environment left little room for error. Life was always on the edge.

Implements were few. Knives, needles and other key implements were made from the bones of animals and birds. Sleds and other devices, of which there were few, were made from seal, whale or walrus bones, caribou antlers and hides. (Metals were only introduced in the last few hundred years, and wood in the early 19th century.) A simple lamp, made from stone and filled with blubber, was an important item at all times. Dried moss wicks were ignited by striking flint.

Inuit sports and games highlight the physical skills necessary for survival, such as foot races, dog sled races, and all sorts of tests for physical strength and stamina.[10] There are song duels and competitive story telling. But the competition is never allowed to damage a person psychologically, so the dominance of the group exerts itself.

Sixth, Inuit religious beliefs are animistic, as are the beliefs of most non-Westerners, as mentioned in the main text. All is imbued with soul. All is alive. The universe is full of demons and forces that could kill, maim, and prevent a successful hunt. Whereas an American will gaze out over the land and see lifeless mountains, trees, rocks, snow, ice and so forth, the animist sees force-filled elements.

Magic was one method of trying to protect oneself and one's group from being afflicted by evil forces. *Shaman*, therefore, had tremendous power over group behavior. Such men were feared, yet respected. They could foretell the future and restore the balance of life in bad times.

Although the polar environment's impact upon Inuit culture building is summarized in the main text, it should be restated here that the harsh habitat set narrow limits on what the Inuit could do. It set narrow limits on the size of the group, lead to infanticide in moments of extreme food scarcity, promoted an equalitarian-collective organization, was intolerant of complex political mechanisms; limited tools to a few carefully crafted ones, called forth a marketless economy of sharing and trading and encouraged people to seek solutions for their dilemmas via magic.

Japan's archipelago land mass is approximately 146,000 square miles,[11] and only about 15% is useful for cultivation. Alluvial soils are rich and the result of centuries of buildup and careful management. Hills and mountains are terraced to maximize food production, as every nook and cranny of cultivable space is used.

The massive forests provide lumber for building and charcoal for fuel. Mineral deposits are minimal and industrialization is fed by the importation of raw materials. While sulphur, copper and limestone have been adequate, zinc, lead, phosphate and potassium, all elements comprising fertilizers,[12] must be imported.

The islands make a crescent configuration as they lie in a northeasterly-southwesterly direction, in what is known as the temperate zone of the middle latitude. This geographic location provides for a varied climate. The southern islands of Kyushu and Shikoku are characterized by long hot summers and mild winters. Honshu, the largest and centrally located island, varies from the southwestern extreme to the northeast. Hokkaido, to the north, is similar to the extreme northeastern United States – cool summers and cold, snowy winters.

The islands experience much rain, with the heavier amounts falling during the June-July and September-October periods.[13] The environmental profile is deeply affected by two main ocean currents, seasonal winds, known as monsoons, and typhoons that sweep up from the south Pacific.[14] Rainfall varies from a low of forty inches in Hokkaido to more than one hundred fifty inches on the southeast coasts of the southern islands.[15]

Japan is now occupied by some 124,000,000 people, which translates to a density of 864 people per square mile, and is, as noted in the main text, one of the heaviest in the world. And, what is more, most of the population is crowded onto 16% of the land, or an area similar in size to that of West Virginia.

As for the social habitat, Russia's Kuril and Sakhalin islands lie a few miles north of Hokkaido, and Korea lies to the west of Japan's southwest tip, about one-hundred twenty-four miles away. In today's terms, with rapid jet travel, these distances may seem minor and inconsequential, but the Japanese still continue to think of themselves as historically isolated. This idea dominates Japanese thinking and forms a powerful rationale for their unity and cultural differences from those of nearby neighbors.

Compared to the cultural history of the *Inuit*, the portrait of the Japanese is more difficult to sketch. It takes a brief historical review. The earliest written histories are the *Kojiki* (Record of Ancient Matters), ca. A.D. 712, and the *Nihongi* (Chronicles of Japan), dated A.D. 720.[16] These comprise old myths and legends that were previously passed on orally through the generations, and they establish Japanese presence on the islands around the 3rd century. Archaeological records show people were fishing, hunting and gathering as early as B.C. 4500, a period known as the *Jomon* (meaning corded).[17]

Sedentary, or non-migratory sites, do not show up until the *Yayoi* period, around B.C. 200. The *Yayoi* were irrigated rice farmers who migrated from regions of south Korea.[18] They brought the technologies of weaving, domestication of horses and cows, wheel-made pottery and simple iron tools. The *Yayoi* either spawned a group that developed significant political awareness, or such awareness came from a new wave of immigrants from the Korean or Chinese mainlands.

Whichever, the records show the emergence of a late 3rd or 4th century A.D. group who left large tombs housing hereditary chiefdoms (emperors), more sophisticated pottery, jewelry, armor and an array of weaponry indicating the presence of a military calvary.[19] These people had already perfected the technology of rice irrigation. The fact that specialists were developing shows their technology was supplying a surplus far beyond household needs.

In the following centuries Japan borrowed heavily from China (Buddhism, writing, etc.), while still exhibiting much independent creative cultural development. The history of Japan from the 3rd century is marked by political struggle for control between its various factions. Early kinship clans, or *uji*, evolved into tribes and chiefdoms, as they tried to "adapt to the local social habitat conditions." [20]

Until unification in the late 16th century, Japan's history is marked by battles between feudal lords, *daimyo*, which led to the development of a warrior group called *samurai*. Irrigated rice continued to be the staple crop and the basic unit of wealth and exchange.

A class structure developed and flowered in the 12th to 16th centuries that closely paralleled that in Europe.[21] Differing from European feudalism's dependence on legal concepts, Japan's feudalism operated on the basis of an ethical loyalty rooted in Confucian thought. As Reischauer points out, "Japanese feudal relationships were commonly phrased in absolute terms and described in terms akin to the relations between father and son; while in the West an emphasis on feudal rights proved to be the background for the development, in time, of democratic institutions." [22]

The 16th century saw political unification led by three powerful *shogun* or military lords, the last of whom was one *Tokugawa Ieyasu* (surnames are given first in Japan).[23] The *Tokugawa name* is used to characterize the shogun rule during the period from 1600 to 1868.[24] *Tokugawa* shoguns ruled by controlling the distribution of land and privileges to a network of vassal lords, *daimyo*. These various daimyo spent most of their time in *Edo* (now Tokyo) taking care of the *shogun's* needs. Their families were considered as hostages when the daimyo returned to their feudal territories.[25]

It should also be noted that the Tokugawa shoguns effectively shut out the rest of the world for the next two hundred and fifty years as the feudal system developed internally.[26] As stated earlier, travel outside the country was not allowed. The only contact with foreigners took place in Nagasaki, where the Chinese were allowed a trading presence, and on a nearby island where the Dutch were allowed a small trading presence.

A monetary system replaced rice as the basic medium of exchange.[27] Paper money and credits were standardized. Although fluctuating prices for rice prevailed, fixed prices for goods and services were common as the system moved toward a market economy.[28] By the latter part of the Tokugawa rule, people were used to working for wages.[29] The daimyo were busy draining swamps to increase agricultural productivity.[30] Agricultural improvement was important enough to warrant written books on the subject.[31] The merchant class expanded and trade between domains grew. Urban dwellers became dependent on products from around the country. The arts flourished, and literacy grew. Class distinctions still prevailed as privilege was socially distributed first to the samurai, then to the peasants or farmers, then to the craftsmen, and lastly, to the merchants.[32] The people were effectively controlled by a benevolent ruler. In present day terms, the benevolent rulers are government bureaucrats, ministers, politicians and corporate senior executives.

Yet, the Tokugawa changes sowed the seeds of its own demise. The emerging urban sites drew the political authorities and their warriors, leaving the peasants to fend for themselves.[33] As the merchant class prospered, it threatened the preeminence of the samurai class, a conflict that has never been totally resolved. So, the samurai, tradi-

234

tionally related to the old agricultural feudal system, was gradually diminished in stature. The old fiefdoms gradually evolved into fairly independent villages, and became the key unit of social organization.[34] And as villages grew, the neighborhood became an extended kin system.[35] Local affairs came under the control of village assemblies, comprised of landowners and tenant farmers.[36] Like the old hunting/ gathering groups, they chose their spokesman from among the upper strata of the village's families. Generally, the higher status families were descendants of the old samurai who stayed with their land rather than move to the urban centers in service to their daimyo. The resulting changes produced a stable village organization of wealthy farmers and merchants. The latter Tokugawa was marked by citizen protest and general unrest.[37]

Perry's visit to Japan in 1854, designed to force Japan to open its market to trade, fortuitously coincided with the *Tokugawa* decline. Yet, the government's failure to keep foreign influence out was a great embarrassment and the old fears of foreign influence did not vanish easily (and many will argue that they still persist). There was a period when Westerners were fair game for *ronin* (masterless samurai), and there were reprisals by American and French military contingents.[38] Members of the samurai forced the resignation of the last Tokugawa shogun and they opted to restore the centrality of the emperor.[39] In fact, the samurai rebels used the idea of an emperor as their main rationale for change. The emperor died in 1867, leaving a fourteen-year old heir, who was enthroned in 1868, as the first emperor of the new *Meiji* (illustrious rule) restoration period.[40]

As noted in the main body of the chapter, the new emperor was not the ruler de facto.[41] Collegiality via an imperial council provided the guiding hand, and many will argue that this is still the case. The Council issued a statement of operating principles, called "The Charter Oath," which stated that government policy would be decided after much public discussion and urged all to unite behind the new nation as it moved toward the goal of being a "rich country" with a "strong army."[42] Second, all things foreign were no longer viewed as dangerous. The Meiji leaders encouraged new ideas from outside. Third, the council urged that a national army replace the samurai. Although difficult to implement, it prevented further samurai coups. But the old samurai value of *bushido* (way of the warrior) has never died. Fourth, class structure was to be eliminated in favor of a meritocracy. In 1871 all class restrictions were lifted, and legally all were equal. Peasants could now choose their own occupation, live where they desired and take a family surname.

Industrialization was rapid. Large company combines grew, such as Mitsui, Mitsubishi and others. And corporateness has always been the key feature in Japanese organization, whether kin, tribe, daimyo, shogun, village, neighborhood, nation or corporate enterprise. *Most important, as Japan moved through these changes, she always carefully grafted the new onto the old traditional culture.*

As one reflects on Japanese history the dominance of early rice irrigation systems certainly stands out as the key to the Japanese culture. It freed people from a certain dependence on the weather and was a giant leap beyond the most advanced forms of horticulture. Interestingly, many of the world's most complex cultures evolved in conjunction with irrigation technology – Middle Valley of Mexico (floating gardens, *chinampas*), the Indus River Valley, Nile River Valley and Yellow River plains of China. In each case people were faced with the challenge of insuring a dependable water supply. This requires significant engineering skill, a good labor pool and some strong bosses, for someone in the group has to be able to coordinate people, land and water. Briefly put, in Japan, as with other groups who developed complex centralized cultures, there was a stratified and autocratic management bureaucracy. This has led one social scientist to label such populations *hydraulic societies*.[43]

Rice growing, as a total complex of activities, is a labor intensive corporate technology and demands a compliant labor force. It shapes an extreme group-oriented personality, which has certainly continued through modern Japanese culture. As stated in the summary of the main text, the historic culture built around rice irrigation farming continues to drive Japan's contemporary industry.

Finally, it should also be stated that the Japanese were never behind the West with regard to the other components of their culture. They lagged only in technology. The importance of the Tokugawa period of isolation, that allowed the Japanese cultural system to reach such an unmatched state of homogeneity, cannot be overemphasized. Significant diversity has only existed in the stratification of occupations, roles and family lineage. The cultural codes historically shaped by the interplay between the environment, with its limited cultivable space and island isolation, and rice irrigation technology were well developed and internalized in the deep mental recesses of the people. The end result is an extremely strong ethnocentric view of the world which translates into a powerful sense of nationalism and an unyielding racial and cultural homogeneity. Some have even described Japan's cultural singularity as akin to *tribalism*. [44]

It is important to emphasize that the most amazing part of Japan's evolution has been its ability to accept new ideas, processes and products within its traditional cultural environment. Cultural continuity, and thus political control by bureaucratic functionaries, is an important part of the Japanese focus. These two elements are now fused.

References Cited

1.   *The New Encyclopedia Britannica* (Chicago: University of Chicago Press, 1989), Volume 1, page 533.

2.   *World Book Encyclopedia* (Chicago: World Book, Inc.), Ibid., page 637.

3.   Sam Hall, *The Fourth World: The Heritage of the Arctic and Its Destruction* (New York: Alfred Knopf, 1987), pp. 10-70; *Living on the Planet Earth* (Washington D.C.: National Geographic Society, 1988), p. 63.

4.   Nelson H. H. Graburn and B. Stephen Strong, *Circumpolar Peoples: An Anthropological Perspective* (Pacific Palisades, California: Goodyear Publishing, 1973), pp. 19, 64.

5.   Donald S. Connery, *The Scandinavians* (New York: Simon & Schuster, 1966); T.K. Derry, *A History of Scandinavia: Norway, Sweden, Denmark Finland and Iceland* (Minneapolis: University of Minnesota Press, 1979); Graburn & Strong, Ibid.

6.   Norman A. Chance, *The Eskimo of North Alaska* (New York: Holt, Rinehart and Winston), 1966, pp. 77-79.

7.   Jean Briggs, *Never in Anger: Portrait of an Eskimo Family* (Cambridge: Harvard University Press, 1970); also, Jean Briggs, *In Search of Emotional Meaning* Ethos 15 (1987), pp. 8-15.

8.   Briggs, *Never in Anger*, Ibid., p. 234.

9.   Ibid., p. 286.

10.   Ibid., pp. 10-12, 35-45.

11.   Frank E. Blair, editor, *Countries of the World and Their Leaders Year Book 1991* (Detroit: Gale Research, Inc. 1991), p. 735.

12.   Mikiso Hane, *Modern Japan: A Historical Survey* (Boulder, CO: Westview Press, 1986), p. 5

13.   Ibid., p. 4.

14.   Ibid.

15.   *Collier's Encyclopedia* (New York: MacMillan Educational Company, 1990), Volume 13, p. 452.

16.   Hane, op. cit., page 15-21; Hendry, *Understanding Japanese Society* (London: Croom Helm, 1987), pp. 6-11; Edwin O. Reischauer, *Japan: The Story of A Nation* (New York: Alfred A. Knopf, 3rd Edition, 1981), p. 13.

17.   Hane, Ibid, page 6f.

18.   Hane, Ibid., pp. 15f; Edwin O. Reischauer, *Japan: The Story of a Nation,* op. cit., p. 13.

19.   Hane, op. cit., p. 7.

20.   Reischauer, *Japan: The Story of a Nation,* pp 14-26.

21.   Ibid.

22.   Ibid., p. 53.

23.   Hane, op.cit., p. 21f; Reischauer, *The Japanese Today.,* pp. 64-70.

24.   Reischauer, *Japan: The Story of A Nation,* op cit, pp 74-105.

25.   Gibney, op. cit.

26.   Hane, op.cit., p. 45.

27.   Reischauer, *Japan: The Story of a Nation*, op.cit.,p. 71.

28.   Ibid., p. 93.

29. Ibid., p. 21f.

30. Hane, op.cit., page 46f; Reischauer, *Japan: The Story of a Nation,* op.cit., p. 92f.

31. Reischauer, Ibid, p. 93.

32. Ibid., p. 96.

33. Ibid., p. 97f.

34. Hane, op.cit., p. 45f; Reischauer, *Japan: The Story of a Nation,* op.cit., p. 71.

35. The unique Japanese family, or i.e., includes all past and future members with the corporate head being the present senior male. For a fuller discussion on this subject, see suggested readings following:

Hendry describes it as a house, like the House of Windsor. See Hendry Ibid., p. 21.

Kitano explains it as a corporate unit, see Kitano Seiichi, "Dozohu and Ie in Japan: The Meaning of Family Genealogical Relationship."

In Robert J. Smith & Richard K. Beardsley, editors, *Japanese Culture, Its Development and Characteristics* (London: Methuen & Co., p. 963), pp 42-46.

Nakane agrees, but thinks it's like a residential managing body, similar to today's *uchi-no* (work place). See Chie Nakane, *Japan Society* (Berkeley: University of California Press, 1970), p. 7f.

Gibney also sees the Japanese family as corporate structure, see Frank Gibney, *Japan: The Fragile Superpower* (W.W. Norton & Company, 1975), pp. 68, 214-219, 351-354.

36. Reischauer, *Japan: The Story of a Nation,* op.cit.

37. Ibid., p. 103f.

38. Ibid. p. 114f.

39. Ibid., p. 117.

40. Ibid., p. 118.

41. Ibid.

42. Ibid., p. 119.

43. Karl A. Wittfogel, *Oriental Despotism: A Comparative Study of Total Power,* (New Haven: Yale University Press, 1957).

44. Gibney, op.cit., p. 38.

Bibliography

BOOKS

Andrews, George F., *Maya Cities: Placemaking and Urbanization* (Norman: University of Oklahoma Press, 1977)

Auden, W.H., *Prologue: The Birth of Architecture, About the House* (New York: Random House, 1965).

Barth, Fredrik, *Nomads of South Persia* (New York: Humanities Press, 1965).

Bayliss-Smith, T. P., *The Ecology of Agricultural Systems* (Cambridge: Cambridge University Press, 1982);

--------------, *Ethnic Groups and Boundaries* (Boston: Little, Brown & Company, 1969).

Berger, Peter, *The Capitalist Revolution* (New York: Basic Books, 1986).

Black, C.E. *The Dynamics of Modernization: A Study of Comparative History* (New York: Harper & Row, 1966).

Blair, Frank E. editor, *Countries of the World and Their Leaders Year Book 1991* (Detroit: Gale Research, Inc., 1991).

Blaxter, K., *People, Food and Resources,* (Cambridge: Cambridge University Press, 1986);

Briggs, Jean, *Never in Anger: Portrait of an Eskimo Family* (Cambridge: Harvard University Press, 1970).

Brown, Ina Corinne, *Understanding Other Cultures* (Englewood Cliffs, NJ: Prentice-Hall, 1963).

Burch, Ernest S., Jr., *The Eskimos* (Norman: University of Oklahoma Press, 1988).

Campbell, B., *Human Ecoology* (London: Heinemann Press, 1983);

Campbell, Joseph, *Myths to Live By* (New York: Bantam Books, 1973)

Chance, Norman A., *The Eskimo of North Alaska* (New York: Holt, Rinehart and Winston, 1966).

Chayanov, A.V., *The Theory of the Peasant Economy* (Homewood, IL: Richard D. Owen, American Economic Association, 1966).

Claiborne, Robert, *Climate, Man and History* (New York: W. W. Morton & Company, Inc., 1970);

Cohen, Erik, et. al., *Comparative Social Dynamics* (Boulder, CO: Westview Press, 1985).

Condon, John C. *Good Neighbors: Communicating With the Mexicans* (Yarmouth, ME: Intercultural Press, 1985).

Connery, Donald S. *The Scandinavians* (New York: Simon & Schuster, 1966).

Critchfield, Richard, *Villages* (New York: Harper & Row, 1981).

Daniken, Erich von, *Chariots of the Gods* (New York: Putnam Press, 1970).

Derry, T.K., *A History of Scandinavia: Norway, Sweden, Denmark, Finland and Iceland* (Minneapolis: University of Minnesota Press, 1979).

Dobyns, Henry F. et al, editors, *Peasants, Power and Applied Social Change* (Beverly Hills, CA: Sage Publications, 1964).

Donne, John, *Devotions Upon Emergent Occasions* (Ann Arbor: University of Michigan Press, 1959).

Eickelman, Dale F., *The Middle East: An Anthropological Approach* (Englewood Cliffs, NJ: Prentice Hall, 1981).

Eliot, George, *Daniel Deronda* (New York: The Hovendon Company, 1876).

-------- *The New Encyclopedia Britannica,* (Chicago: University of Chicago Press, 1989, Volume I).

Evans-Pritchard, E.E., *The Nuer* (Oxford: Oxford University Press, 1940).

Forde, C. Daryll, *Habitat: Economy and Society* (London: Methuen & Company, 1934).

Foster, George, *Tzintzuntzan: Mexican Peasants in a Changing World* (Boston: Little, Brown and Company, 1967).

Fraser, J.T., *Time: The Familiar Stranger* (Amherst: University of Massachusetts Press, 1987).

Fukuyama, Francis, *Trust: The Social Virtues and the Creation of Prosperity* (New York: The Free Press, 1995).

Geertz, Clifford, *Agricultural Involution* (Berkeley: University of California Press, 1963).

----------- *The Interpretation of Cultures* (New York: Basic Books, 1973).

Gibney, Frank, *Japan: The Fragile Superpower* (New York: W.W. Norton & Company, 1975).

Graburn, Nelson, editor, *Readings in Kinship and Social Structure* (New York: Harper & Row Publishers, 1971).

Graburn, Nelson H.H. and Strong, B. Stephen, *Circumpolar Peoples: An Anthropological Perspective* (Pacific Palisades, CA.: Goodyear Publishing Company, 1973).

Hall, Edward T., *The Hidden Dimension* (Garden City, NY: Anchor, Doubleday & Company, 1969).

Hall, Edward T., *Beyond Culture* (Garden City, NY: Anchor Press, 1976).

Hall, Sam, *The Fourth World: The Heritage of the Arctic and Its Destruction* (New York: Alfred Knopf, 1987).

Hane, Mikiso, *Modern Japan: A Historical Survey* (Boulder, CO: Westview Press, 1986).

Hardoy, Jorge E. *Pre-Columbian Cities* (New York:Walker & Company, 1964).

Harris, Marvin, *Cannibals and Kings: The Origins of Cultures* (New York: Random House, 1977).

Harris, Marvin, *Cultural Materialism: The Struggle for a Science of Culture* (New York: Random House, 1979).

Harris, Marvin *Our Kind* (New York: Harper Collins Publisher, 1989).

Harvey, David, *The Conditions of Postmodernity: An Enquiry Into the Origns of Cultural Change* (Cambridge, MA: Basil Blackwell, 1989).

Hendry, Joy, *Understanding Japanese Society* (London: Croom Helm, 1987).

Huizinga, J., *The Waning of the Middle Ages* (New York: Anchor Doubleday , 1956).

Hunter, David E. & Whitten, Phillip, editors, *Encyclopedia of Anthropology* (New York: Harper & Row, 1976).

Ishihara, Shintaro, *The Japan That Can Say No,* translated by Frank Baldwin (New York: Simon & Schuster, 1991).

Jones, Loyal & Billy Edd Wheeler, *Hometown Humor, USA* (Little Rock, AR: August House Publishers, Inc., 1991).

King, Leslie J. & Golledge, Reginald G., *Cities, Space and Behavior: The Elements of Urban Geography* (Englewood Cliffs, NJ: Prentice-Hall, Inc., 1978).

Leacock, Eleanor & Lee, Richard, *Politics and History in Band Societies* (Cambridge: Cambridge University Press, 1982).

Levy, Marion J., *Modernization: Latecomers and Survivors* (New York: Basic Books, 1972).

Lewis, Oscar, *Five Families: Mexican Case Studies in the Culture of Poverty* (New York: Basic Books, 1959).

Lightfoot, Charles Robert, *Handbook of Business Quotations* (Houston, TX: Gulf Publishing Co., 1991).

Malthus, T.R., *An Essay on the Principles of Population* (London: Mac-Millan Press, 1926).

Manchester, William, *A World Lit Only By Fire: The Medieval Mind and the Renaissance* (Boston: Little, Brown and Company, 1992).

McLuban, Marshall, *Understanding Media: The Extensions of Man* (New York: McGraw, 1964; NAL, 1966).

Middleton, John, editor, *Studies in Social and Cultural Anthropology* (New York: Thomas Y. Crowell Company, 1968).

Mumford, Lewis, *Technics and Civilization* (New York: Harcourt Brace, 1934).

Oliver, Chad, *The Discovery of Humanity: An Introduction to Anthropology* (New York: Harper & Row Publishers, 1981).

Oster, Patrick, *The Mexicans, A Personal Portrait of a People* (New York: William Morrow & Company, Inc., 1989).

Pasternak, Burton, *Kinship and Community in Two Chinese Villages* (Stanford, CA: Stanford University Press, 1972).

Patterson, James & Kim, Peter, *The Day Americans Told the Truth* (New York: Prentice Hall Press, 1991)

Plog, Fred and Bates, Daniel G., *Cultural Anthropology*, 2nd Edition, (New York: Alfred A. Knopf, 1980).

Post, Don E., *Ethnic Competition for Control of Schools in Two South Texas Towns* (Las Cruces: New Mexico State University, ERIC-CRESS Press, 1975).

Potter, Jack K., Diaz, May N. & Foster, George, editors, *Peasant Society, A Reader* (Boston: Little, Brown, and Company, 1967).

Rappaport, Roy, *Pigs for the Ancestors: Ritual in the Ecology of a New Guinea People* (New Haven: Yale University Press, 1968).

Reischauer, Edwin O., *Japan: The Story of a Nation* (New York: Alfred A. Knopf, 3rd Edition, 1981).

Reischauer, Edwin O., *The Japanese Today* (Cambridge, MA: Belknap Press, 1988).

Ricks, David A., *Blunders in International Business* (Cambridge, MA: Blackwell Publishers, 1993).

Rosman, Abraham & Rubel, Paula G. *The Tapestry of Culture* (Glencoe, IL: Scott Foresman & Co., 1981).

Selby, Henry A., *Zapotec Deviance* (Austin: University of Texas Press, 1974).

Shakespeare, William, *As You Like It,* (Act II, Scene 7).

Shapiro, Michael, *Japan: In the Land of the Brokenhearted* (New York: H. Holt, 1989).

Smith, Adam, *The Wealth of Nations* (Oxford: Clarendon Press, 1976).

Stoll, David, *Is Latin America Turning Protestant?* (Berkeley: University of California Press, 1990).

Tasker, Peter, *The Japanese: A Major Exploration of Modern Japan* (New York: E.P. Dutton, 1987).

Taussig, Michael T., *The Devil and Commodity Fetishism in South America* (Chapel Hill: University of North Carolina University Press, 1980).

Tax, Sol, *Penny Capitalism: A Guatemalan Indian Economy* (New York: Octagon Books, 1972).

Thurow, Lester, *Head to Head: The Coming Economic Battle Among Japan, Europe, and America* (New York: William Morrow and Company, Inc., 1992).

Tobin, Joseph, editor, *Remade in Japan: Everyday Life and Consumer Taste in a Changing Society* (New Haven: Yale University Press, 1992).

Vayda, Andrew P., *Environment and Cultural Behavior* ((Garden City, NY: The Natural History Press, 1969.

Wallace, Anthony F.C., *Religion: An Anthropological View* (New York: Random House, 1966).

Weber, Max, *The Protestant Ethic and the Spirit of Capitalism,* translated by Talcott Parsons (New York: Charles Scribner's Sons, 1958).

Weber, Susan, *USA By Number, A Statistical Portrait of the United States* (Washington D.C.: Zero Population Growth, Inc., 1988).

Whitehouse, Ruth, *The First Cities* (New York: E.P. Dutton, 1977).

White, Leslie A. and Dillingham, Beth, *The Concept of Culture* (Minneapolis, MN: Burgess Publishing Co., 1975).

White, Leslie A., *The Concept of Cultural Systems* (New York: Columbia University Press, 1975).

Worf, Benjamin Lee, *Language, Thought and Reality* (New York: MIT & John Wiley & Sons, 1956).

Wolf, Eric R., *Peasants* (Englewood Cliffs, NJ: Prentice-Hall, 1966).

Wolferen, Karel van, *The Enigma of Japanese Power* (London: MacMillan Company, 1989).

------ *World Book Encyclopedia* (Chicago: Volume 1, 1990).

Wittfogel, Karl A., *Oriental Despotism: A Comparative Study of Total Power* (New Haven: Yale University Press, 1957).

Zall, Paul M., editor, *Mark Twain Laughing* (Knoxville: University of Tennesee Press, 1985).

ARTICLES

Roberts, Paul Craig, "Problem Isn't Tokyo, It's Washington", in Houston Chronicle, Outlook Section, Wednesday, November 27, 1991, p. 10C.

Bakerjian, Ramon, and Patricia P. Mishne, "A Whole New Ball Game", in Manufacturing Engineering, Vol. 101, Issue 4, October, 1988, pp. 61-62.

Barnathan, Joyce, et al, "Has Singapore Got What It Takes To Be a Finance Power House?" in Business Week, March 20, 1995, p. 54.

Brown, Donna, "The High-Tech Debate: Can America Keep Pace?", in Management Review, Vol. 78, Issue 12, December, 1989, pp. 30-36.

_____, "Crossed by Jordan, Men Press Case", in Houston Chronicle, February 5, 1992, p. 10A.

Dallas, Sandra, "Rule No. 1: Don't Miss the Locals", in Business Week. May 15, 1995, p.8.

Hughes, Beth, "Japan's America-Bashing Book Stuns, Angers its United States Readers", in Houston Chronicle, December 18, 1989, p.48.

Inkles, Alex, "Making Men Modern," in American Journal of Sociology, Volume 75, pp. 208-225.

Kroeber, Alfred L., "Relations of Environmental and Cultural Factors", in Environment and Cultural Behavior, Andrew P. Vayda, editor (Garden City, NY: The Natural History Press, 1969).

Lee, Valeria, "Chewing Gum Ban Sticks In Singapore's Craw", in Houston Chronicle, January 10, 1992.

Peters, Tom, "Our Real Trouble Is, Asia is Asian", Houston Chronicle, Outlook, Section 4, Sunday, July 31, 1988.

Piturro, Marlene C., "How To Blow a Billion-Dollar Deal", in World Trade, June/July, 1991, p. 56f.

Schiller, Zachery, "P & G Is Still Having a Devil of a Time", in Business Week, May 15, 1995, p. 8.

Ullman, John E., "From Bubble Traveler to Country Expert: Knowledge, Ideology and the Conduct of International Business", in Lehman, Cheryl R. and Moore, Russell M., Multinational Culture: Social Impacts of a Global Economy (Westport, CT: Greenwood Press, 1992), p. 81f.

Index

A

Adams, Henry 61
Africa 24, 78, 88, 127, 128, 132, 181, 190
  Ashanti 137
  Egypt 31, 137, 190
  Dhomey 137
  Nigeria 48
  Uganda 137
  Yoruba 137
agriculture
  hoe 111, 132, 133
    characteristics 130, 131
    see also horticulture
    intensive 51, 124, 134-138
    characteristics of 135, 136
    differences from horticulture 134
    impact on culture 136
  plow
    varieties of 52
Al-Assad, President Hafez 103
America 35, 102
  cultural diversity, unique to 27, 28, 63
  historic culture 111–112
Americans
  egalitarian values 77
  ethnocentricism 30–42
    bluntness 30, 40
    body language 30, 37-39
    colonialism 30, 89
    communalism 25, 33, 35, 37
    entrepreneurial and combative inclinations 111
    impatience 30, 40

Indians, see Native Americans
    manifest destiny 30, 37
    radical individualism 30, 37, 111
    self-sufficiency 111
    speech patterns 30, 39
  illegal discrimination 77
Antarctic 227
Arctic 114, 115, 227
Asia 4, 5, 28, 33, 78, 166
Asian (s) 5, 6, 7, 37, 154, 158
Ashvaghosha 93
  see also Buddhism
Auden, W. H. 209

B

bakshish (see also bribery, payola, kickbacks, *mordida*)
  definition 152
Berger, Peter 34
Bhagavadgita 91
  see also Hinduism
body language, see Americans, body language
bribery(see also *bakshish*, payola, kickbacks, *mordida*)
  American prohibition 153
  definition 152
Briggs, Jean L. 198, 230
Brown, Ina Corinne 6
Buddhism 87, 92–94
  Buddha, see Gautama, Siddhartha
Bunker, Archie 82
Burke, Kenneth 46, 59
business
  competitiveness 5, 7
  cross-cultural relationship 2
  managing flaws 28-42
  economics
    differences 165-170

personnel 74, 173-175
Philippines 7
relations
    managing time 200-201
Southeast Asia 4

C

Calvin and Hobbes 49, 87, 106, 110, 138, 152
Calvin, John 154
Campbell, Joseph 22
capitalism 150, 154
    Asian 170
    definition 175
    state-managed 157, 158, 169, 170
Central America 27, 194, 195
    Guatemala 30, 31
China
    People's Republic of 166
Christianity 87, 88–89, 107
church and state, separation of 85
classification
    differences, traditional vs modern people 21–25
    hybrids bridge modern & traditional 22
    modernism and capitalism interchangeable 43
    modernism drives America 26
Clinton, President William J. 32
Confucianism 94, 97–98
Confucius 85, 97
    Confucius, see also Confucianism
Critchfield, Richard 13
cross-cultural
    engineering 9
    equip to understand 10
    home-stays 216-220
    illiteracy 8
    inquiries 220-222
    literacy training 9
    literature 216, 217
    misunderstanding 3
    observation 222, 223

cross-cultural perspective 11-15, 56
    definition 213
    understanding 3, 4, 14
    See also cultural perspective
cultural bias
    anti-modernizing sentiments 53
    baggage 21
cultural differences
    traditional vs. modern
        communalism 25, 33, 35
        fatalistic world view 25
        how change and progress are viewed 23
        mythology 22
cultural lens
    basic focal 12, 13
    main focal 11, 13-1 48-53
    skepticism 47, 56
        debunking motif 46, 47
cultural organization
    economic 55
    environmental 55
    political 55
        clans 131
    religious 55
    social (kinship) 55
    space/time 55
    technological 55
cultural perspective
    accessing a culture 214
    definition 11-15, 56
    for acceptable behavior 10
    lack use of 21
    optic analogy 13, 15
    tools provided for questioning 220
    use of 3, 16
cultural portrait
    continuum 22
    equip to sketch 2
    how to use 14–15
    perspective tool 15
    purpose 14

sketching 12, 214-223
  basic contours 213
  business factors and inter-
    relating to cultural
    scenes 214
  Inuit 116
  socio-cultural scenes 214
  political codes and rela-
    tionships 191
  pursuit strategies 214, 223
cultural tool
  need to be equipped with 11
  use of 12, 13, 14
cultural understanding
  obstacles 21-45
culture
  adaptive capability 51, 125
  Asian 6
  benefits of understanding 3
  common courtesy 8
  composition 49
  decoding v, 2, 3, 21, 61
  definition v, 10, 12
  demystify. See culture, decoding
  device to demystify 11
  differences affect business 14
  dharma, see Hinduism
  European 6
  European, modern 18
  inability to understand others
    3, 6
  Japanese 14
  knowledge of 27
  Latin America
    patronage (*patronismo*)
      190
  need to understand foreign as-
    sociates 4
  screening and adaptive capa-
    bilities 50, 51
  understanding others 6
cultural examples
  Bedouin camel herders, mix-
    ture of two technologies
    128

  Guatemala, attempt at social
    reform 31
  Iran, traditional Islamic 24
  Mexican pottery makers, tra-
    ditional design 24
  Middle East, market codes
    150
  Navajo sheepherders refuse to
    take up farming 24, 150,
    151
  New Hebrides, pig culture
    patterns 56
  pastoralism (herding)
    Africans refuse new breed
      of cattle 24
  upper Rio Grande River Indi-
    ans, traditional corn 24

D

daimyo (feudal lords)
  Japan 118, 233
Dalton, George 159, 163
decoding 213
democracy 171,
despots 189
Donne, John 196

E

economic issues 171–175
economic thought
  differences between Western
    and non-Western think-
    ing 153–156
  differences in 150–157
economics
  bazaar market 165
  capitalism, see capitalism
  *global economics, see global
    economics*
  just-in-time production 157
  market-dominated economies
    159
    characteristics 163, 164
    implications for business
      persons 165
  see also peasantry

marketless economies 159
  feast exchanges 160
  functions of 160
  guanxi (Chinese) 166
  mass production (old system) 157
  modern capitalistic markets 167–170
  peripheral markets 159, 163
  reciprocity rules 133, 161, 162, 164
    types of 161
      balanced 161
      generalized 161
      negative 162
  redistribution exchange systems 162
  standards of exchange 159
  strategies
    working in tightly-controlled markets 171–175
  traditional modes of exchange 151, 159, 163
  traditional views 157, 158
  treasure tales 154-155, 161
economy
  definition 149
  modern capitalistic markets characteristics 167–169
  pastoral 129
  profit 154, 160, 162, 165, 171, 172, 174, 175
  traditional modes 150, 151
Edo, see Tokyo, Japan
Egypt, see Africa
Eliot, George 82
Ellis, William 154
Emersonian
  view of self-reliance 112
environment, see Inuit
  case history, environment
Eskimo, see Inuit
Europe 5, 38, 78, 86, 88, 135
  pre-industrial 163, 190

European 6, 18, 25, 35, 73, 132, 158, 166, 181, 197
European Economic Union 157
Evans-Pritchard, E. E. 195
extended kinship, see kinship

F

face, see honor
familia 67
  definition 33
  Mexican family structure 67
    colonia 72
    compadres
      definition 70
    machismo 69
    patrons 70
    nepotism 68
feng-shui 96
feasts, see also fiesta, luau, pig feasts
fiesta 160
folk religions 105–106
foreigners, as devils 73, 137
French 47, 75
  concepts of time 201
Frost, David 75

G

gaijin 73, 101
Ganges River (India) 90
  see also Hinduism
Gautama, Siddhartha (Buddha) 92, 93
Geertz, Clifford 11, 135
German (y) 17, 75, 96
  concepts of time 201
Ghandi, Mahatma 154
global economics
  economic domination 157
  impact on 8
  incentive 14
  leadership 2
global executives, need to develop 7
global transformation 204
globalization 143

multinational companies 143
products 143, 145
transnational companies 143
Goethe 109
Gorbachev 158
Greeks (Greece) 38, 75
gringo 73, 193, 194
Guatemala (n) 30, 81, 89
see also culture examples, Guatemalan

H

habitat 17
definition 109
*see also Inuit and Japanese case
histories*
habitats
as affect technology 125
culture relations 111-113
influence on ways of extracting food and resources
149
Halberstam, David 190
Hall, Edward T. 201, 203, 206,
208, 209
harnessing energy 52, 53
Harris, Marvin 57
herding, see pastoralism
high technology, see technology
Hinduism 90–92
social codes 91, 92
history
rice irrigation technology 235
Hong Kong 6, 96
honor, face 29-31
horticulture 51, 124, 130
division of labor
domestication of plants 130
shifting cultivation
swidden, definition 132
Hughes, Beth 74
Huizinga, J. 180
hunting and gathering 51, 124,
130, 131
Hussein, President Saddam 103

I

immigration
pull of individual freedom 27
United States 26
impatience, cross cultural impediment 40-42
example of patience 42
imperialism, Western 24
Inca (Peru) 113, 135, 163
India 90, 92,93, 105
sacred cows 220-221
individualism, radical 31-37, 39,
111
Indonesia 78, 105, 107, 138
Inkles, Alex 198
Inuit
case history 111, 114–117,
226-229,231
environment 114, 227, 228,
229
environmental effect on cultural development 228
equalitarian social system
115, 229
Eskimo 111
habitat 114, 115, 117, 231
implications for doing business 116
marketless economies 115,
229
political control 115, 229
religious beliefs 115, 231
technology 115
Iran, Shah of 158
Iraq 86, 103
irrigation 52, 136
Olympian, definition 137
origins of 134
rice, Japan 235
rice, Java 135
Ishihara, Shintaro 74
Islam 86, 87, 102–105
Allah 86
anti-modernization feelings of

102
  five Pillars of 104
  Mohammed, Prophet of Islam
    103
  Moslem (Muslim) 102
  pilgrimage to Mecca 104
  Qur'an (Koran) 103
  Ramadan 104
  Shi'ite 104
  Sunni 104

J

Japan 117
  Yayoi 120
  early history 119, 230-234
Japanese 111
  case history 111, 117–121,
    231–236
    Arctic 118
    characteristics of success
      120–121
    environment 232
    habitat 117, 231-232
    hydraulic societies 236
    Meiji (illustrous rule)
      119
    political control 233, 234,
      236
    political struggle 233
    rice irrigation 118, 119,
      120, 231-233, 235
    social organization 234
  implications for doing busi-
    ness 119
  rice irrigation system, Yayoi
    118
  societal development 33
Jay, Anthony 75
Johnson, President Lyndon B. 36
Johnson, Samuel 4
Jordan, Barbara 77
Judaism 87, 107

K

kami, see Shinto
Khomeini, Ayatullah 104

kickbacks (see also payola,
bribery, *mordida, bakshish*)
  definition 152
Kim, Peter 167
kinship 25, 55
  definition 63
  fictive kin 70-72
    extra-kin 63, 67
  intimacy continuum 62, 64
    age 68
    fictive kin 67
    gender 68
    roles 64
    statuses 64
  Mexican kin system
    chart 65-67
      first tier intimacy 65-70
      patrons 70-72
      second tier intimacy 70-
        72
  strangers/outsiders, see separate
    heading for strangers/outsiders
Kobe, Japan
  earthquake 110
Korea 29, 38, 93, 96, 180, 231
  the Yayoi 118
Kroeber, A. L. 121
Kyoto, Japan 118

L

Lapps (Scandinavia) 126, 226
Lec, Stanilaw 124
lens, see cultural lens
Levy, Marion 21
Los Angeles
  ethnic gangs 33
luau (Hawaiian) 161

M

machismo 29-30
  definition 69
    see familia, Mexican family
      structure
MacLaine, Shirley 105
man, anthropological view 48-49

Manchester, William 35, 196, 205

manifest destiny, see Americans, ethnocentricim

Marcos family of the Philippines 153

marketless economies, see Inuit, case history, marketless economies

marketplace
    government role in 5
    groups in 79
    images and views of people 8

Marx, Groucho 179

Maya (n) 77, 86, 113, 135, 164, 198

McArthur, General Douglas 107

McDonalds Corporation 144

McLuhan, Marshall 200

Mecca 104
    see also Islam

Mesopotamia 31, 113, 163, 190

Mexican 56, 57, 68, 77
    family 65-72
    for role of family members, see chart on page 65-67.

Mexico 17, 27, 73, 77, 78, 161, 194, 195

Middle Ages 25, 181

Middle East (ern) 5, 78, 103, 128, 137, 151, 153, 182

Mississippi River, flooding 110

modern culture
    class 141, 142, 143
    definition 21-29
    modernism 16-37, 109, 159
        lack of order 26
        materialism 26
        secular world 26
    nationality 141, 143
    technology of 109-113, 139-145
    vs. traditional 25-28

Mohammed 103

monarchs 187, 189, 190

money 160, 169, 180

mordida
    definition 152

Mother Teresa 154

Mt. Fuji 98

Mumford, Lewis 197

Muslim, see Moslem

mythology 115

myths
    definition 22
    modern 23
    religious 86
    traditional 23

N

Native Americans 27
    Hopi 196
        concept of time 197
    Navajo 24, 152, 197
    Pueblo Indians
        Eastern 132
        Western 131
    purification ritual 33, 34
    Sioux, concept of time 197

nepotism
    definition 68
    see familia, Mexican family structure

New Ageism 105

Nirvana 91, 92, 93

Northern Rio Grande River Indians, use of traditional corn for tortillas 151

non-Western 18, 26, 32, 34, 35, 76, 85, 89, 136
    buying influence 153-154

O

Olympian
    definition 137

Osaka, Japan 118

Oster, Patrick 69, 77, 78

Ottoman Empire 103

P

Pahlevi dynasty 24, 102

Pasternak, Burton 138

pastoralism 124, 129
   characteristics of 129–130
   tools of 129
   tribal affiliation, as protective
     association 129
patron, see kinship, Mexican kin system
Patterson, James 167
Paulson, Pat 193
payola (see also bribery, kickbacks, *mordida, bakshish*)
   American prohibition 153
   definition 152
   influence on American busi-
     ness people 153
   leveling device 153
Paz, Octavio 69
peasantry 155, 156, 164
   ancestral background 112
   definition of 163
   European, serfs 164
   implications for business per-
     son 165
   peasant communities in exist-
     ence 165
   traditional economics 155
   see also market-dominated
     economy
Perry, Admiral Matthew 234
Peters, Tom 6
Philippines 6, 7, 30, 154
Pickens, T. Boone 152
pig feast 160
pigs and culture 56, 161
plow agriculture, see agriculture, plow
polar regions, see Artic, Antartic
politics 55, 85, 180-192
   chiefdoms 186-190, 232
   colonialism 181
   definition 179
   early political systems 180
   headmen 126
     bands/headmen 186
   historical political systems
     (chart) 186
   human rights abuses 179

key integrative features 187
monarch 188, 189
nation states 186, 190
nationalism 181
order
   definition 179
political culture
   definition 181
political risk analyzed 191
power
   definition 183
power authority
   definition 185
power relations 182
   definition 183
state structures
   characteristics 189
   definition 189
stratification
   definition 187
   tribes, see separate heading for
     tribes
Portillo, President Luis 68
profit, see economy, profit

Q

Qur'an (Koran), see Islam

R

Rabin, Yitzhak 86
race 55, 85
reciprocity rules,see economics,
   reciprocity rules
Reischauer, Edwin O. 231
religion
   animism 86, 130
   monotheistic 137
   Olympian, see separate listing
   philosophical theism 137
   as cultural scene 55, 88-108
   myths, see mythology or myths
Rio Grande River 24, 152
Rogers, Will 213
Romulo, President Carlos R. 6
Russia 48

S

Sadat, President Anwar 103
samurai (warriors)
    Japan 118, 234
scenes 55-56
Schlain, Ben 39
Selby, Henry A. 28, 72, 160
Shakespeare, William
    Ages of Man 59
shaman 116, 231
    definition 96, 126
    see also yin and yang
Shinto 86, 98–102
    kami 86, 99-102
    shrines 98, 100
shoguns
    Tokugawa, Japan 118, 234
Shula, Don 223
Siberians 126, 229
Singapore 4, 26, 32, 169, 170
    criminal justice 32
Smith, Adam 170
social distinctions
    boundary mechanisms 75, 76
    insider/outsider 75
    rules of behavior 64
    strangers/outsiders 36, 72,
    75, 136
        see also under separte listing
    tension-releasing mechanism
        avoidance 80-81
        humor 80, 81, 82
        xenophobia 75
social organization
    communal 134
    core of 131
    graph 62
    household 133
    work groups 79
social relations 25, 62, 64
    honor 29
    machismo 29
    social amenities 28
social relations, see kinship

South America
    Boliva 155
    Columbia 155
    Peru 190
space 17, 55, 140, 194, 205-211
    cultural use of 206
    social space 207
    social space distances (chart)
    208
    spatial codes 210
    spatial differences 206
    spatial dimensions 204
    spatial limitations 205
    spatial view
        cause for conflict 206
    world view 193
space orientation
    cultural code 194
Spanish 67, 75, 135, 221
speech patterns 39-40
strangers/outsiders 137, 166
    kwa lo (Chinese) 137
    neisi (Japanese) 137
    social codes 35, 153
strategy
    for assessing cultural mean-
        ing 56
    for sketching cultural portraits
        214-223
swidden, see horticulture, shifting
    cultivation

T

Taiwan 26, 85
Tao Te Ching, Book of the Virtue
    of the Tao 95
Taoism 94–96
Taussig, Michael T. 154
technology
    definition 125
    horticulture
        reduced need to roam 131
    hunting and gathering 52,
        126–127

industrial to modern high-technology 138–145
industrialism
 definition 138
 influence on shape of culture 124
 influence on ways of extracting food & resources 149
 irrigation 124
 rice 120
 rice, Japan 118
modernism
 characteristics of 140–143
 definition 139
 high technology (hi-tech) 124
 industrial 124
 post-industrial 124
pastoralism 127–130
 as adaptive strategy 127
 as affects population 128
 as cause of wars 127
 definition 127
 post-agricultural 139
 post-industrial 139
technology, agriculture, see agriculture
Thailand 38, 93, 138
Thurow, Lester 3, 158, 170
time
 calendars 199
 concepts of
  French and German (chart) 201–202
 Gregorian calendar 198, 204
 life rhythms 198
 light-years 194
 managing 197
 M-time (moonochromic) 200-204
  definition 201
 non-Western view of clock-time 199
 passage of time 194
 P-time (polychromic) 200-204

 definition 201
 time rhythm 200
 time-keeping devices 197, 198
 world view 193
time orientation
 cultural code 194
Tokugawa, see shoguns
Tokyo, Japan
 formerly Edo 118, 234
tortillas
 definition 44, 152
traits
 American 21
treasure tales, see economics, treasure tales
tribalism, Japan 237
tribes
 definition 188
 Nuer (Sudan) 195
 social organization of 188
tropical forest 53, 109
Trump, Marla Maples 105
Twain, Mark 40, 85, 149

U

United States 7, 11, 29, 32, 78, 103, 167
 immigrants 26, 27

W

Wallace, Anthony F. C. 137
Weber, Max 154
Western
 colonialism 30
 dress 58
 imperialism 25
Westerners 101
Whorf, Benjamin Lee 196
Wolf, Eric R. 164
world views 22-23
 modern 25-28
 traditional 25-28
World War II 24, 181

Y

yakuza (Japanese)50, 51
Yayoi, see Korea; see also Japanese,
  rice irrigation
Yew, Prime Minister Lee Kuan
  32, 169
yin-yang principles 95–96
  see also Taoism

Z

Zapotec 72, 161